LYNN TELFORD~SAHL

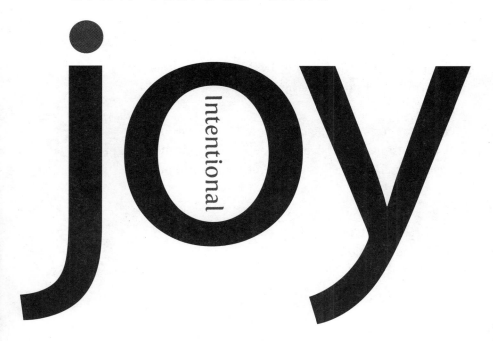

joy
Intentional

How to Turn Stress, Fear and Addiction into Freedom

Book Design by
ILLUSIO / Chuck Spidell
illusiodesign.com

ISBN: 1-56025-154-9

Library of Congress Card Catalog Number 97-61889

To Dave, my heart

To all my clients, past and present,

who have touched me deeply and

taught me oh so much. It's been my privilege.

Acknowledgements:

I truly understand what other authors mean when they say the creation of a book is always a team effort. I give thanks to—

My dedicated writing group of Marianne Peck, Gay Walker, Jennifer Grainger who listened, praised, critiqued, and laughed (and did we laugh) for the four years this endeavor took.

Bill Manville, our fearless leader, for his wisdom, wit, and *Cosmopolitan* experience—and for pushing me to include more of myself in this book.

Barbara McNichol, my editor, who straightened out my tenses, tightened up my wordiness, and made me love this book even more.

Phyllis Kelly, my favorite aunt, who demonstrates what true recovery is all about.

Jennifer Grainger, an extra thank you for the editing support so freely given.

Lane for being yourself, no matter what.
Lee, my sweet brother.
Rich, my fearless son.

Suzann, my beautiful daughter with whom I am so grateful to have reconnected.

All who encouraged me, asked me "how's it going?" and trusted in its completion.

Contents

10   FOREWORD: "And Everything Will Be All Right?"

13   CHAPTER ONE: What The Bleep Do We Know Anyway?!
13   My Epiphany
15   Good Girl/Bad Girl
16   The Pony Man
18   Stretched to the Limit
20   Fear—It's Like Breathing Air
20   Escape, Over-thinking, and Anxiety
22   Making the Mind-Body Connection
23   Is the Sky Falling?
24   What I've Always Wanted
25   Transforming Our Relationship to Fear

27   CHAPTER TWO: The End of the World
29   Big "T" and Little "t" Traumas
32   Our Unconscious Can Hurt Us
33   We Live in a Culture of Fear
38   Advertisers Prefer Us Uncomfortable
41   The Consequences of Fear
42   Get It All Done RIGHT
44   We Can Choose Between Fear and Love
45   Can We Find a Safe Harbor?

Contents

48 CHAPTER THREE: The "Lite" Addictions

50   Shopping as a "Lite" Addiction

54   Internet Porn as a "Lite" Addiction

55   Gambling as a "Lite" Addiction

57   Fast Food as a "Lite" Addiction

58   Sugar as a "Lite" Addiction

59   Emotional Freedom Technique

63   Aspartame–Worse Than Sugar?

64   Addiction Isn't Black or White

66   My Own "Lite" Addiction to TV-Watching

67   My Own "Lite" Addiction to Sugar

70 CHAPTER FOUR: Addiction–Facing the Dragon

71   Afraid of Being Destroyed

72   Better Not to Feel

73   How Addiction Gets Started

74   From Pattern to Habit to Addiction

77   Not "Good Enough" at the Root

79   The Suffering We Know

81   Brain's Neural Pathways and Addiction

83   New Energy Therapies

87 CHAPTER FIVE: Addiction–The Set Up

90   The Traumatized Brain

95   How Often Does Trauma Occur?

96   How Addiction Relates to Trauma

98   Blocked Trauma Causes Disconnection

98   Trauma Lowers Stress Threshold

99   Denial of Trauma

100 Trauma Makes Us More Vulnerable to Stress

104   **CHAPTER SIX: Chronic Stress and Addiction**

 109 Toxic Stress: A Set-Up for Addiction

 109 We're Even Competitive About Stress

 110 Change: The Faster We Go, the Better?

 114 Self-Care: The Antidote to Stress

 115 What is Self-Care?

 118 Prevention = Love and Gratitude

 120 The Heart Knows the Way

 121 Relaxation Response

124   **CHAPTER SEVEN: Emotional Wisdom Defined**

 127 Prodigal Daughter Needs to Come Home

 129 Getting to Know Ourselves Inside

 130 Bump Up Against Avoidance

 131 Lying to Avoid Pain

 133 The Nature of Emotions

137   **CHAPTER EIGHT: The Power of Emotional Wisdom**

 142 How Emotional Pain Drives Behavior

 143 When Buttons Get Pushed

 145 The Iceberg Theory

 148 Addictions "Sort of" Work

 152 What's an Authentic Person?

 154 Applying Emotional Wisdom in Everyday Living

164   **CHAPTER NINE: Touch, Accept, Release, Action**

 166 TARA—A Movement Psychology Technique

 168 Finding My Adopted Daughter

 174 More Tools for Resolving Pain

Contents

177 CHAPTER TEN: Emotional Freedom Technique

182 How Emotional Freedom Technique Works

188 How Traditional Therapy Compares with EFT

189 More Benefits of EFT

191 Taking Care of Yourself

193 Trauma and EFT

195 Addiction and EFT

198 CHAPTER ELEVEN: Imagery

203 Imagery Takes Us Within

205 Teaching Imagery

205 How Imagery Can Heal Trauma

207 Freeze Frame Technique

210 CHAPTER TWELVE: The Mind Thinks It Knows

213 We're Not Victims of Our Minds

215 Retrain the Mind –The Rest Will Follow

216 Over-thinking Mind + Negative Mind = Stress

217 The Relaxation Response

219 Changing Negative Thoughts

221 Our Beliefs: The Lens Through Which We See the World

224 CHAPTER THIRTEEN: The Body Really Knows

226 Body Wisdom

227 Non-Verbal Communication

231 Breath As A Power Tool

234   CHAPTER FOURTEEN: There's No World Without Love

235   The Concept of Loving Ourselves

237   But Isn't Loving Yourself Selfish?

238   What Is Love, Anyway?

239   When Love is Missing

242   Resisting Love

245   The Scientific Side of Love

247   Chemical Components of Love

249   Willingness to Go After Love

254   CHAPTER FIFTEEN: Love's Leap into Higher Consciousness

255   What Is Consciousness, Anyway?

256   Consciousness and Addiction Like Oil and Water

258   The Principle of Opposites

258   A Conscious Choice: Love or Fear

261   AUTHOR'S FINAL NOTE

262   ABOUT THE AUTHOR

264   INTENTIONAL JOY RESOURCES

268   ENDNOTES

278   AUTHOR BIO

Foreword

"And Everything Will Be All Right?"

by Bill Manville, author of *Cool, Hip & Sober:*
88 Ways to Beat Booze & Drugs

OT LONG AGO, a guest on my radio show, Addictions & Answers, walked into the studio eating a candy bar. I asked her to leave it outside, knowing that talking with her mouth full would make her hard to understand and the sound of crinkling wrapping paper would be distracting. As she put it down, she said sadly, "I hope I won't be too nervous. Whenever I unwrap a Hershey Bar, I have this feeling that nothing bad can happen to me while I eat it."

Don't laugh. It's a symptom of today's obesity addiction in America. Calling it a "public health nightmare," the *San Francisco Chronicle* noted that . . ."Servings have grown exponentially in recent years; 7-ounce muffins, for example, are equal to 7 slices of bread . . . At the movies, patrons typically consume huge 64-ounce soft drinks (500-900 calories) with half-gallon buckets of buttered popcorn."

Nor is overeating our only plague. Every day, millions of Americans—overwhelmed and exhausted—distract themselves with nostrums that advertisers say will give "relief." But the anxiety goes on. My own feeling is that the mantra "Will everything be all right?" comes closer to being our national anthem than "The Land of the Free and the Home of the Brave."

One thing my years as an alcoholic (long over now, thank you very much) taught me is this: If you try to fill the hole in your stomach (which means the hole in your life and soul) with the wrong stuff, you can never get enough. What's the wrong stuff? Food, money (ah there, Enron), TV, dope, sex, work, religion, shopping, gambling, cars, entertainment, gin, applause, game, and too many marriages or roller coaster rides.

Lynn Telford-Sahl has appeared frequently on my radio show as a guest expert with impeccable credentials. But what I especially like about Lynn is that she doesn't play the superior doctor, cool and aloof, removed from the fray. When she talks about overeating, overdrinking, overworking, or living in a wretched family, she makes no bones about it—she's been there herself. It's a quality that I think gives her book *Intentional JOY* its unique power. Whoever created the slogan, Doctor Cure Thyself! must have had Lynn in mind. And in these pages, she tells you how you can Cure Thyself! too.

* * *

Bill Manville writes the column "Addictions & Answers" for the *New York Daily News*. In addition to being a radio talk show host, he's been a columnist for New York's Village Voice and contributing editor for *Cosmopolitan*. His novel *Good-bye* was a Book-of-the-Month Club selection. Currently living in California, Bill says his hobbies are "maligning my friends and working on a new novel—or is that the same thing?"

" **If you can't control**
your emotional state, you're
addicted to it. "

- What the Bleep Do We Know Anyway

CHAPTER ONE

Chapter One:

What The Bleep Do We Know Anyway?!

THANK GOD, I woke up next to my husband Dave. My head was pounding, fuzzy. Images of the night before flooded in: Dancing with some loser guy who Dave and I'd met at a bar—drinking too much, doing one line of coke, and another, and more later—Dave finally telling me "we're going home" and making sure I got in the car.

Lying in bed that morning, I knew I'd crossed a line that I hadn't crossed before. I also knew I'd made an ass of myself with that stranger—couldn't even remember his name—dancing and flirting with him—my husband looking on. The guy even told Dave, "I think your wife wants to go home with me." That's when we left.

I felt scared, ashamed, and finally, resolute. I was used to feeling bad about myself, but this was the deepest level of misery ever. I knew I'd hurt Dave badly. So before he woke up, I made a decision—one that I finally kept. *I would find a way to quit running and start facing what I was most afraid of—myself.*

My Epiphany

That moment of truth occurred more than 25 years ago. That's when I began getting honest about how miserable I felt and how much I loathed myself.

At first it was slow-going because self-hatred kept me searching outside of myself—looking to everyone else to see if I was doing it right. I couldn't look within for direction; there wasn't a rudder inside me. Honestly, I felt too bruised and beaten and ashamed to be able to realistically look at who I really was.

Little by little, I gained the courage to pull back the covers and trust that I wouldn't die if I admitted I was far from perfect—if I admitted I was angry, guilty, and full of shame. I took stock of how out of balance everything in my life had become, although from the outside it looked pretty good. I sweated out the answers—worked and reworked them—to heal from the fear I felt inside. Because fear is what drives all addictive behavior.

I could see that as a child, I longed to be like Dorothy in The Wizard of Oz, my favorite childhood movie. While I may have looked like the original blonde Dorothy of L. Frank Baum's book, Dorothy's tornado happened in Kansas while my childhood *was* the tornado. I landed not in friendly, magical Munchkinland wearing ruby red slippers, but in the dark forest totally terrified of the wicked witch.

"Heh, heh, heh, heh, heh. I'll get you, my pretty," cackled the Wicked Witch of the West. My best friend Victoria used to tease me with that line, which made me cringe whenever I heard it. Now I know why it bothered me so. The Wicked Witch, whom I both hated and feared, lived inside me. Facing the witchy places inside myself (and seeing how I'd always avoided those places) was the magic that brought me home— not to Kansas, but to the natural, loving, loveable self I'd left behind in my childhood.

For years I lived in extremes. The face I showed at work, in my relationships, and at home (for the most part) was a happy, fairly together, little flighty from time to time, busy young wife and mother. The face I showed the world was the good girl doing what was expected, what she thought she *should* do to make others happy.

The other me lived mostly inside where I was so disconnected from my real feelings, I felt numb—except when I got angry. And I got angry and then depressed, quite a lot. I didn't know (and wouldn't have admitted it anyway) that I was afraid. I lived behind a façade made up of survival—a fine line of survival—because I didn't have much inner strength to lean on.

Good Girl/Bad Girl

My parents used to joke that I was like the little girl in the poem about the girl with the curl in the middle of her forehead – "when she was good, she was very, very good and when she was bad, she was horrid."

I now know that living in the extremes is a set-up for addiction, but I didn't then. Until I hit 14, I was the perfect good girl—good grades, compliant, sweet, available for everyone else. Then I flipped to the other extreme—the bad girl, sexually acting out, experimenting with alcohol and drugs, smoking cigarettes, running away, spending time in juvenile hall, getting pregnant.

At 19 when I got married, I flipped back to being the good girl. Throughout my 20s, I mostly maintained the external image of the good girl—married, working, going to school, cleaning house, raising our son. But inside was the witchy, bad girl who lived like the troll under the bridge, waiting for her time. The bad girl would take over once in a while. She'd stay up late drinking with her girlfriends, playing pool, dancing, or raging at her husband or son. Then, feeling guilty and ashamed, back underground she'd go.

It's said that a girl's self-esteem is assured if her dad

adores her and sees the best in her—the good girl. My dad usually saw the worst in me—the bad girl.

With an angry voice and a look on his face that blared disappointment, Dad simply had to accuse me of something and I'd flush and feel guilty—whether I was guilty or not. In contrast, Grandmother and Mom always noticed the best in me. They saw the good girl.

Before my moment of epiphany, I was only aware that I was unhappy and missing *something*, but didn't know *what*. I had all the externals that are supposed to make us happy—loving partner, home, child, and career. I eventually realized that the emptiness inside could never be satisfied with "stuff." It could only heal by being like Dorothy, and finding the path home to myself rather than Kansas.

If we're lucky, we'd have one or more positive guiding forces just as Dorothy did with her guides—the scarecrow, tin man, and lion along with the Good Witch Glinda—all available to oversee our journey. If we're not lucky, we struggle the best we can, leaking stuffing, rusting up from time to time, and puffing up our chests to convince the world we're fearless. Mostly, we quake inside and feel guilty and ashamed.

And we hide.

The Pony Man

My mother told me that before the age of seven I was a contented child, interested in everyone and everything. That all changed when I, who was crazy about horses, met the "pony photographer" who visited our suburban neighborhood. A trail of children followed this man with the camera, hoping to pet his ponies or maybe even ride one. He seemed to like me especially and allowed me to ride one of his ponies. He talked to my mother who gave permission for me to ride with him as he made his rounds in the area.

But what started as a joyful experience became terrifying as he molested me in a drainage ditch and left me unconscious. When I woke up, it was dark and I didn't quite know where I was. I made it home on my own, wandering until I found my way.

IS THIS BOOK FOR YOU?

As you read about my experience, perhaps you're thinking, "I wasn't molested so I don't think this book is for me." First let me say I'm happy you weren't. Research shows that 1 in 4 women and 1 in 7 men have been molested, and that most abuse is initiated by people we know, not by strangers, as happened to me. Beware: While molestation is an extreme example of fear that changes our thinking and feeling, many smaller fears occur in "normal" childhood that you may likely relate to.

When I walked in the door, Mom was furious that I was out late. I couldn't tell her what had happened. She sent me to bed. I fell asleep and when I woke the next morning, I didn't remember a thing about it—until 30 years later.

I was in my 30s when I told my mother I'd been molested. As any mother would, she felt guilty and responsible for not knowing. Looking back, though, she recalled that I changed at that time. Today I know that I disconnected from myself and that's what she could see without understanding why.

When a certain level of trauma happens, we shut down emotionally. We block out our feelings because they're so scary or so uncomfortable. We sense that they won't make someone else happy or we simply don't know what to do with them. Robert Bly, poet and author of *A Little Book on the Human Shadow*, says that by age 18, children are no longer the golden, dynamic orb of energy they were at birth.[1] Rather, they're full of holes, having given parts of themselves away during their childhood. Somewhere between the extremes of teaching our children to be safe or scaring them into abandoning themselves, there must be a balance point.

The rebellion of my teen years finished off what little self-esteem I had left. When these years are filled with pain and confusion, teens run as fast as they can into adulthood and slam the door shut. Perhaps you decided that if you couldn't feel good about yourself, you could at least *look* as if you did— like I did.

Yes, I bought into the façade of perfection and held it up in front of myself like a shield. That shield kept me from seeking help until I was in my early 30s. Like Marilyn Monroe— who looked like a goddess but felt like a fake—too many in our culture believe we will never be smart enough, rich enough, beautiful enough, or certainly thin enough. As for me, I lived with the unconscious fear that I would never be loved or accepted as I was. I didn't believe I deserved to be loved, anyway. So not really knowing how to live, I'd get out my list of shoulds, can'ts, and judgments that disconnected me from myself and from the relationships I longed for.

It's common to forget that the human condition is "perfectly imperfect" (in the words of author and substance abuse counselor Pia Mellody). We're like Dorothy and her friends, all searching for the piece of our "self" that will make us whole again.

Now I know. It's not outside us but within us. It has been all along.

Stretched to the Limit

Since my click of recognition described at the beginning of this chapter, our culture has had another 20 plus years to refine the extremes. By now, more people have gotten the drift that we're out of balance, but we're not sure how to change it! Why? Because our addictive parts don't want to give up the adrenaline rush sparked by a substance like caffeine or the mellowing effect of whatever we're using to make us feel better—temporarily.

DO YOU EVER FEEL STRESSED?

I don't mean a little stressed; I mean overwhelmingly stressed, exhausted, helpless? Has your stress gone on and on with no relief in sight? Have you ever become ill and said, "Thank God. Now I can stay home for a couple of days." Have you ever reached for a glass of wine to help take an edge off your stress? Or taken out your credit card to buy something, believing it will reward you because "after all, I work so hard."

I remember coming home and ritually drinking a glass of wine while I fixed dinner. I remember my mother doing that, too. Except in the back of my mind, I could envision her years later living in a skid-row, single-room-only walk up, penniless, cut off from family, and near death. That vision—and the misery she existed in for years—led me to find other ways to cope with my baggage of fears and stresses.

In the 1970s, researchers predicted that, by the turn of the century, we would work a lot less—perhaps only 32 hours a week. Today, the average person works just over 50 hours a week and has less buying power than people did 30 years ago. In fact, Robert Reich, Secretary of Labor under President Bill Clinton in the 1990s, states in his book *The Future of Success* that the average American works 350 more hours a year than the typical European, ". . . more hours than the notoriously industrious Japanese."[2] In material goods, the United States is the second wealthiest nation on earth (only Norway has a higher standard of living) but emotionally we're like the national debt—stretched to the limit. The old ways of just ignoring the problem no longer work; the new ways of paying attention to how we feel and what we need haven't gained enough credibility.

Fear—It's Like Breathing Air

Fear, and the negativity it inspires, insidiously becomes the under-the-surface motivating force in our lives. Spiritual teacher Eckhart Tolle, in *The Power of Now*, says we're not talking about the fear we need to avoid danger, but psychological fear that shows itself as "...worry, anxiety, nervousness, tension, dread, phobia, the psychological fear that something *might* happen, not of something that is happening now."[3]

Living with a background of fear dulls our senses and dampens our aliveness. Like the drone of traffic for new city dwellers, we cringe at first but adjust over time, although our bodies pay the price with stress, illness, and addictions. It's easy to forget we are whole beings comprised of a mind, body, emotions, and—for many—an awareness of a spiritual element.

Many in this culture have become out of balance, top heavy. It's as if we carry around a huge head on our out-of-shape and (likely) overweight body. Thousands of thoughts pour out of our heads every day about what needs to be done and by when. We curse what will happen if it's not done. The feeling is one of pressure and worry. To cope, thinking, thinking, thinking has become the main way we experience the world.

Escape, Over-thinking, and Anxiety

I often hear from clients how they'd like to "turn off the mind" or "escape from thinking." Ads for Lunesta, a sleep drug introduced in 2005, touts its ability to turn off thinking so

you can get a good-night's sleep. It must work; the American
public spends $650 million a year on sleeping pills.[4] A guest
on The Today Show[5] reported that 42 million prescriptions
were written in the previous year for the three main sleeping
pills: Lunesta, Ambien, and Sonata. Are we really more sleep
deprived or are we influenced by advertisements, or both?

HOW CONNECTED DO YOU FEEL?

Take a moment to ask, "How connected do I feel to my own
body and emotions?" Do you have a daily practice of meditating,
or checking in, so you can pay attention to your feelings and
deep thoughts? Is your mind telling you that you don't have time
for quiet or to meditate?
Does it criticize you because you don't know how?

Harvard research scientist Dr. Gregg Jacobs, author of *The
Ancestral Mind,* writes that over-thinking and anxiety are linked
to what he calls the "Thinking Mind," which is the verbal,
analytical, detached-from-experience and socially conditioned
part of the self.[6] He explained that the human brain developed
in three parts. The oldest part of the brain, which he calls the
Ancestral Mind, is the brain stem or reptilian, instinctual brain.
The next part of the brain to develop was the mammalian
or emotional brain. The newest part is the neocortex, the
reasoning part of the brain in which abstract thinking takes
place.[7] Dr. Jacobs states that the Thinking Mind's future
orientation and constant worrying makes adults more fearful
than children. It also produces chronic anxiety and has led
to an explosion in depression, social isolation, and an over-
reliance on money as the key to happiness.[8]

We're not born with the Thinking Mind as our dominant
brain. When we observe babies and toddlers, we see that

most are born with loving hearts, curious, open minds, and extremely forgiving natures. Our well-meaning parents train children in what's right/wrong, good/bad, important/trivial (often based on the question "what will the neighbors think?"). These become a framework for how we "should" think and behave. What we actually "do" think, feel, or believe takes a back seat, it seems.

Our parents naturally socialize us as they'd been socialized by their parents, using warnings and criticisms to keep us safe and mold our characters. As training continues through childhood, we often get the message (spoken and/or modeled) that the world is a frightening place and there's little we can do about it—except get good grades and go to a good school and land a good job and grow up to have a successful life. That means we get trained to use the Thinking Mind in an attempt to control everything. While this kind of training isn't wrong *per se*, how does it connect today with our overly scheduled, stressful, and increasingly addictive lives? Is this really the best we can do?

Making the Mind-Body Connection

We're born with the awareness of the Ancestral Mind—the emotional, intuitive, non-verbal, present-in-the-here-and-now part of our brain. It's what Robert Bly meant by the "golden orb" of awareness children naturally have at birth in *A Litle Book on the Human Shadow*.[9] After 18 months or so, the Thinking Mind starts to come into play.

Naturally we don't want to get rid of the Thinking Mind and its critical, analytical nature. Rather, we want this part of ourselves to balance with our hearts (mammalian brain, emotional self) and our bodies (reptilian brain, instinctual awareness). That means feeding our Thinking Mind less and our Ancestral Mind more through the practices presented in this book. This creates what scientist Dr. Candace Pert[10] coined the bodymind connection. Specific skills like conscious breathing, emotional awareness, Emotional Freedom Technique (EFT), and imagery serve to reconnect our bodies with our bodies. These practices support our nervous systems to stay balanced, allowing us to manage demands of hectic living more easily and making addiction less appealing. (See Chapter 10 for more on EFT and Chapter 11 for Imagery.)

Children get trained away from their Ancestral Mind through criticism and negativity. My husband has told me more than once, "Lynn, you're so critical." I replied, "I had a great teacher, my dad." Like bees fleeing a broken hive, my criticisms would escape my mouth and hurt Dave, hurt our relationship. Dad was a sweetheart to outsiders, but filled with judgment and anger toward his family. Until age seven, my emotional reservoir was full of enough love to counter Dad's "be carefuls" and guilt-inducing accusations. I'm not sure when his fears overwhelmed my adventurous nature, but by age eight or nine, I started holding back my energy around him. I'd look to see if he approved before I'd play softball with the boys (he'd say no) or I'd read (he'd say yes). After a while, I had no protection from Dad's criticisms. His rejection picked away at my self-esteem. On the outside, I'd look like I didn't take him seriously, but to do that, I had to get small and quiet so I wouldn't be noticed.

Is the Sky Falling?

When we look at survivors of abuse (whether it's physical, emotional, or sexual), it makes sense that fear results from the traumas experienced. As mentioned earlier, beyond the big traumas, it's the day-to-day negativity—the criticisms, perfectionism, irrational expectations—that push us to abandon ourselves. Our once-trusty inner compass gets steered by an invisible web of fear that makes us tune out our own intuition and needs.

That's what is so damaging and pervasive.

That's what we don't want to face as a society.

You see, if we admit the sky is falling, *we might have to address it.* Kids are the ones who'll say the emperor has no clothes, but we adults teach them to pretend, just as we were taught. Eventually those parts of ourselves that we give up create a vulnerability to fear, an emptiness we try to fill, and a false need for ever more stimulation or a need to escape. This addictive coping may come in the form of hard drugs and alcohol or appear subtly as a constant need for entertainment, food, glamour, sugar, diet sodas, or caffeine.

Fear stresses and overloads our mind and body systems. It makes us more vulnerable to illness and less able to tune in to our needs for rest, relaxation, and replenishment—and our need for joy. Fear causes us to believe the addictive illusions of constant advertising. It makes us afraid to unplug because we feel uncomfortable being quiet and listening to the call of our hearts and souls.

What I've Always Wanted

At five, I knew what I wanted. I wanted to dance. I started dance lessons with Percy Venable, 80, of Chinese descent, with a thin, downward curling mustache. He had worked with some of Hollywood's best hoofers. He'd hobble in on his cane when it came time to teach a new routine, then hand the cane to his assistant and demonstrate the new steps. For a few moments, he'd float across the floor, magically lithe and I'd imagine how he looked at 20. Mr. Venable had presence and conveyed his respect and love of the art through his kind words of encouragement. I blossomed under his wise tutelage and worked hard at perfecting my performances. For a year and a half, I looked forward to Saturday morning class and practices during the week. Then, we moved and my next instructor was like a dime store imitation of Neiman Marcus. I didn't like this new instructor and she didn't like me. I quit. By then, I was eight and had lost that part of myself that believed I could be graceful and special. Although I was coordinated, I came to think of myself as being a klutz. I forgot I loved to dance and was good at it. I forgot the part of me that was totally in the moment, vivacious, thrilled to be alive.

WHAT DO YOU REALLY WANT?
WHAT DO YOU MOST WANT OUT OF LIFE?

After the basics are taken care of, most of us want love, belongingness, meaning or a sense of purpose. We also want to enjoy life and make a contribution. We certainly don't *plan* on living in fear or getting trapped in our emotional pasts.

Too many of us do.

The joy that came from feeling powerful and performing well had fed my soul during that time. I'd felt wildly interested in everything. But, fear and negativity chipped away at my enthusiasm and belief in the goodness of life. Today, I realize this is an unconscious process; a child doesn't realize what's happening and adults are often too conditioned to realize that what's wrong is not only an individual problem but a cultural limitation.

Transforming Our Relationship to Fear

It wasn't until my 30s that I was able to melt away the fear that drove my life—like the Wicked Witch melted when Dorothy threw water on her. I re-trained my thoughts and feelings by moving *into* my fears rather than avoiding or denying them.

Despite the fears constantly being broadcast out into the world and those we feel inside, fear is really about perception. Fear is only as powerful as we allow it to be.

We're not going to eradicate fear, but we can create a different relationship with it. We do this by tuning up our heart-strings to rebalance our mind and body and reclaim the energy, vitality, and passion we once had. We can learn to choose how much we allow fear to dominate our lives. We can heal the bodymind split that sets us up for addiction.

Bruce Lipton M.D., a cellular biologist and author of *The Biology of Belief,* says we're always *either* growing and changing *or* protecting ourselves, but we can't do both at the same time.[11] The good that comes when we switch our focus from fear and negativity to love and optimism are astounding. However, first we have to recognize the grip that fear can have over us.

EMBRACE THE FEAR

As you do the exercises in this book, you will realize it's easier than you think to embrace fear. By going into your feelings, you regain the energy, vitality, and aliveness you desire. As you accept the imperfectness of yourself and humanity, you become more loving and compassionate. The Thinking Mind relaxes its hold on you.

Most important, once you learn to manage fear and negativity, you can focus on what you want: more joy, peace, hope, creativity, and vitality. And guess what? Love and optimism promote your growth rather than allow you to stagnat.

"We think we see the world as it is. But we see the world as we are."

~ A Course in Miracles

CHAPTER TWO

Chapter Two:

The End of the World

I F YOU'RE LIKE I WAS, you're probably unaware of much how fear runs your life.

I remember the exact moment I slipped beneath my well-protected façade of "what, me afraid?" I was watching a TV show in the mid 1980s about the 16th-century physician and philosopher Nostradamus. In the program, Nostradamus predicted the end of the world in the year 2000. Since many of his predictions such as both world wars, the rise of the Nazis, and technological advances had materialized, I found myself both mesmerized and terrified. The unconscious floodwaters of fear I'd been holding at bay since childhood rose up and carried me off. As the program continued, I became more and more frightened. By the end, I was convinced that the END of the world was imminent. We were all doomed!

Because Dave was my Prince Charming, I often looked to him to feel safe. But this time, his reassurances weren't working. I didn't want to live feeling terrified that our world would end in 20 years. I didn't want to continue pretending I wasn't afraid. Yet, I had no clue how to get rid of the anxiety that was choking me. That's all I wanted to do: be free of that panicky, out-of-control, the-end-is-coming-any-minute feeling.

At the time, I was an atheist and had developed no spiritual place within me for comfort.

That wasn't always true. Before age seven and the "pony man" molestation, I knew I had a magical golden "light" inside that I could touch—not something I thought about but something that was just there. Now I know that magical place was my connection to Source—a blissful, effortless, body-and-mind experience many young children have. After the "pony man," though, I'd been thrown into the abyss. Glimmers of peace lingered, but they gradually withered until, by age 14, I lived in what seemed like a black hole.

Still, I kept searching for the warmth and comfort that was missing. I filled up with what was available. As a kid, I'd sneak over to the Red Barn and buy a few cents worth of candy, then steal a few cents more. The Red Barn seemed like a setting in a scary movie—a huge dilapidated barn converted to a dirty, smelly store. The man behind the counter frightened me because he had a hole where his nose was supposed to be. I had to be brave to steal candy from him.

As a teenager, I couldn't depend on my parents to guide me and tell me the truth; they were too wrapped up in their drinking and their failing marriage. Thankfully, my grandmother kept me from getting totally lost. No matter what trouble I was in, she always saw the best in me. She shared bits and pieces of Christian Science philosophy, but the words made no sense at the time and my mother's atheistic distrust of all things Christian interfered. My self-esteem trashed, I found myself hanging with my peers on the "fringe"—I deemed them a better fit than the smart, achieving teens around me.

Big "T" and Little "t" Traumas

Trauma has been defined by experts as a *perceived* life-threatening event in which our ability to respond is inhibited and the meaning we create about it damages our ability to connect with ourselves or with others.[12] The big traumas include child abuse, major car accidents, the death of a parent or sibling. These life-changing events make it easy to understand why a child might act out or use substances to escape. Society accepts that children who endure these experiences will have more trouble managing the stresses of life than those who don't.

However, most children experience a subtle yet steady diet of small traumas. According to Dr. Robert Scaer, these little traumas include "motor vehicle accidents, parental alcoholism or mental illness, racial, gender and job discrimination, violence in the media, bullying in schools, personal debt, the insurance industry and the legal system."[13]

Francine Shapiro, Ph.D., the inventor of eye movement desensitization and reprocessing (EMDR), writes that trauma can come in the form of a big "T" or little "t" trauma, with the big "T"s referring to abuse and neglect.[14] More insidious are the small "t" traumas we're taught to *not* pay much attention to. But the little painful events of childhood pack a bigger punch than we realize. These include overly critical or demanding parents, the big brother who beats up his siblings, or the "not enough" feeling when a sibling gets praised. Also included is the guilt and shame used by parents to make their children behave. (I certainly used these "weapons" of child management when I was raising my son, though I notice with my granddaughter, my parenting skills have vastly improved.)

Dr. Scaer also defines trauma as " . . . an experience that involves a threat to life while the victim is in a state of relative helplessness."[15] Whether someone becomes traumatized or comes away unscathed also depends on the meaning the victim gives the event. For example, Dr. Scaer notes that the female corporate executive whose male superior harasses her feels and responds differently if she bears the burden of having an abusive father.[16]

Certainly we think we survive the hurtful little "t" events just fine. However, depending on the degree of pain we bring into adulthood and the amount of energy it takes to keep our pain in check, some of us develop a prick in our natural resilience. It's like that small tear in a piece of fabric weakening the whole. As little traumas accumulate, they affect the way our brains process stress, which in turn generates a vulnerability. We seek to fix what bothers us with something outside ourselves—food, alcohol, drugs, work, and so on. As my friend and empowerment coach Leah Silvestre says, "We try to fix the internals with the externals."

But I now know that trauma rips away love, trust, and comfort; it leaves fear in its wake. Like a lion trainer whose whip was his critical tongue, my dad was a fear-trainer— and a master at it. If my dad hadn't installed in me a variety of fear buttons, I might have made it into adolescence emotionally intact.

As a little girl, I remember feeling my dad's anxiety emanate from him like heat waves off hot concrete. Like most magical thinking children, I wondered why I made him feel that way—what was wrong with *me*. I noticed his bitten-to-the-quick bloody fingers from chewing his cuticles. I remember my mother yelling at him about it. "Bob, knock it off," she'd yell. He'd wait for her to leave the room and then frantically bite, bite, bite.

I also remember his constant smoking and nervous squints, his drinking, and especially his immersion in sports of all kinds. He'd have the TV tuned to football or golf, the radio plugged into his ear announcing baseball, and the sports page of the newspaper spread out before him. If we kids made noise or disturbed him, we were in big trouble. I feared him because he'd lash out at the slightest real or perceived mistake. And worst of all, he suspected we were always doing something wrong. That made me feel so guilty, I'd confess to "crimes" I hadn't even committed.

In contrast, my mother lived much the same day to day—numb or depressed with occasional bursts of yelling, "Be quiet; just go outside and play." My dad, though, could be really funny and silly, especially with people outside the family who saw him as a great guy. Fueled by a couple of beers, he sometimes initiated wild water fights that my peace-loving mom did her best to keep outside of the house. He played games with us, built us stilts, and made us kites to fly on windy days. He found a way to buy our first horse with his gambling proceeds. And when we were little, he tucked us into bed with a prayer.

However, the "good stuff" never balanced out his quick-tempered behavior. And we couldn't predict which Dad would show up on any given day.

PROGRAMMING OCCURS BEFORE AGE SIX

Let's say you're four years old and witness your father hitting your mother. It's not the only time your dad has hit your mom. Petrified, you feel helpless to do anything about their behavior. You grow up and forget about these painful times. You get married to a nice man who, after a few years, starts hitting you. This reflects what biologist Dr. Bruce Lipton stated in his audio program The Wisdom of Your Cells—that most of our subconscious programming occurs before the age of six.

Our Unconscious Can Hurt Us

Like an iceberg that's 90 percent under the surface of the water, the big "T" and little "t" fears accumulated on the road to adulthood remain unseen until an event triggers an awakening—like my Nostrodamus night of terror or the terrorist attacks of 9-11. Fear could result from divorce, job loss, illness—anything that disrupts habitual patterns and brings up issues we've valiantly run away from. How frightened and alone we feel! How much we long to be loved, comforted, and accepted for who we are!

As an addiction counselor, I work with women dealing with food and weight concerns through my Take Loving Charge™ groups. One woman I'll call Jill was startled to realize she was a food addict. In a group session, Jill laughed as she said, "I know it's silly because I weighed over three hundred pounds, but I only felt afraid after I had gastric by-pass surgery and was unable to eat the type of food I was used to eating. It threw me into a tailspin. I wanted to die and stopped eating entirely. Only after my doctor's intervention and forcing myself to eat according to the plan could I tell that the anorexia I was now in was the flip side of the binge eating I'd done for most of my life. It wasn't eating or not eating I was afraid of; I was afraid of facing life without my buffer—food." Eating gave Jill the comfort she had longed for all her life.

We Live in a Culture of Fear

In 1994, I knew my mother was dying, the doctor confirmed it, but she could never acknowledge it. Trying to give her the chance to talk about her death, I asked her if she thought she was dying. She said emphatically, "No, I'm not dying." End of discussion. She passed away within two weeks.

I believe humans have at least a vague, existential fear of death. Intellectually, we know and accept that we will die—someday. But as my mother experienced, the concept isn't real; it's out there and far away.

We Americans pride ourselves on being tough, fearless, and, above all, independent. When I see the bumper sticker NO FEAR proudly displayed on a truck or SUV, I can always predict that it belongs to a young man. I wish I could sit down with him and say, "Hey, so what if you're afraid once in a while? The big secret is *so is everyone else*." Yet if I'd been asked if I was afraid at age 25, I would have puffed up my braless, feminist chest and emphatically stated, "No way."

Intellectually, we deny what our hearts know is true. We think too much to cover up our feelings because to admit being afraid is to admit being vulnerable. Vulnerability isn't valued in American culture. In fact, we beat ourselves up for being afraid because admitting it messes with our carefully constructed self-image of bravery. We assume that others hold a secret that we don't. "They aren't afraid; I must be a wimp."

Fear is nothing new in this culture—with much to be afraid of from terrorism alerts to new varieties of cancer, from violence to flesh-eating diseases, from obesity to avian bird flu. With the prevalent influence of mass media, fear is fed by the daily headlines about crime and the constant "if it bleeds, it leads" programs.

Barry Glassner, author of *The Culture of Fear*, states that a fear mongers' focus on crime makes the average person believe crime has increased in the U.S. while it actually plunged in the 1990s. Their statistics about school violence, breast cancer, teen drug addiction, and more terrify us. Glassner points out that this false fear distracts us from real social problems—lack of health care, the increasing gap between rich and poor, the prevalence of guns. As Michael Moore spelled out in his movie *Bowling for Columbine*, The United States has about the same number of guns per capita as Canada does, but about 15,000 Americans are killed with guns each year versus a few hundred in Canada.[17] The average 18 year old has witnessed 200,000 acts of violence (including 40,000 murders) on TV and movies.[18] But we don't really let ourselves absorb the subtle effects that visual images have on our psyches. A University of Washington professor of psychiatry estimated there would be 10,000 fewer murders each year in the U.S. and 700,000 fewer assaults had TV never been invented.[19]

John Bradshaw, guru of the adult children of alcoholics movement and author of *Homecoming*[20], says that addiction is a need for control. I agree.

But exactly what are we trying to control?

Our feelings in general; our FEAR in particular.

In my experience, we do anything to avoid fear because it makes us feel vulnerable.

An addiction to fear keeps us in an emotional never-never land—not too alive, not too dead. Connie Mugas, a shaman, calls this state the "walking dead." To me that means we hate feeling caught by our addictions, but we're afraid of making of a change because we want to feel safe and in control.

REAL-LIFE EXAMPLES OF FEAR-BASED ADDICTION

Geri's alcohol addiction is a symptom of the fear she feels underneath. Because fear, her primary addiction, unconsciously tells her that she's bad, she lives within a narrow emotional band of "bad" that feels safe and familiar. It feeds her addiction to alcohol. While in recovery, Geri gets anxious when she moves too far into feeling happy. So she cycles between months of sobriety (and feeling okay) and going back to drinking (and feeling bad). Although Geri didn't realize it, she was addicted to the very fear she hated.

* * *

Janet, an addicted shopper, primarily felt unlovable and invisible. The fourth of five girls, she grew up in a stable home but didn't receive much individual attention and what she did get was material—clothes, toys, horseback riding lessons. As a child, she often felt empty and sad. She married a man who repeated the dynamics of her family; he made good money, but rarely paid attention to her needs. She had the American dream—a beautiful home and two healthy children—but still felt cheated, unfulfilled. That couldn't make up for the dread she felt inside.

* * *

My friend Bill Manville, author of *Cool, Hip, and Sober*[21] told me about his ex-girlfriend Joanie, a successful architect whose addiction was work. Growing up, Joanie adored her father and felt loved by him. Even 50 years later, she couldn't say a negative thing about him. Bill surmised that while her father loved Joanie, he criticized her a lot. As a result, in her relationships with men, she couldn't take criticism at all. The unconscious pain from being criticized still had power over her because she'd never addressed it. And if she faced the pain, she'd have to re-evaluate her relationship with her father. So by avoiding it, she remained addicted to her fear of being criticized. This addiction both protected the ideal image of her father and kept her from changing. When fear is unconscious, addiction takes charge.

As Bill was telling me this, I felt an immediate kinship with Joanie because my dad was also critical. In the early years of my marriage to Dave, I wouldn't let him say anything that was remotely critical because I'd immediately get defensive. Defensiveness doesn't make for good problem solving or for closeness. To Dave, I wouldn't let him say anything that was remotely critical because I'd immediately get defensive. Defensiveness doesn't make for good problem solving or for closeness.

* * *

My client Dwayne, returning to me after a year's absence, told me once again his doctor insisted he lose weight. He clearly described his addiction to fear when he said, with a look of anguish on his face, "This (eating problem) is all I know. I'm afraid to give it up. I've been to Weight Watchers, but I gained it all back. If I keep going like this, I'm going to get sick and then I'll have to do

The more we reach for the doughnut without being conscious of how we're feeling—anxious, stressed, unhappy— the more we cement in the fear that's driven us to reach for it in the first place. In fact, the more we deny our fears with distractions, the more compulsive we become. The simple act of repetition forms a habit and wires into our physiology the "need" for more distractions, in whatever form they may take.

The movie *What the Bleep Do We Know?*[22] features research demonstrating that the brain's neural pathways are stimulated by repetitive emotions. With repetition, some neural connections (fear, anger) deepen while possible connections that are unused (peace, hope, love) wither. The more we feel stressed and afraid, the more susceptible we are to those states and the more addicted we become to them.

Pamela Peeke, M.D., author of *Fighting Fat after Forty*, backs up this idea by saying, "When Toxic Stress (chronic, uninterrupted stress) is allowed to permeate your daily existence, it can result in self-destructive behaviors. These behaviors include anything perceived as an antidote to emotional pain such as inappropriate eating, excessive alcohol consumption and the use of tobacco and drugs."[23]

The addictive cycle is so powerful because it creates a feedback loop. It works like this: First we experience an uncomfortable feeling, often unconscious, such as anxiety. Next, to make the barely registered anxiety go away or to avoid it, we work, watch TV, smoke pot, or eat. Working stimulates an adrenaline rush and makes us feel useful;

watching TV and smoking pot zone us out; food comforts us and makes us feel nurtured or soothed. "Ah, now I don't feel a thing," we think. Anxiety feelings get muffled, but only until the next day when the cycle starts over. Of course, the longer we put off dealing with anxiety and problems, the more they accumulate. With a reservoir of repressed feelings inside, we're more easily affected by stress and more likely to seek the relief of a quick fix.

Here's the kicker. The act of running from our fears by taking or doing something to get rid of them makes us *more* fearful. Our physiology both responds to fear and becomes wired for fear. Attempts to avoid or numb out anxiety don't work. What does work? To go into our feelings by acknowledging them, releasing them, and replacing them with peaceful, neutral, or loving thoughts and feelings.

Advertisers Prefer Us Uncomfortable

People get bombarded with images of wonderful things to buy that will "transform" our lives. According to Olivia Mellan in her book *Overcoming Overspending*, "By one estimate, American kids have seen an average of 360,000 ads by the time they graduate from high school."[24]

ARE YOU ADDICTED TO FEAR?
You may accept that people, maybe even you, are stressed and resort to addictive coping. But perhaps you question if it's possible to actually be addicted to fear. Fear is something everyone experiences but hates to admit to. Deep down, they believe they aren't supposed to feel it anyway.

How do you perceive fear in your life?

Nothing sells like fear. Advertisers amplify normal human fears and worries; it makes them lots of money.

Before television, we'd see advertising in magazines, on radio, and on billboards. But TV, with its colorful storybook images and familiar themes, has made the biggest impact on our psyches. They penetrate our subconscious without our even being aware.

In 1997, federal regulations governing advertising changed and gave pharmaceutical companies the green light to advertise on television. These ads now dominate. Picture this scenario: Sunday evening, the family is watching a favorite TV program. Next commercial break, a loving couple embraces on a sandy beach gazing at the dark blue ocean. The message? If you want what this couple plans to have all weekend long— wink, wink—you need Cialis, a drug for erectile dysfunction (ED). More programming, then another commercial. A handsome 30-ish man wakes up after a restful night's sleep and happily yawns. The message? Ask your doctor about Lunestra, a sleeping pill.

Advertising like this supports our consumer culture. It also feeds addiction. For some, going shopping quells anxiety, but it can set up the problem of overspending. Says Mellan, "We've created a culture that not only fosters overspending, but makes it almost impossible to kick the habit."[25]

HOW DOES TV ADVERTISING AFFECT YOU?
To become more aware of how advertising affects you, see what types appeal to you. Notice if you get up to have a snack during commercials. Pay attention to how many food commercials have been playing during your favorite TV shows. Then for the next two weeks, mute all TV commercials. (If you have TiVO, you can just zip through the commercials.) Be observant. Did you snack less during those two weeks or feel any different by not paying attention to commercials?

Are we never supposed to feel afraid? Of course not, and it's not black or white. Fear is good because it can alert us to danger or cause us to search for new solutions. But fear too often makes us run away from ourselves and to the nearest mall to buy, buy, buy. Advertisers know that Americans have bought into the ideal that "more stuff" equals "happiness."

According to the National Opinion Research Center, though, the "apogee of happiness in America, was in 1957, when the average American family had one car, one TV, a smaller house with one bathroom, no air conditioning, no clothes dryer, no stereo—in fact, less than half the stuff we have now." The article states that the correlation between wealth and happiness pretty much disappears once basic human needs are met.[26]

Isn't it time to be aware that just hearing advertisers say "newer is better" simply doesn't make it so?

The Consequences of Fear

Why should we make this shift? Are you stressed, exhausted, your blood-pressure too high? Do you eat or drink too much or struggle to get out of bed to go to a job you hate, just for the paycheck? Researchers state that over 80 percent of doctor visits are stress related.

Preventable illnesses affect the quality of life of large numbers of Americans and cost us billions. And that's not even addressing all of the addictive coping we do. Illnesses signal being out of balance, out of love with ourselves, and disconnected from the true needs of our mind, our body, and our spirit.

The consequences of living in fear—whether it's conscious or not—affect every aspect of our lives. I realize that fear locked up my joy and humor and passion. It put these emotions in jail where the most vital, creative parts of myself languished for years. Then, in seventh grade, I met Vicky (now Victoria, who is still my best buddy 40 years later). She teased me mercilessly about being "so serious." Still, it was serious work surviving in my household where I never knew if my mom would be gaily dancing to Barbra Streisand songs when I got home from school or holed up in her bedroom yelling at us to be quiet.

Yes, the happy-go-lucky kid I'd once been was already turning in to what my husband later dubbed The General. But there really isn't much funny about this part of me. The General is the taskmaster—the critical, demanding, controlled and controlling part of myself that gets a lot done in a joyless way. Today, when I find myself less than happy, I know I need to say good-bye to the list-making General and hello to the non-scheduled, lighthearted "Goldilocks" who helps me play.

Get It All Done RIGHT

I'm not alone in having The General rule me. I think most adults possess a driver that pushes them to get "stuff" done and done RIGHT! (Done perfectly would be even better.) This driver is motivated by fearful thoughts—"I won't have enough, I won't be liked, I won't look good enough." It makes us feel guilty if we don't cross everything off the list.

But we can only take being locked in jail so long. We want to break out. And that's what addictions do. They break us out of jail, even though we may only have a weekend pass.

The Goldilocks part of me doesn't need to break out of jail. She lets me know she wants to sit out in the backyard on a spring day, bask in the sun and look at the wind rustling through the trees. Too often The General doesn't let her. Back to jail I go. On Fridays when my granddaughter visits, Goldilocks takes charge and gently ignores the General. The child inside me laughs with delight as my granddaughter and I watch the bubbles float over the house and disappear. We play hide and seek under the covers and run madly around the house. (I confess: The rest of the week, I have trouble letting Goldilocks come out to play—but not on Fridays.)

When the General used to run the show full-time, my stress levels went way up. Stress is like compounding interest; it carries over from day to day, but instead of accruing something positive like money, the body goes into debt. Unless the body is given the chance to replenish and restore itself, serious illnesses like heart disease and psychosomatic illnesses can occur. It works like this: unresolved negative emotions create and exacerbate stress. Stress reduces the effectiveness of our immune system. When the immune system is impaired, it reduces the body's ability to protect itself from illness. At age 20 or 30, we bounce back quickly. At age 40 or 50, the accumulated strain shows in the lines on our faces, the stoop of our backs, the extra weight we carry, and the lists of ailments we take to our doctors.

When I'm in my General mode, my body tenses, my shoulders tighten, and my body contracts. This tension blocks my ability to feel. In the past, I had shut down to deal with the pain inside—joy, vitality and aliveness were also blocked. Although it acted as a sort of protection, an equal and opposite reaction always occurred. By suppressing the painful or "negative" feelings, my capacity to experience the "positive" feelings became muted as well. Numbness was not an escape; it was a wasteland looking to be filled.

In his book *Living, Loving & Learning*, Dr. Leo Buscaglia says the opposite of fear is not hate but apathy. Apathy limits us from trying new experiences.[27] I see this in teens who are so afraid of failing that they won't try to learn to ride a motorbike or play a sport. "I won't be able to do it right. I'll feel humiliated," they protest. So they lapse into apathy and depression. They feel numb. Then they cut themselves with a knife to feel *something*, anything, to relieve their emotional pain. Their concerned parents take them to a doctor who prescribes anti-depressants.

Because we're afraid, we allow ourselves to be victimized. I see this over and over in our current work environment with layoffs and mergers and offshore hiring. Today, companies expect a smaller number of people to do the same volume of work as before. Statistically, productivity has increased in this country—but at what price?

A friend who has an already demanding job was asked, and then told, she had to add a big project to her schedule. She said no at first and the manager told her to either do that or get fired, so she said yes. But every time I see her, she's overwhelmed and stressed with the demands of her work. When we are this afraid of losing our jobs, our self-esteem and our self-care goes right out the window.

We Can Choose Between Fear and Love

My Nostradamus wake-up call launched me on my own quest to get rid of fear. An impossible quest, as I discovered. I've learned that as long as we try to get rid of something, fight it, overcome it, control it (think "War on Drugs"), we attract more of the same. But turning our attention to what we want—love, peace, joy, even a new boyfriend—begins to neutralize what we *don't* want and create what we *do* want.

Eventually, I discovered the perfect antidote to fear. It's love.

After weeks of sleeplessness, anxiety, clinging to my husband, and feeling sick to my stomach, I declared, "No. I won't live like this. I have to find a better way." By divine timing, my sister-in-law Diane gave me a Christian-based study book (the agnostic within me freaked out) called *The Course in Miracles*. I spent the next few years studying and practicing how to turn my attention away from fear to focus on what I wanted—love.

It was hard work, but I learned to change my relationship to fear. Not to get rid of it because that's an illusion. I learned to face my fears and release them using the skills I teach in this book. I learned to focus on increased peace, joy, love, connection with my own heart and soul, and deeper connections with the people I care about.

At the time of the Lacy Peterson murder in our hometown of Modesto, California, my 27-year-old daughter-in-law and new mother, Gina, talked about her fears of being kidnapped or harmed. She had gone to school with Lacy, so Lacy's murder was more than an anonymous name in the paper to her. She told me she couldn't stop thinking about what happened to Lacy. I nodded and listened for a while, then I said, "Yes, scary things happen. Life is precious and things happen over which we have no control. But we do have a choice about what we focus on and I've learned that focusing on fear makes me more afraid."

Can We Find a Safe Harbor?

Growing up challenges even the most loving of families. We all bring a certain level of anxiety with us to adulthood. The world is a more volatile place than it was 30 years ago. I believe people feel less protected and more aware of life's fragility. Aren't we more nervous about war, terrorist attacks, stock market drops, safety of our children, social security, retirement funding? Like quicksand, everything we hold dear can change quickly. The unknown prevails. Will I walk out my front door and get shot—have a heart attack—come down with cancer? What can I hold on to? Where can I place my trust?

DOES LOVE HAVE A FOOTHOLD?

Turn on any news channel and you'll catch the top stories of the day about the current weather disaster, school mayhem, drug busts, murders, rape, and torture. It appears that love doesn't have much of a foothold in our scary, dangerous world. But stop, think, and observe. "Do I see mayhem in my family or neighborhood? How much am I letting the media's obsession with drama color my world?"

Can you go to the other side? Can you shift from relying on the *external* and a belief that "I'm okay only if everything out there is okay" to an *internal* safe harbor?

I remember how alone, frightened, and confused I felt before I decided to find a way to be happier and less self-destructive. It's been a long hit-and-miss road to nurture the courage and skills that have helped me let go of my addictive traps—so I could trust myself and humanity more—and so I could love more.

I know, I know. Love? What does love mean, anyway? How can love make everything better? It can't in the sense that love will *not* make life perfect. If we look to TV sitcoms as models, love is cynically talking to your best friend and scheming to "get" the guy who is hot. Or, we believe it's the steamy sex of a romance novel (the absolute biggest fiction sellers) with the hero rescuing the damsel and living happily ever after. In real life, steamy passion sometimes gives way to mundane things like working, cooking dinner, and cleaning poopy diapers.

I'm talking about a deeper meaning of love. In *A Course in Miracles*, fear means all negative feelings such as anger, judgment, cynicism, resentment, and especially guilt. Love is the other side: trust, gentleness, joy, generosity, patience and acceptance. Wouldn't love go over well in a boardroom?

Learning to love is a practice of choice. It's tough to choose to be patient rather than demanding, generous rather than stingy, kind and appreciative rather than cranky. I hung out in my well-worn groove of negativity and it was familiar, but not very peaceful. With practice, I discovered that love gave me a rudder that steered me through the rough seas of life—much more than fear ever could.

Choosing to love the best in myself while accepting my warts and bumps and spurts of bitchiness encouraged me to rise above the pettiness. Love gave me a place of safety inside and reconnected me to that soft, magical place in my heart. Love allowed me to trust that no matter what happens OUT THERE, I know I'm okay.

Choosing to love was hard work because it was different than what I was used to. But doing so taught me to become gentle and accepting more than critical and demanding. Rather than hopping from crisis to crisis like a Mexican jumping bean, love created a sweet leap of faith so I could face the dragon *and* be more selective about what I allowed in from the world's constant barrage of fearful messages.

How can you, too, learn to choose love over fear? Hint: the exercises in this book await.

" **Americans are addicted** to being something they're not. They're addicted to **things**.

- Oprah Winfrey

Things and conditions can give you pleasure, but they **cannot** give you joy.[29] "

- Eckhart Tolle

CHAPTER THREE

Chapter Three:

The "Lite" Addictions

HAVE YOU EVER been so stressed that you've reached for the closest piece of chocolate or run down to the corner to get a latté to feel better?

If so, you're not alone. Every day, millions of Americans are overwhelmed and exhausted. They seek to distract themselves with what advertisers say provides "RELIEF."

You may be familiar with the challenges of being fully addicted to alcohol and drugs, but what is a "lite" addiction? If you or I eat chocolate, go shopping, or stop off at McDonald's when we feel stressed, does that mean we're addicts?

Most of us don't think about addiction much—unless it affects the "other" guy. The mocha I drink every day to get through the afternoon (Starbucks, 400 calories and 22 grams of fat), the three hours of zoning in front of the TV to unwind, the Saturday shopping binge—these *don't* make us addicts, right?

We believe addictions are only the ones easy to spot— you know, Sam, the guy at the end of the block who keeps changing jobs and wives. We see him drinking a beer at 9:00 a.m. and know he has a problem. However, the insidious monster we live with (but don't see) is the layering of a little addiction here, a bit more there. Together, they add up to a "sort of alive, but sort of not" kind of life.

We coast along keeping our greatest passions and our deepest pains at bay. It's not the lattés or the TV or the shopping that presents the problem. It's what drives a desire to numb out—to live life in a "not really happy, not really sad" but emotionally detached manner. Or, opposite to numbing out, we create the next adrenaline high by blasting through our days with as much caffeine or diet soda as possible to keep us wired.

We're dealing with what Judith Wright calls "soft" addictions or habits, compulsive behaviors, or recurring moods or thought patterns.[30] I call them "lite" addictions. They satisfy a surface desire but ignore or block finding satisfaction at a deeper need. These soft addictions numb us to our feelings and our spiritual awareness. How? By substituting a superficial high or sense of activity for genuine feeling or accomplishment. Let's look at a number of these.

Shopping as a "Lite" Addiction

In 2002, Myvesta, a web-based financial health center, conducted a random survey of 1,000 people and found 52 percent of those surveyed experienced mood changes before or after shopping. Myvesta found that 49 percent of them spend money to escape problems or relieve stress. Even more startling was that most women who were stopped on the way out of a department store didn't even know what they had in their bags. Steve Rhode, a financial expert and founder of Myvesta, states: "Half of American adults are struggling to control excessive spending and debt, and are failing."[31]

In *I Shop, Therefore I Am*[32] April Lane Benson, Ph.D., notes that likely 5 percent of the population in the United States are full-fledged compulsive shoppers. A Merck Family Fund poll found that 72 percent of Americans say people buy things as a substitute for something missing in their lives and 80 percent believe too many people are "addicted" to shopping.[33]

REAL-LIFE EXAMPLES OF "LITE" SHOPPING ADDICTIONS

Joan, stressed at the end of a long week at work, goes into Target to get school supplies for her daughter Maggie. An hour and a half later—and $150 lighter—she leaves the store feeling elated. When she gets home and her husband asks her where she's been, she says, "Shopping," but proceeds to lie about how much she spent. The rest of the night, she feels guilty. She swears that "next time" she'll be better.

* * *

Another client I'll call Sharon told me that when her adult daughter visited at Christmas time, she told Sharon that she wanted her to be more of a mother to her. Sharon looked at me, shrugged, and said, "I don't understand. I take her shopping. What does she want from me?" Sharon's daughter is asking for connection with her mother, the kind of connection it seems hard to find in our mad-rushing-around world of separate activities and little face-to-face time.

Connection comes when we share enough realness with each other to break the barrier of separation experienced in our individual lives.

Note these statistics:[34]

- 40 percent of women say they lie to their spouses about what they've spent on their purchases.
- The number of women seeking bankruptcy in the past 25 years has increased 662 percent. In 2003, more women sought bankruptcy protection than graduated from college.
- Almost three-quarters of Americans admit that their home lives suffer because of debt.
Here are more statistics of note:[35]
- The Roper Organization found 3 out of 5 women owning up to shopping to relieve stress.

- The number of shopping centers in the U.S. outnumbers the high schools.
- A Merck Family Fund poll found that 72% of Americans say people buy things as a substitute for something missing in their lives; 80% believe too many people are "addicted" to shopping.
- Publicis, an ad agency, found 55% of men and women acknowledge buying while feeling depressed, only to regret their purchases later.

Writes Olivia Mellan in *Overcoming Overspending*: "Overspending can also be a way of numbing ourselves to past or present fears, anxieties, or injuries. Like eating, spending is often the solace we learn to seek when we're feeling lonely, sad, frightened, helpless, unfulfilled, or unlovable. Maybe it's not really love or happiness, we may admit to ourselves, but it's better than nothing."[36]

Janet, 32, a wife, mother of a two and five year old and business owner came to my office fashionably dressed and clutching a 32-ounce Diet Coke in her hand. Later she told me she drank four of those a day. (I wanted to ask how much time she spent in the bathroom, but didn't think she'd appreciate my humor at this stage of counseling.) When she made the appointment, she said she was having relationship problems. What came out was the tremendous amount of pressure and anxiety she felt trying to keep all the balls in her life going.

Our conversation went like this:

"There's never enough time. The only relief I get is when I'm shopping. I buy things I don't even need. When I'm at Nordstrom and I see the perfect pink bag to go with my new outfit, it's like all my problems disappear and I'm not boring little Janet from the Central Valley, but Paris Hilton or Ivana Trump. My husband doesn't know how high our credit cards balances are and if he did..." A few tears slid down Janet's face and I offered her the tissue box.

"Do you know what they are?" I asked.

"I don't want to know. I just keep paying the minimum. If I was any more out of control...God what is wrong with me?" Janet looked at her lap, a pile of tissues gathering.

"Even though this will sound like an odd question, how is the shopping helping you?" I asked.

Janet's eyes closed for a moment and her face flushed. She said, "It makes me feel like somebody. If my friends see all my things and I look happy to them, I feel okay. Sometimes I know that's not true. Sometimes I feel horrible because I'm putting our family in debt. We could lose everything."

I learned toward her and said gently, "It sounds like shopping relieves stress and makes you feel better, for the moment. If you take the judgment out of it for a moment, you can always come back to it."

Then I looked her in the eye and we shared a small smile. "What you said is, shopping is the one thing in your life that makes you a 'somebody.' But the real question is finding out how to be you. What's going to make you truly feel good about yourself? Who are you, really, underneath all the purchases? Let's work together to find healthier ways to deal with stress. Let's find out who you are and what you need. It's probably hard to imagine, but learning to go within to nurture yourself is a great antidote to stress. More than that, it's the yellow brick road to find the person you were meant to be. You'll also find that, as you learn to love and accept yourself, your urge to shop addictively will diminish. You'll discover a joy in life that shopping can never provide."

Internet Porn as a "Lite" Addiction

"Internet porn is the crack cocaine of sex addiction,"[37] reports Robert Weiss, LCSW, CAS, director of the Sexual Recovery Institute in Los Angeles, California. He says that if sugar or food is what women reach for, Internet porn is often the guy's choice and it has reached epidemic portions. Weiss's sexual recovery website states that 40 million Americans watch porn a year.[38]

Kirk Stockham is the forensic investigator who discovered maps of the Berkeley Marina in the computer of Scott Peterson, convicted for the murder of Lacy Peterson. Stockham told me that almost every computer he searches doing his investigations has Internet porn on it.

According to Patrick Carnes, Ph.D., sex addiction expert, in the United States alone, Internet porn is a $10 billion industry and worldwide, it's $57 billion. To give a sense of how it's grown, in 1998, there were 14 million sites and in 2003 there were 260 million sites. One quarter of all Internet search requests are porn-related and 40 percent of those who have an addiction problem are women. Significantly, 70 percent of Internet porn is accessed on work computers.[39]

I can think of half a dozen women who've told me their partners have an Internet porn addiction problem. What do I mean by "problem"? Wives request that their husbands not sit and watch porn for hours, which they agree to but rarely keep their agreements. This activity harms and even destroys marriages. As reported in Utne magazine, "At the 2003 meeting of the American Academy of Matrimonial Lawyers, some two-thirds of attending lawyers said the Internet played a significant role in divorces that year, pointing a finger at online pornography. Seven or eight years ago, pornography had an almost nonexistent role in divorce..."[40]

It looks like this addiction is about sex, but it's not really. It's about getting high, altering how you feel. And it carries all the components of any other addiction--isolation, lying, hiding, denial, damaged love relationships, lost jobs, money problems. Yes, it may start out as innocent stress relief and stay there as a "lite" addiction, but for millions of people, it becomes more than an occasional quick fix.

ASSESS YOUR BEHAVIOR

Go to the Addictive Coping Assessment at the end of the chapter and check out your own addictive behavior. Although you may find it hard to get honest with yourself, it can be freeing to do so. Also ask someone close to you to assess your behavior.

Think of addiction as a continuum. (Go to page 58 for explanation). Experiment with what it's like to shut off the computer and not watch any porn , or not shop, or not have a drink, for two weeks. If you can't make it for even two weeks, seek professional help. Go to a Sex Addicts Anonymous meeting, visit an AA meeting, seek counseling, or both. If you determine you're moving toward the out-of-control side of the addiction continuum, you must get help. That means contacting an addiction professional and taking action now.

Gambling as a "Lite" Addiction

Gambling, like many addictive behaviors, is sometimes a "lite" addiction, sometimes a serious one, depending on where the user falls on the continuum of addictive behaviors.

Think of it this way. When we're pushing the buttons of a flashing slot machine, we don't have to deal with the anxiety of an unhappy marriage. The rush we feel makes problems go away, at least temporarily. I like to gamble occasionally, averaging once or twice a year. My dad loved to gamble; in the

1960s, he played poker in Gardena, California, one of the few legal poker places at the time. But he only spent his budgeted amount, didn't put us into debt, and was lucky enough to buy our horse with his winnings. With the easy availability of casinos and Internet gambling today, I wonder if he might have developed a problem.

Gambling has become big business. An article in *The Modesto Bee* states, "In 2004, more than 200 tribes in 28 states grossed an estimated $18.5 billion from more than 400 bingo halls and casinos. The Bureau of Economic Analysis reports Americans spent about 1% of their total after-tax income in 2003 on gambling."[41] California's gambling revenue exploded to more than $13 billion in 2004, according to a report released by the state attorney general's office, and puts gambling as one of the state's largest industries.[42] Gaming industry advocates say that only 2% to 3% percent of the population develops a pathological relationship to gambling.[43] Another gambling expert, Carlton K. Erickson, Ph.D. who is Director of the Addiction Science Research and Education Center at the University of Texas at Austin's College of Pharmacy states that pathological gambling affects 1% to 2% of the population with roughly 4% to 6% of all gamblers.[44]

Dorothy, 78 years old and a retired school teacher whose husband of 52 years had passed away, discovered that going to the gaming casino made her feel better. She said, "When I put those nickels or dimes into the slot machine, I feel a little thrill. I don't just sit there though, I talk to people. And I egg 'em on when they're winning and cheer 'em up when they're losing. It makes me feel less lonely than just sitting around at home missing Bill." Dorothy's friends and family became concerned because she was spending more money on the slots and less time with them. While she was okay financially, they were concerned that all this spending would jeopardize her future finances.

According to the authors of *One More Time*, Dorothy (and women in general) are particularly vulnerable to slot machine addictive tendencies because they've been caretakers all their lives. The elderly are also more vulnerable because of the loneliness and emptiness they face as their partners and friends die.[45][46]

Fast Food as a "Lite" Addiction

Who doesn't like fast food once in a while? On any day in the U.S., 25 percent of the adult population visits a fast food restaurant. In 1970, Americans spent $6 billion dollars on fast food. In 2001, we spent more than $110 billion.[47]

The surprise movie hit *Super Size Me*[48] documented writer/ director Morgan Spurlock eating nothing but fast food for 30 days. Because he ate 90 meals in 30 days, the effects of the high fat and sugar on his body were concentrated. He gained 30 pounds (a pound a day) and had such toxic changes in his liver that two of the three doctors who supervised his experiment wanted him to stop before the month ended.

While fast food is only part of the whole food issue, it's a significant factor. Eric Schlosser, author of *Fast Food Nation*, writes that about half of the money families use to buy food gets spent at restaurants, mainly fast food restaurants.[49] Combined with diets that are high in fats and sugar (highly addictive), people today are less active and work longer hours than the older generation did.

The medical literature classifies a person as obese if he or she has a Body Mass Index (BMI) of 30 or higher...' BMI is a measurement that includes both weight and height. A woman who is five-foot-five and weighs 132 pounds has a BMI of 22, which is considered normal. If she gains 18 pounds, her BMI rises to 25 and she's overweight. If she gains 50 pounds, her BMI reaches 30 and she's considered obese. Today, about 44 million American adults are obese.

Sugar as a "Lite" Addiction

It's not only drugs or alcohol or work that we become addicted to. One of the biggest unaddressed addictions is *sugar* in its various enticing forms. When I go into my husband's office, I find piles of donuts or jars of candy around. At Christmas time, I go to Starbucks and order a decaf eggnog latté. It's syrup, milk, and coffee—and it's yummy. Nurse and guided imagery practitioner Maureen Minnehan-Jones says lattés are like mother's milk—sweet and warm. No wonder this treat tastes comforting. It makes sense that, in the midst of our hectic, busy, never-enough-time lives, we need some motherly comfort.

My client Jessica always had a happy smile always and at age 55, she looked 45. In her first appointment with me, she told me she was addicted to Snickers bars and had to lose at least 40 pounds or her doctor was going to "fire" her. Here's Jessica's story.

"Jessica, why do you think you're addicted to Snickers?" I asked.

"Because I can't stop—even when I know it's really bad for me."

Jessica said it started innocently enough when she was a secretary for a large insurance firm. She liked her job yet she got tired and bored in the afternoon so she'd have a Snickers to break the tedium or reward herself for a project well done. The candy gave her a welcome lift. In the beginning, she'd have a Snickers two or three days a week. No big deal.

"But then every day after lunch, I'd start obsessing about the yummy, nutty, carmel, chocolaty taste. I'd imagine how it would feel in my mouth. I'd soon find myself with an empty wrapper in my hand."

"Did you try resisting the craving?"

"I've tried everything. I'd make myself go out for a walk on my break and right up to the time I gobbled the Snickers, I'd think, 'Okay, you're doing well. Dr. Grace will be proud of you.' The cravings were strong. I'd tell myself to eat the carrot sticks I brought and I would. Then I'd wait a few minutes and eat the Snickers, sometimes two or three. I even tried calling a friend—you know, like they tell you to do in AA. Ha! I guess I should have called someone who doesn't like chocolate as much as I do. I'm hopeless. I just give in. I can't stop."

I took a deep, slow breath. Jessica talked quickly and sweat beaded on her forehead. I was starting to feel anxious.

"You're describing addiction alright. The definition of addiction is not being able to stop doing something, even though it's causing harm. Did you bring a Snickers with you like I asked when you called?"

"Yeah, but I don't understand why. Is this some kind of aversion therapy?"

At this point, I told her about Emotional Freedom Technique and why it's such an effective tool to reduce or eliminate cravings. It deals with what's really driving the addiction—the feelings we're either not aware of or don't know how to deal with.

Emotional Freedom Technique

Emotional Freedom Technique (EFT) is known as an energy or power therapy because it moves people so much more quickly than traditional talking therapy. It's based on acupuncture theory, that is, when an acupuncture point is stimulated by tapping, energy (whether physical or emotional) gets released. EFT uses tapping with two fingers on particular meridian points on the body. For example, the meridian or energy river under the eyebrow relates to feelings of sadness or trauma. Tapping on that point affects the meridian circuit that runs up and down the body, stimulating and releasing stored emotional energy.

Emotions register in the nervous system when we experience either little "t" traumas (for example, my dad's constant criticism) or big "T" traumas, (the molestation I experienced at seven). Because of the need to survive, these feelings often get repressed and become unconscious. Then an event happens to trigger our emotions, like the boss says something in the exact tone of voice that dear old dad did. Or a spouse withholds love because something not done right echoes dearest mom's critical words. Rather than deal with the upset, people who have addictions check out or eat or drink or overwork. Not the best strategy for managing feelings.

I know EFT may sound like impossible magic, but it's the *most* effective process I've worked with in 20 years of counseling. I use EFT myself for anything from stress to grief and I've taught it to hundreds of people. I'd say it works for more than 90 percent of those who try it. Even skeptics become converts once they've experienced the relief of reducing a problematic feeling to almost nothing. You can use it anywhere for anything—from cravings to driving phobias to test anxiety.

Here's how EFT worked in Jessica's situation.

After my explanation, Jessica looked intrigued but she laughed. "Right, I could just see myself sitting at my desk tapping on my face and my boss walking by. He'd think I was crazy."

"Well, you may want to go into the ladies room then."

"You're telling me that tapping on my body can stop my cravings?"

"Be as skeptical as you want. It works anyway. Why don't you get out the Snickers and set it next to you? As you look at it and imagine eating it, I'd like you to rate the intensity of the craving on a scale of zero to ten, with ten being the most intense."

"Ten plus."

"Okay. And where do you most feel that craving in your body?"

"In my stomach. I feel everything in my stomach."

"Can you think of any reason not to let this craving go?"

"No. I need to quit eating Snickers before I weigh three hundred pounds."

"Jessica, how would you like to feel instead of this craving?"

"I'd like to feel calm and relaxed."

Next, I led Jessica through the tapping process. (See diagram and instructions in Addendum A for an explanation.) After a round of tapping, I checked in with her and asked her to notice any feelings or any thoughts that had surfaced and to again think about her craving for the Snickers still sitting next to her.

"How would you rate the intensity from zero to ten now?"

"It's lower. I don't feel as anxious and the knot in my stomach isn't as tight. I'd say it's a six or seven. This is bizarre. But, I still don't want to give it up and I'm afraid I'll feel deprived."

Two more rounds of tapping and the craving rating slid down to a two. At this point, Jessica became aware of her specific fear—being deprived of her dad's love because her mom was jealous. She'd experienced tremendous fear and anger as a child because of their constant power struggle. Yet, because she's a nice person, it's hard for her to admit she's angry, even to herself. At work, a situation rang a similar bell in Jessica's emotional body. Her boss, whom she liked and respected, had a wife who was jealous of their professional relationship. Whenever the wife called (and she did frequently), that childhood button got pushed and stirred the cravings. Bingo.

"You mean my cravings for those Snickers are all because I couldn't have Dad's love like I wanted?" Jessica asked.

"The most important thing for a child is to receive their parents' love. Did you use food as a child to help you feel better?"

"God, yes. I'd sneak into the kitchen in the middle of the night and eat the candy Mom kept in the drawer. She never said anything to me about it. I think she did the same thing."

"There may be additional feelings attached to these cravings. As you go through the next few weeks, notice when you have cravings and what you're feeling. Why don't you keep a journal at the office and just jot down a note? Then when you come in next time, we'll work on those specific triggers.

"And something else. Remember what you said you'd like instead of the cravings, to feel calm and relaxed? It's important to replace what you're letting go of with what you want. So remember to tap 'calm and relaxed' into the same points we just released."

Six months later, Jessica came in to see me about one of her teen-aged children. When I greeted her in the waiting room, she was wearing a soft green sweater and slacks. She smiled as soon as she saw me.

"Jessica, you look fabulous."

"Thank you. I've lost twenty-five pounds, I'm exercising regularly, and I'm eating lots of fruits and vegetables. I still have cravings once in a while, especially when I'm stressed, but if I tap, I can manage them. I don't keep sugar in the house any more and when I want to treat myself, I buy one Snickers and eat it on the way home. I don't feel guilty afterwards. I think I'm finally free."

Aspartame–Worse Than Sugar?

Is aspartame, an artificial sweetener that goes by the name Nutrasweet or Equal, an effective diet aid or is it poison?

Cori Brackett, who was diagnosed with multiple sclerosis and now uses a wheelchair, links the two or three cans of diet soda she was drinking daily to her illness. Cori was so convinced that she became co-producer of a documentary called *Sweet Misery: A Poisoned World.*[52]

Seemingly a friend of the diet-conscious, aspartame is highly toxic because it converts to methyl alcohol or wood alcohol in the body. According to Dr. Candace Pert, aspartame, an amino acid that's an excitotoxin (isn't that a scary word?) can cause neurons in the brain to get overexcited to the point of burnout or even death. Methanol, another component of aspartame, breaks down in the liver forming formaldehyde, the chemical used to embalm dead bodies.

Dr. Pert writes in her book *Everything You Need to Know to Feel Go(o)d* that the National Cancer Institute has reported an increase in rates of brain cancer since 1985. It jumped 10 percent two years after aspartame was introduced. She also notes that aspartame is the most complained-about substance reported to the Federal Drug Administration (FDA). More than 10,000 official complaints reporting a range of side effects from aspartame, including neurological ones.[53]

What good is it to drop an addiction to sugar and substitute it with poison?

Addiction Isn't Black or White

Getting pregnant is a black-or-white issue but addiction is not. Think of addiction as being on a continuum. At one end are people who aren't addicted at all; at the other end are those who have out-of-control addictions. Most of us with our "lite" addictions fall in between. We're more *addictive* than addicted. That means we take in a little caffeine in the morning to wake up, a soda or two in the afternoon, a few hours of TV at night to unwind from all the caffeine or just to zone out. As Judith Wright says, these addictions "become a problem when we overdo them and when they are used for more than their intended purpose."[54] And the rate of "lite" addiction is growing exponentially in the U.S. because of a constant pressure to look outside ourselves for intimacy, excitement, comfort, or escape.

If we had to give up our sugar and our lattés, it would be annoying, maybe uncomfortable, but we could do it. The challenge is not switching to another "lite" addiction to fill that gap. After all, Alcoholics Anonymous meetings are filled with sober caffeine/nicotine/sugar addicts.

REAL-LIFE STORY OF BRAD'S RECOVERY

Meet Brad, who introduced himself to me on the telephone by announcing, "I'm addicted to shopping, internet porn, and fast food." He sounds so American, I thought. Most early twenties young clients don't announce their addiction concerns when I first talk to them. I couldn't wait to meet this aware and honest young man. The good news is that within a month, using the skills I teach in this book, Brad was able to break the hold his addictive behaviors had on him. That doesn't mean he was cured. But it does mean he'd acquired new skills to cope with the fear, stress, and negativity that drove him to stare for hours at the images of women, or go hit the McDonald's drive-up window for snacks several times a week.

Six months after starting his counseling, Brad experienced only occasional cravings to overeat at McDonald's or distract himself from his pressures using Internet porn. The important difference? He learned to use his built-in "pause" button. Instead of giving in to his cravings, Brad remained aware of what he was feeling and fearing. He released the fear by practicing his new skills. As a result, he felt stronger, happier, and more motivated to go after what he wanted.

Having spent years berating myself for every little real and imaginary offense, I make it a point to help clients see both sides of the situation. Yes, they're over eating or under eating, or shopping too much, or drinking in a way that's harmful. No, it doesn't mean they need to be tarred and feathered. I want them to see they're not alone.

We've all done things we feel ashamed or guilty or stuck about. It's those who are willing to confront the "why" underneath the desire for escape and take responsibility that I cheer for. It takes a lot of courage to pull off the blinders and say, "I'm looking in the mirror"—even if it's not pretty.

My Own "Lite" Addiction to TV-Watching

When I quit smoking and chose to be more conscious of why I was drinking, I started school and funneled my obsessive nature into getting "A"s. Better choices, same intensity, *and* my relationship with myself and those around me didn't change. I still felt emotionally isolated. I didn't have friends, but I did have tasks that I committed to do *right*.

For my addictions to heal, I needed to change. What actually changed was my relationship with myself. I had to face the real me, not just the "pretend" me I showed the world. I had to learn how to notice and honor my feelings, my negative thoughts, and the past I dragged around behind me like a stinky garbage bag. The emotional work of reconnecting to a loving self set me free from alcohol and drugs.

Yes, I still have some "lite" addictions, including TV-watching and sugar. (Over-exercising isn't a problem any more because I'm more focused on balance than on how I look.) Do I use TV and sugar in a way that's harmful? Yes and no. (Denial!) I see my TV watching as more non-productive than harmful, but still mostly a waste of time. I use TV as an entertaining way of zoning out at the end of a tiring day. I resisted watching "Desperate Housewives" because I thought it'd be just one more schlocky show. But when a friend I respect called it a fun romp, I tried it and put it on our TiVo list.

Do I drop other activities to watch TV? No. If I'm working on a project, I'll get to it first. I don't watch TV during the day. On the weekends when my husband is home, it bugs me when he has it on all the time. My granddaughter seems surprised she can't watch TV at our house any time she wants, but that's my rule. No TV during the day. I don't like the noise.

I'm still struggling with changing my relationship with TV. In fact, I'm amazed when others say they don't even own a TV. Either I'm in awe or I think they're lying! I even have friends who only watch educational videos, but for me that's going too far. My commitment is to change my relationship to TV by completely refraining from watching a couple of evenings a week. I'll keep you posted.

TV WATCHING AND YOU

Are you like the average American who watches six hours of television a day? Answer these questions:

How much TV do I watch every day?
A) less than 1 hour
B) 2-3 hours
C) 4 or more hours
D) TV is on all my waking hours

How do I feel when I'm watching TV?
Empty? Bored? Restless? Relaxed? Happy? Connected? (There's no right or wrong answer.)

Try this experiment: Watch one less hour of TV a day for a month. Use this newfound time for relaxation or to develop a healthy pleasure. Read a book, start a hobby, get outside and walk, breathe fresh air, give or receive a massage, listen to a guided imagery tape. Now answer this question: How do I feel after doing this new behavior compared to how I feel after watching TV?

Research shows that we feel bored by TV but don't notice until it's turned off. Boredom doesn't come from turning off the tube; it really comes from allowing yourself to feel the existing boredom after you turn it off.

My Own "Lite" Addiction to Sugar

Sugar is another "lite" addiction not just for others. I like it and I use it as a reward. When I have an afternoon cup of tea, I like to have two pieces of candy or chocolate. In the last year, I've developed a cozy affection for Trader Joe's dark organic chocolate. I'll have two small pieces.

Notice how I discount the amount of sugar I eat? I barely have any. I don't really have a problem, but the proof is this: *I don't want to go without my little afternoon fix.* If I don't stop eating sugar, will it negatively affect my life? Probably not, since I don't eat much. But how would it be to eat fruit instead of a sugar treat? Well, I'm not ready to let go of this one. As a friend of mine says about her morning coffee, "I've got to have *some* bad habits" (although this friend recently switched her morning coffee to tea because the caffeine caused stomach problems).

The important questions are "What's my overall quality of life? Am I in touch with myself emotionally? Do I practice healthy habits more than unhealthy habits? Do I tell myself the truth most of the time?"

This is where the 80/20 rule comes in. It changes the question to become: "Am I being loving and real with myself about 80 percent of the time?" No, I don't have to be perfect all the time; there is *some* give.

I use this 80/20 rule to break the perfectionist/failure cycle. If I'm eating healthy 80 percent of the time, that's good enough. Then, when I do something off my intended plan, it's not "failure" and I don't have to go "back to jail." Often people who have weight issues use a "bad food day" as an excuse to give up completely. Using this 80/20 rule makes failure not a black-or-white issue.

IS YOUR BRAIN BEING HIGH-JACKED?

An antidote to "lite" addiction is learning to support yourself in a healthy, loving way. Examples include talking to a friend, journaling, staying present with my feelings and not judging them, getting some exercise, yoga, getting outside for a walk and fresh air. But if you're really out of control with food, sugar, substances—whatever—these activities may not work for you because you're dealing with a hard addiction. Your brain has been high-jacked, which means the substance or activity controls you. Your freedom of choice is gone. Get professional help.

Self-Assessment on Addictive Coping

Gently and honestly answer these questions for yourself:

1. When I'm stressed or anxious, do I have a variety of healthy coping skills to turn to? What are they?

    _____.

2. Do I have only one or two behaviors, like watching TV or eating chocolate, that I always go to for temporary relief?_____.

3. On a scale of 0-10 (10 high), how guilty do I feel when I engage in these behaviors?

4. Do I avoid feelings of anger, sadness, anxiety, or guilt? How often do I feel numb?

5. Have others (e.g., boss, significant other, friend) ever said my addictive coping behaviors posed a problem for them?

    _____.

6. What do I *really* need? Time, attention, rest, nurturing, fun, socializing, rewarding work, spiritual connection, something else? (Write down one or two needs here

    _____, _____).

7. What is one action step I am willing to take to meet these needs *this week*? _____.

" Most people use an **artificial** vehicle to create certainty and comfort and that's why the live in **fear**.[55]

~ Tony Robbins

In my mind, both kinds of user—the one who gets the drugs from a doctor and the one who buys the from a dealer—are **doing the same thing**: altering their chemistry with an exogenous substance that has widespread effects, many of which are not fully understood, in order to change feelings they don't want to have.[56] "

~ Dr. Candace Pert

CHAPTER FOUR

Chapter Four

Addiction—Facing the Dragon

THERE ARE only three ways to deal with a dragon—avoid it, run from it, or face it. When we're addicted to eating or drinking or shopping to change how we feel, nothing changes until we have the courage to face the dragon— ourselves.

In a dream I had while in therapy, I was walking down dark, narrow stairs with two small children clinging to my legs. As I got closer to the bottom of the stairs, a frightening man wielding a club came toward us. I quickly placed the children behind me on the stairs and went to meet this man. Terrified, I knew I had to protect the children. I raised the stick I found in my hand and went forward to confront him. All of a sudden, even though I didn't really want to, I told him I loved him and forgave him. Instantly he was disarmed and—poof like smoke—he disappeared. Instantly, I was flooded with contentment and peace.

I never dreamed about the molestation by the "pony man" again.

Afraid of Being Destroyed

Addiction always involves running from or avoiding our feelings and problems. At the bottom of all addiction is fear, and fear generally provokes one of two responses—avoidance or attack. We're afraid that if we face the pain within us, we'll be destroyed. We defend ourselves by tuning out and ignoring the messages of our heart and body. But the threat of fear is always there, waiting for a vulnerable moment.

The most basic of human needs are avoiding pain and seeking pleasure. Pleasure and pain are both driven by feelings, but feelings *aren't* the bad guys; it's *not dealing with feelings* that gets us in trouble. We don't always know how we feel or what our emotions mean—and that can confuse or frighten us. We do what we've been taught to do—avoid, deny, minimize, blame others—anything to escape feeling uncomfortable.

As adults, we think we're supposed to know everything, and of course we don't. If faced with a plumbing problem, we don't believe we should know how to do plumbing, right? But feeling comfortable with our emotions seems as foreign as flying to the moon. Think of it this way: If we weren't taught to read, we'd need someone to help us learn how. It's the same with feelings. If we haven't developed our emotional skills, we need education. Without it, we shove our fears and anxieties down deep.

Better Not to Feel

What can be more revealing about a family than witnessing their rituals at the dinner table? One year, just a few days after Christmas when I was nine or ten, members of my family were sitting at their places quietly eating. Mom, head down, cigarette in one hand, was pushing food around her plate with the other. Then the phone rang. The caller from the hospital told Mom that her infant daughter Lisa, who had been born prematurely on Christmas Eve, had just died. She hung up, sat down, and told us our baby sister was gone. Nothing else. She didn't look at us; she just went back to pushing food around on her plate. My dad, also mute, looked sick. I sat there feeling blank and waiting for *something* from Mom or Dad. Nothing. That's when I ran into the living room and sobbed on the couch. Mom came in and patted me on the back. She quietly said Lisa was just too little to make it. I noticed that no one else budged from the table.

I was so angry that no one seemed to feel *anything*. Of course, after Mom's brief reassurance, we never talked about Lisa again. When I was an adult and thought about Lisa's death, I wondered if a factor had been the loud, pounding fight a few months before that ended when Mom ran up to our bedroom. She'd often run to the kids' rooms as a last resort because she knew Dad wouldn't hit her in front of us.

How Addiction Gets Started

After reading the following section, my friend and writer Marianne Peck, a marriage and family therapist, said, "People are dumber than rats." She's referring to the experimental rats that go through a maze once and, when they don't get food, change directions or stop. Not so for people. They start out with a pattern that can turn into a habit and grow into an addiction.

A *pattern* is if Jessica ate a Snickers bar only a couple of times a week. She likes the treat, but could easily choose something else. When I was a pattern smoker, there were times I'd smoke and times I wouldn't. I quit during both my pregnancies. I didn't smoke during my first marriage because my husband asked me not to. But when my life would change (that is, get more stressful or chaotic), I'd pick up smoking again. A pattern is defined as something we do, yet we have control of when and where we do it. We can take it (the Snickers or the cigarette) or we can leave it.

A *habit* means we still have choice about whether to eat the Snickers or smoke the cigarette. However, we use these treats more frequently to make ourselves *feel better*, to distract, or to numb ourselves from our real feelings. Because our brains get trained by our repetitive behaviors, we feel less in control and our cravings get stronger.

An *addiction* takes that a step further. Jessica came to me when she was finding it harder to go without her afternoon sugar reward. She'd think about the Snickers more often and earlier in the day. When she said, "If I'm bored at work, I can eat a Snickers," I knew it had become a buddy to her. For me, smoking moved from "occasionally" to "every day" and provided ever more relief from the irritability I felt inside.

I remember the first drag of my first cigarette at age 14. It burned my eyes and throat and made me nauseous. But I felt a rush followed by a calmness that I was unaccustomed to. That rush penetrated the numbness layered over the ever-present anger and anxiety. "Ah, I feel something, I'm alive," I thought. Later, a line of cocaine evoked the same response.

I've learned that every intense emotion produces a chemical reaction experienced in the body. The substance or activity screens the real addiction. *We're really addicted to the emotions that feed the behavior.* More than that, we become addicted to a particular fear pattern that operates like a set of double lines through our lives. It keeps us from going too far up or too far down. Unfortunately, we can get stuck in this emotional comfort zone.

From Pattern to Habit to Addiction

How does "lite" addictive coping (as in the Snickers and smoking examples) become a full-blown addiction? As we move along the addiction continuum, patterns become habits and habits become compulsions. Our brain chemistry actually changes the more we repeat a behavior.

A compulsion happens when our freedom of choice is going, going, almost gone. There isn't total surrender to the addiction, but it's a lot harder to let go of in this stage and we usually give *in* to the craving. In Jessica's case, she doesn't consider doing something else to deal with her boredom and has no awareness of the feelings underneath her Snickers hit. She'd bonded to the Snickers bar because it's been "there" for her in ways she hasn't learned to support herself. *It* takes care of her feelings; *denial* takes care of any consequences that might crop up (like the weight she's been gaining).

Even though the doctor told Jessica she was pre-diabetic and 40 pounds overweight, she couldn't stop. She'd start obsessing about the Snickers bar at the mere hint of boredom and check out by going into the addiction trance. "I won't feel better until I eat the Snickers . . . must eat the Snickers . . . I'm eating the Snickers." Only later when she's out of the trance does she feel guilty and remorseful. She makes those promises we've all made: "I'll never do that again." By this time, Snickers is no longer just a buddy, it's become Jessica's best friend. (This is known as a pattern to addiction formula noted by Craig Nakken in *Women, Sex and Addiction: A Search for Love and Power.*[57])

In my case, at the compulsion stage, I was smoking after lunch, after dinner, and always when I went out for a drink with friends. I didn't want to quit because I told myself I needed it. Besides, I believed smoking was better than not smoking. That it was no one else's business. I couldn't have cared less about how I felt inside.

I was a smoking addict when I started dating my current husband Dave. When he asked me to quit, I laughed. He kept asking. I ignored him. He bought me packets of "Quit Smoking Filters" to help me quit. (These filters were numbered from 6 to 1; theoretically, when I got to 1, I should be able to easily stop smoking. So I humored him. I'd use them and then accidentally "lose" them one by one until I was back to smoking regular cigarettes.)

By this point, I had fused my identity with smoking. I was a smoker. I'd get angry if he talked to me sternly about my health because, even though I was running a few miles a day, his pro-health argument didn't compute. I wouldn't let it. I couldn't let go of smoking until I was ready. That was in 1979.

I vividly remember the weekend I quit smoking. Dave was celebrating the opening of his new business called ComputerWare. My sister and I were the hostesses. Champagne flowed during the event and cocaine afterwards. I smoked so much, I made myself sick. That was it; I was done with cigarettes for good.

GERI'S REAL-LIFE STORY

Geri and her husband, Sam, came in together for their first counseling session with me. Blonde, petite, and extremely thin, Geri sat down and shrank into the couch. In contrast, Sam filled all the space in the room. His voice boomed out of his six-foot five-inch, well-padded body as he declared: "Geri drinks too much." What did Sam want? "For her to control her drinking and be a better mother to our three children."

"Oh boy," I thought. "This dynamic will be fun."

Geri, her head down, hadn't said a word for the full 20 minutes Sam and I talked. I requested that Sam give us time together without him. When I asked Geri in private if she agreed with what Sam said, she nodded but denied that her drinking was "that big a problem."

Over the next few sessions, Geri reluctantly told me about her childhood. "Everything's my fault. It's all my fault. My parents gave me everything. I don't do anything right." When she described her mother as big, loud, and bossy, I could see why Sam seemed so comfortable to her. She was extremely loyal to her parents, as abused children often are. Geri described her mother's "ups" as lots of loud talking, drinking and eating, and spending money.

Her "downs" involved not getting out of bed for weeks.

I learned that Geri's mother had given her alcohol at ages two, four, and eight to calm her down, shut her up, or help her anxious daughter socialize. I also learned that, in her family, Geri played the part of the bad child who could do no right while her sister played the adored child of perfection. Everything Geri did was criticized by her mother who emphasized the importance of what other people thought. The message she received? "I'm not good enough."

I suggested to Geri, "Maybe you drink because it's the one thing in your life you have choice about. That helps you feel less afraid." She looked at me with a funny expression. I explained I wasn't saying alcohol was the best way to cope, just that I could understand why she'd chosen it. First, she'd been taught to drink by her mother, and, second, it helped blur the anxiety and the "I'm bad" beliefs running through her.

During the time Geri was counseling with me, she was drinking every day to the point of blackouts. Because she was also suicidal, I encouraged in-patient treatment for her, which she adamantly refused. A few sessions after that, she came in drunk. I stated emphatically to both Geri and Sam that she needed in-patient treatment. He agreed, though I wasn't sure he meant it. I could see that Geri was mad about the idea, her jaw firmly set, her arms folded. I knew it would probably be the last time I'd see her, but I had to take a chance and push her toward a breakthrough. Until she realized she needed help, even a veteran addiction counselor couldn't help her.

Happily, I heard from Geri a few months later, following her stay at The Meadows in Arizona. (The Meadows is a multi-disorder trauma facility that treats people with addictions.) She was in recovery and no longer drinking to hold off the panic she felt.

Situations like Geri's always remind me that we're not "bad" because we run from fear by using a substance to make ourselves feel better. Unfortunately, as with Geri, drinking (or any other addictive behavior) simply doesn't achieve that result.

Not "Good Enough" at the Root

When I was raising and showing Morgan horses, my trainer and friend, Lydia, would go on and on saying, "If things were different in my life, I wouldn't have to drink." Lydia had it "bass-ackwards," because later, when she got sober, she realized drinking not only caused most of her problems but gave her the excuse she wanted to keep drinking.

Yes, our addictions help us cope, but they never solve the real problem—fear of our imperfect selves. As Bill Manville said, "That's why addictions seem like our only friends—the ones who tell us what we *want* to hear, not what we *need* to hear."[58] If we're lucky, we wake up before too much damage has been done. We begin to realize (or a loved one pushes us to realize) that we have to face the truth. We're imperfect— maybe even really screwed up—but we're still worthy of love and acceptance.

When I was a teen, using alcohol and drugs helped me deal with the shame and craziness in my family. In my 20s, I continued to be out of touch with how I felt. But when I grabbed a cigarette because I was stressed or pissed off, I'd relax. Going for a cigarette and denying my anger rather than feeling it—"I'm not angry, I'm fine"—gave me the illusion of controlling my emotions. I didn't have a clue *how* to deal with my anger. And I preferred to believe it was *their* fault, anyway.

Underneath my need to "control" my anger was my fear that I wasn't "good enough." *I was completely unaware of this fear.* When I look back, I can see I was terrified of not doing life *right*—as if I just had to follow the perfect recipe for everything to fall into place. Like Geri, I had a belief that I wasn't "good enough." Fear had grabbed me early. I ran harder and faster to escape it, though I could never have named what I was running from then. In the process, I became addicted, not only to the cigarettes, but to the very fear I was running from.

Yes, what we do repetitively, whether positive or negative, gets programmed into our physiology. Like the legendary Sisyphus who gets trapped endlessly pushing a boulder up a mountain, I could neither face my fears nor escape them. They kept me in a hellish limbo—afraid, acting out with anger, and using substances to numb the pain. Feeling stuck, mostly I was afraid to break the patterns.

To say it another way, even though I was anxiety-ridden, the bad feelings were uncomfortable but I needed them to feel like a normal human. I became addicted more to the feelings than the substances, which became a vehicle to keep the "not good enough" feelings in place. If people had told me, "Hey, you're addicted to feeling not good enough," I would have said they were crazy. But those feelings drove my addictions. I couldn't allow myself to experience the underlying fear because I thought it would swallow me. I couldn't let myself overcome my "not good enough" behavior because that would set up my highly conscious fear of changing.

The Suffering We Know

With my smoking, I didn't have the skills to feel safe and move through my emotional baggage from the past. I, like anyone struggling with an addiction, was compelled to repeat the same old comfortably uncomfortable patterns, habits, and behaviors. After all, what would take their place?

Being forced to deal with the unknown makes it challenging to break addictive patterns. For example, a compulsive eater looks in the mirror and feels failure, rejection, and self-hate. The feelings themselves barely register in her awareness; what registers is her drive to eat the donuts—all of them—NOW. It shows how choosing the suffering we know becomes easier than what might lie ahead.

In recovery, the feelings and thoughts that drive a person's addiction have to be addressed or relapse follows. Most professionals consider relapse part of the recovery process. Relapse rates are high for addictive diseases and range from 50% for resumption of heavy use to 90% for a brief lapse.[59] The Baldwin Research Institute, whose statistics are found at the National Institute of Chemical Dependency's website (http://www.nicd.us), states that the success rates for AA and treatment programs range from 3 to 10 percent. Its studies found that brief intervention was more successful than either AA or in-patient treatment. However, I have doubts about the long-term success of brief interventions for hard addictions. I do know that bodymind techniques (such as those taught in this book) work. Why? Because they begin the process of re-wiring a brain traumatized by alcoholic parents, neglect, abuse, and so on.

In *Awakening Intuition,* Dr. Mona Lisa Schulz discusses a famous study of rats raised in boxes where they regularly received electric shocks from birth.[60] Once the rats reached maturity, they were given the choice to move to other boxes where they wouldn't be shocked. What did they do? To a one, they chose to stay in their comfortably uncomfortable but familiar homes. It shows the power of repetition, even in rats. Like many trauma survivors, the rats may have thought something like, "Hey, I can handle (control) this next event since I've lived all my life being shocked."

Like many of us who feel overburdened at work or suffer miserably in relationships, the idea of leaving or doing something different terrifies us. More than that, we come to believe that fear is our friend. Me, too, until I finally learned the difference. We hold onto it like it's a safety net. No friend would treat us as fear does—causing us to harm ourselves by excessive dieting or tricking us into believing that if we make more money, own a bigger house, drive a more luxurious car, or have a thinner body, then we'll finally feel loved and be "good enough."

Brain's Neural Pathways & Addiction

Addiction gets cemented in the brain through the repetition of feelings. For me, the record groove of habit began with the anxiety and judgment I learned at my father's knee and the depression at my mother's.

We unconsciously act out the emotional patterns we have laid down from our most potent experiences. From the time we're little children, we're experiencing the world and reacting to it emotionally. Through these experiences, the brain lays down neural pathways like train tracks that makes connections with similar pathways. The brain's neural pathways are stimulated by emotions like fear, anger, and so on when they are repeated often. With repetition, these neural connections deepen (e.g., fear and anger) while other possible connections (e.g., peace, hope, and love) wither from lack of use. That results in us seeking the same feeling experiences over and over. Thus, if the majority of our experiences are negative, we program ourselves toward similar pathways, leaving out connections to positive experiences. Later, we wonder why we see the world through such a negative lens.

For example, when I was criticized by Dad and Mom as a child, a criticism "track" formed. It was reinforced in my brain every time Dad implied I was stupid because I didn't understand a math problem, or when Mom re-cleaned an area I'd already cleaned. Criticism, fear, negativity, and trauma experienced in childhood often set us up to seek those same emotional experiences.

The anxiety that depressed me, made me irritable, and ran my life didn't feel good, but it was oh, so familiar. It would periodically peak into rages followed by guilt and shame—hmmm, just like Mom and Dad experienced. I couldn't seem to stop banging my head against the same old wall of anger and fear no matter how much it hurt. That is, until I learned how to release the emotional patterns with therapy, meditation and Emotional Freedom Technique.

Because whatever emotional climate we're raised in becomes familiar, we tend to seek a similar environment as adults—until we wake up, that is. For example, my first husband, John, came across as a great guy to everyone else but was highly critical of me—just like my dad was. Everyone thought Dad was likeable and funny; the same was said about John. At the time, I never consciously linked John with Dad. Yet he'd criticize everything about me including the miniscule size difference between my eyes. Even at age 22, I knew to draw the line there. If only I had to tolerate John's negativity, I may have hung in longer, but I could see how it affected my son, which gave me the push to get out of this marriage.

AMANDA'S ADDICTION

Amanda, the main character played by Marlee Matlin in the film *What The Bleep Do We Know?* is a 40-ish, single, anxiety-ridden woman whose marriage ended disastrously. Just after the wedding vows and still at the altar, Amanda saw her new groom flirt with an attractive blonde in the congregation. Soon after, she walked in on them in bed. Forever after, every time she went to any wedding, she believed the groom to be a cheating bum. Wouldn't you know it, her job as a photographer forced her to attend weddings.

Over and over again, the brain's neural programming caused Amanda to re-experience the emotional addiction that had been set since her own wedding. Although she hated how she felt, she didn't want to give up the anger, shame, and judgment because it also made her *right*. She couldn't control those feelings even though they were harming her. That's addiction.

So at the current wedding she's photographing, Amanda believes she sees the groom having sex with a bridesmaid. Her expressions of pain and anger show she's reliving her past. When she tells the man next to her how disgusting the groom is, he lets her know the groom definitely wasn't being unfaithful. She doesn't believe him and yells at the groom, who is dancing with his new wife. Everyone in the room stares at her, wondering, "Who is that crazy woman?" Then she sees a mussed-up couple coming out of a back room and realizes, oh, oh, it's not the groom. Feeling sick about her mistake, she finally "gets" how much her past was controlling her present.

New Energy Therapies

But good news abounds! Energy therapies, like Emotional Freedom Technique (EFT) that was introduced in Chapter 3, can shorten the whole recovery process. EFT condenses and contains upsetting feelings and makes therapy safer. For example, my early therapy included going into great detail about being molested. With EFT, that wouldn't be necessary because talking about pain often re-traumatizes us. Emotional charges can now be eliminated or greatly reduced in a few sessions. (See Chapter 11 for a full description of how EFT is done.)

Before getting trained in Emotional Freedom Technique, a part of me kept going back to my familiar emotional landscape. I tried everything to escape my feelings, but they clung like moss to a rock—reinforcing the vicious cycle of addiction. Experiencing fear and/or pain sets up the neural pathways, solidifying the behaviors we use to avoid the feelings. These behaviors eventually become addictions that control our lives—most often unconsciously.

What's the set up for addictions? None of us consciously set out to become addicts. And while we may believe addictive problems "just happen," that's not correct either. At the core, I think we go to outside fixes because we haven't been taught how to seek comfort and love from within ourselves. Specifically, we have not been taught a set of skills to manage and move painful emotions through us so we have the choice to *feel good* in healthy ways.

None of us grow up without some amount of pain. This is an accepted part of life — perhaps too accepted. Many of us have been much more affected by the neglect and abuse of caretakers, school systems, and corporate environments than we let ourselves know. Trauma sets up addiction. To heal the effects of fear, stress, and addiction, we need to be on the lookout.

Most of us know, deep down, if we're having a problem with our addictive behaviors, we just don't want to admit it. If you answer affirmatively to each question, you're likely experiencing addictive issues. How extreme the problem is depends on the number of consequences to your health, relationships, and finances.

If you're able to admit you're having a problem, I recommend you seek help through AA or NA 12 Step Meetings (found in local phone books) or seek professional counseling. As Ernie Larsen, founder of Stage Two Recovery, says "If nothing changes, nothing changes."

SELF-ASSESSMENT ON FULL ADDICTION

List any health problems you're currently having: for example, frequent heart burn, acid reflux, irritable bowel syndrome, migraines, other: _____

_____

_____

List any relationship problems: for example, my spouse says I drink too much, I've lost friends because of my addictions, I've had job problems related to my use, and so on:

_____

_____

List financial problems: for example, I have trouble making my credit card payments, I've filed bankruptcy, I never have enough money for bills but seem to have enough for gambling, drinking, drugs, binge foods, Internet porn, and so on:

_____

_____

_____

List any attempts you've made to stop the behavior: for example, I quit drinking for a month but felt miserable:

_____

_____

_____

List any excuses you use to maintain the behavior: for example, I only drink on weekends, my wife's (husband) just a nag, I'm only thirty-five, I'll slow down when I'm fifty, etc.

_____

_____

_____

Note: This is not meant to be a complete substance diagnosis. If you're able to admit you have a bigger problem than you thought, please take the next step and seek counseling, AA, NA, or visit your company's Employee Assistance Program. For those who are having full addictions rather than the "lite" addictive coping behaviors, the solutions in this book are not enough to promote recovery. However, after treatment, the bodymind skills in Intentional JOY will support you to a fuller enjoyment of life.

Note:

This is not meant to be a complete substance diagnosis. If you're able to admit you have a bigger problem than you thought, please take the next step and seek counseling, AA, NA, or visit your company's Employee Assistance Program. For those who are having full addictions rather than the "lite" addictive coping behaviors, the solutions in this book are not enough to promote recovery. However, after treatment, the bodymind skills in *Intentional JOY* will support you to a fuller enjoyment of life.

"" All **addiction** comes from a **child** state."

\- Pia Melody

CHAPTER FIVE

Chapter Five:

Addiction—The Set Up

ALL ADDICTION is driven by psychological or emotional issues, particularly a feeling of helplessness or humiliation. Helplessness is the feeling of powerlessness.[62] These words came from Lance Dodes, M.D., psychiatrist and assistant clinical professor of psychiatry at Harvard Medical School, who wrote in *The Heart of Addiction* that trauma, powerlessness, and addiction go hand in hand. Whether it's the big "T" trauma events or a more steady diet of little "t" events, powerlessness and the rage that results, fuels addiction.

Mary, overweight since childhood, was forced to diet from the age of five. Whenever she'd get mad as an adult, she'd stand at the kitchen counter shoveling in chips and other crunchy foods as fast as she could. Working with me, she became aware of the reservoir of anger and humiliation caused by her mother who restricted her food because Mom was fat. Clearly, Mary went hungry because her overweight mother projected her weight issues onto her daughter.

The addictive set-up for me was a little different. When I'd come home from school and my mother was playing her Barbra Streisand records, I knew that when Dad got home, it would go one of two ways. He'd either be mad that she didn't have dinner on the table or he'd join her and they'd take off to the local bar, leaving me in charge of my sister and brother. Either way, I was powerless to make the situation different.

One time, Dad was mad at Mom for flirting with another man at a bar. I took Mom's side, so Dad took out his anger at her on me—by reading my diary. In it, I'd written about "making out" with a friend's brother I had a crush on. Dad charged me with having sex with this boy when it was only innocent kissing. When he made this accusation, I felt like a rabbit caught in a trap. My face flushed and I wanted to disappear. I couldn't put words on the violation I felt. How could Dad betray my trust and assume the worst of me? I was just 13 and definitely not having sex. Of course, not long after that, I started to. And about the same time, my alcohol and drug use began.

Addiction treatment theory says that whatever age the child started using a substance is the emotional age he or she got stuck. But I think the same can be said for emotional trauma. While almost all children experience an amount of shame and humiliation for "inappropriate" feelings, not all become addicts. "Wipe that look off your face, young lady," Mom would say when I got mad. Although she said it often (apparently I got angry a lot), that wasn't enough on its own to set me up for addiction. However, combined with the humiliation, criticism, anxiety, and depression experienced in my home, it all added up.

Today, I don't blame my parents for any problems I've had. My blame rule of thumb is that, yes, my parents' problems affected me, but the pain they inflicted wasn't intentional. They loved us kids the best they could. Once I reached adulthood, I realized it was time for me to take responsibility and heal what needed to be healed. Today, I know they did the best they could.

However, we don't become fully functioning adults by sugar coating feelings that our "kid inside" harbors about what happened in past family life. We need to bring up enough of the grief, anger, and pain, work to release these feelings, and then get on with creating the best life we can. Skills like EFT and imagery definitely help (see Chapter 10 and 11).

The Traumatized Brain

As mentioned in Chapter 1, the brain develops in three stages in humans, with the first being the brain stem or reptilian brain—our instinctual and survival-oriented brain. The second is the limbic or emotional brain; the third is the neocortex or thinking brain. Ideally, all three parts of the brain work together harmoniously allowing instincts, feelings, and thoughts to be conscious.

However, if trauma occurs before the thinking part of the brain develops fully the memory of the trauma is held in the body. Only when our neocortex is more advanced can we try to make sense of what happened. As a consequence—and this is the part that gets us into trouble—we keep acting out the early trauma with no conscious awareness of what drives it.

For example, I acted out the unconscious trauma of being molested and my family dynamics by becoming a promiscuous teen. I knew I was looking for love in all the wrong places, but had no awareness about why or how to stop myself. Although a part of me felt guilty and ashamed, another part liked the attention I received from boys. It felt better than the *nothing* I was receiving at home.

My acting out probably resulted from the early trauma I experienced due to Dad's criticism and neglect and due to Mom's alcoholic self-absorption as well as the molestation at age seven. The trend started early. When my mother was pregnant with me, she smoked and drank because she felt abandoned by my father, who was in Greenland working as a truck driver for the first year and a half of my life.

According to Dr. Arthur Janov, psychiatrist and author of *The Biology of Love*[63] this kind of womb trauma gets imprinted in the brain stem and limbic centers of the brain. As a counselor, when I have an acting-out teen as a client, I look at the family system and what the teen's behavior says about what's working and not working in the family. Acting-out children tend to be the family's "canary in the coal mine" as they strain to get their needs for love, attention, and importance met.

Richard O'Connor, Ph.D. connected the dots between trauma and addiction in the brain in his book *Undoing Perpetual Stress.*[64] The orbitofrontal cortex, a connector part of the brain, plugs into the thinking brain, the emotional brain, the endocrine system, and the brain stem. When childhood trauma happens, it affects the responsiveness of this part of the brain negatively. How? The brain's production of neurotransmitters serotonin, dopamine, and the opiates (which regulate both physical and emotional pain) are reduced by the overproduction of cortisol, the stress hormone. Because the neurotransmitters don't function normally, the traumatized person becomes more susceptible to seeking the relief that's provided by food or caffeine or alcohol.

We know that serotonin levels naturally decline throughout the day, reaching their lows in the afternoon and evening. Food addicts report that their most intense craving time happens in the afternoon and evening. Protein can help regulate serotonin but you have to eat a lot of it. Or you can take a supplement called 5HTP, which is the amino acid serotonin in pill form. Increasing serotonin levels reduces cravings. (I highly recommend Julia Ross's book, *The Mood Cure*, as an excellent guide to using amino acids to reduce cravings and to reduce the depression and anxiety that contribute to addiction and problems with relapse. See Resources.)

Simply stated, fear and stress wire the brain to overproduce and under produce certain neurotransmitters such as dopamine and serotonin. Dopamine is the "gotta have it, go get it" neurotransmitter and serotonin is the "mission accomplished—got it" neurotransmitter. If serotonin levels are low, anything associated with food, danger, or sex causes dopamine to push us to go after it. Dopamine requires us to do what it takes to get whatever survival requires. As a result, it links the behavior with the pleasure of experienced neurotransmitters.[65]

ROSE'S REAL-LIFE STORY

It was easy to see the effects of trauma with my client Rose. Shaking and having trouble breathing, Rose's big blue eyes searched my office to see if it was even safe to sit down.

Rose's story poured out of her in fits and gasps. Her ex-husband had been put in prison for his abuse of her, but was getting released soon, which terrified her. She'd grown up in an alcoholic home where her parents fought all the time and her mother constantly got in Rose's face, yelling at her about how awful, ugly, and horrible she was. Her father's mean, angry looks and constant belittlement made her feel something was wrong with her. She didn't believe either parent loved her and grew up believing she was crazy and stupid.

After many abusive relationships, two treatment programs for substance abuse, and years of counseling, Rose still suffered from nightmares, flashbacks, substance abuse relapses. She felt crazy because of her difficulty breathing and the panic that engulfed her many times each day. I knew it would be a challenge to help her, because Rose displayed many of the classic symptoms of Post Traumatic Stress Disorder. In severe cases PTSD acts to constantly re-trigger the fear and helplessness of the original trauma. For example, every time Rose's husband yelled at her, she re-experienced the fear she felt when her parents fought.

Slowly, guided imagery allowed Rose to feel safer and more comfortable in her body and EFT gave her a skill to combat the panic and anxiety she'd lived with since childhood.

At a 2004 imagery conference, Belleruth Naparstek, a psychotherapist and innovator in guided imagery, healing, and intuition, said that only 12 to 14 percent of women and 6 percent of men will actually develop the debilitating symptoms of post-traumatic stress disorder (PTSD). Those symptoms occur when there is a neurological feedback circuit that keeps the person hypercharged or numb or a mixture of both. The good news is that the same mechanism that makes some more prone to developing PTSD symptoms also makes healing through imagery-based therapies like Imagery and Emotional Freedom Technique more accessible.[66]

John Bradshaw, Claudia Black, and others who pioneered the Adult Child/Co-Dependency movement of the 1980s, helped us see the connection between addiction and trauma. They pointed out that someone raised by alcoholic parents who are abusive and/or neglectful will bear the effects of trauma, which include abusing substances to medicate their feelings. Post-traumatic stress disorder shows up in treatment centers with estimates ranging anywhere from 11 to 59 percent. Interestingly, many people who have no alcoholism in their background experience milder symptoms of trauma. They struggle with anxiety, depression, and chronic illness yet function well enough to go to work, get married, and have children.

DAVE'S REAL-LIFE STORY

Dave talked about his unhappiness and depression as a child, but would never consider himself a trauma survivor. He came to see me for weight issues because his doctor referred him. "I'm really depressed and I've got to do something about my weight. I just sit and eat when I get home from work."

I asked Dave to give me some background about how long he'd been having a problem with weight and a brief history about his childhood. He reported these facts in a flat, monotone voice.

"I'm a business owner. I bought the sporting goods store from my dad and I've been running it myself the last five years. I'm stressed all the time because I work all the time. I worked a lot as a kid helping my dad. I don't remember having fun with him or much fun anytime as a kid. So now when I go home after working all day, I deserve a reward." Strikingly absent in his story was any mention of his mom.

"What kind of foods do you like?"

"I don't eat sweets. But I like fatty foods, like peanut butter and meats like bologna, because they're easy—no prep. I also like hamburgers, steaks, roasts, and cheese. I sit and watch television and eat from the time I get home until I go to bed. And sometimes I get up at night and eat. My doctor says if I don't change my ways, I'm a prime candidate for heart problems."

"Do you know how you're feeling when you're eating? Mad or sad or guilty?"

"I'm mostly numb, though sometimes I feel really guilty that I don't spend time with my son and I wonder how he's going to grow up." Dave is repeating the same pattern of neglect his father and mother did with him. Although he's an outwardly successful businessman with a nice home, a wife, and son, he suffers from depression, anxiety, and hopelessness—all symptoms of traumatic neglect.

Trauma is defined by Dr. Drew Pinksy as feeling and being powerless at the hands of parents or caregivers who were responsible for the safety and nurturance of their children.[67] Certainly, abusive parents cause trauma, but even thoughtless words spoken often enough to a child can produce a little "t" trauma to self-esteem.

In these cases studies, both Rose and Dave received negative messages as children. Although Rose's wounds appear more corrosive, they've both been traumatized—it's a matter of degree. However, I give Rose a better chance of healing than Dave because she knows she's been wounded. She knows it's up to her to heal. In contrast, Dave can't give his parents any responsibility for his trauma because, by societal standards, they did okay by him. They clothed and fed him and sent him to good schools, so materially he was fine. Yet he can't discount the importance of emotional nurturance or the negative effects of emotional neglect.

Rose knows alcohol and drugs are poison for her. For Dave, food may be tougher to battle because, instead of giving it up, he has to change his relationship to it and it's the only nurturing he allows himself. When Emotional Freedom Technique helped him reduce cravings and put him more in touch with his feelings, he quit coming to see me, giving the needs of his business as a reason.

How Often Does Trauma Occur?

It's easy to underestimate the reach of trauma's damage if you're not part of the world of addictions. But more and more evidence is emerging that builds a case for its increasing frequency.

Consider these scenarios:

"...a recent government study involving some fifty-nine thousand respondents found that 'events and experiences that qualified as traumas' had been experienced by 60 percent of the adult men and 51 percent of the adult women interviewed."[68]

"Trauma has become so commonplace that most people don't even recognize its presence."[69] In a study of 1,000 people, 40 percent reported a traumatic event in the past three years. These traumatic events included being raped or physically assaulted, being in a serious car accident, or witnessing someone being injured or killed.[70]

"It is estimated that three-quarters of the general public will experience an event that could cause a traumatic response in their lifetime. Is it any wonder, therefore, that chemical dependence is achieving epidemic proportions?"[71]

How Addiction Relates to Trauma

Just as I visualize addiction on a continuum, I see trauma spread out on a continuum, too. The big traumas like war, rape, domestic violence, and severe car accidents (one of the most common traumatic experiences) are on one end of the continuum. Small accumulated "normal" traumas like shame, humiliation, embarrassment, and minor neglect are on the other end.

While all children experience those feelings to some degree, if they're treated with enough love and stability, their sense of self survives. They may function fine according to societal standards in that they're able to work, marry, and have children. But is "functioning" enough? What about enjoyment, fulfillment, having a sense of purpose and the freedom of a life well lived?

A subtle but pervasive tragedy of trauma is that, in prolonged doses, emotional development gets stymied. We close our hearts to protect ourselves and in the process disconnect from our emotional core. Our bodies—a trusted friend when we're children—often become a battlefield of psychosomatic aches and pains in adulthood. Unfortunately, once we've been blunted emotionally, we become like the participants of the tea party in Alice in Wonderland—*we come to believe craziness is normal.* So until we're aware of who we are emotionally, it's impossible to really grow up.

The experts disagree about how much trauma it takes to cause harm. At a 2004 Guided Imagery Conference, Belleruth Naparstek called trauma a heart-stopping mix of terror and helplessness with a perception of impending annihilation. When asked if she would include in that definition the humiliation, embarrassment, and shame many children experience, she said no. But I disagree. I would side with David Bressler, Ph.D., co-founder of the Academy of Guided Imagery, who said that everyone has been traumatized, and that shame and humiliation murder our souls.

At the conference, Dr. Bressler cited an example of how powerful even one experience can be in creating trauma. In their spearmint-flavored water, baby rats (scientists love those baby rats, don't they?) were given a poison that made them deathly sick for one day. They were never again exposed to the aroma of spearmint until they reached adulthood and were given a choice of water that was either plain or flavored by spearmint. To a one, they refused the spearmint-tainted water.

The work of Bessel van der Kolk[72] shows there is a reward associated with the threat/arousal/endorphin cycle that gets activated in trauma victims. That reward seems to perpetuate seeking abusive relationships, for example, women who were abused as children marrying abusing spouses. Bessel van der Kolk refers to this "reward" system as an "addiction to trauma."[73]

I'm a fairly classic example of the effects of both large and small trauma. After being molested violently one time by a stranger at age seven, I shoved the event into my unconscious and didn't remember anything about it until my early 30s. However, I acted the memory out in my teenage years with promiscuity, low self-esteem, running away (getting me in trouble with the juvenile court system), and, of course, alcohol and drug abuse. The single trauma may have been enough to cause my acting out, but it was fed by the shame, humiliation, and neglect that went on in our family. For example, my dad—in his never gentle way—would yell at me and call me stupid when I couldn't understand a math problem he was helping me with. I remember wanting to disappear anytime he suggested "helping" me. I was terrified to do math until I went to college and actually did quite well in an algebra class.

Blocked Trauma Causes Disconnection

I work a lot with clients who have anxiety. From reports, research, and my own experience, I believe trauma causes most forms of anxiety. This is backed up by Peter Levine who states that when the human body can't discharge trauma (as animals naturally do when they freeze, feint, tremble, and shake it off), it creates symptoms such as anxiety, depression, and psychosomatic and behavioral problems as a way of containing held energy.[74] In a lecture, trauma expert, Dr. Scaer, showed slides of a polar bear tranquilized for medical reasons. As the bear woke up from his chemical nap, he shook and convulsed. Once awake, he ambled off, seemingly unaffected. Dr. Scaer says wild animals almost always complete a traumatic event by physically shaking it off, but humans and animals in captivity don't.

Trauma Lowers Stress Threshold

In my 20s, I was acutely sensitive and often overreacted emotionally. If the dog peed in the house, I might rage for 20 minutes. When my son did something that bothered me, same thing. I never knew what would set me off. Even today I watch my sister Lane have similar overreactions from time to time. She just can't manage the same amount of stress a person with a higher threshold can. Since we grew up in the same family, I believe the main difference is that I've been practicing—more

consistently for a longer time—body-mind practices that
heal stress.

Bill Harris, author of *Thresholds of the Mind*, discusses
research that supports our having a biological thermostat for
stress that can be sensitized by traumatic life events. He sites
a report from Dr. Seymour Levine, Ph.D., that this sensitization
to stress actually alters the physical patterns in the brain. The
body then produces too many of the chemicals like cortisol
and too few of the calming chemicals.[75]

Based on this, Harris has developed a program called
Holosync that uses an audio technology to re-synchronize
the hemispheres of the brain and create the calm, peace, and
happiness that long-term meditators experience. Among other
things, this technology raises the stress threshold. (Information
about Holosync is available at www.centerpointe.com) Bodymind practices such as meditation, EFT, and imagery are
known to balance the hemispheres of the brain over time so
they must also raise the stress threshold.

I believe how you raise your threshold for managing
stress is a matter of choice. I've used the Holosync CDs
and they stir up unconscious feelings, body sensations, and
memories just like meditation does. I've also used Touch,
Accept, Release, Action or TARA (explained in Chapter 8) and
EFT to release the feelings that got activated.

Denial of Trauma

President George W. Bush's childhood training in denial
has created an amazing ability to construct and live his own
version of reality, as Maureen Dowd of the *New York Times*
wrote in *Bush World*.[76] Many trauma survivors go on to self-
medicate with alcohol and drugs. We've been told that Bush
was a great "partier" in high school and college; he would brag
about how much he drank. He didn't quit drinking until he

was 40 and never entered recovery through either a treatment or 12-step program. In fact, though he's admitted he had a drinking problem, he denies ever being an alcoholic.

Dr. Justin Frank makes the case that Bush's childhood grief caused by his sister's illness with leukemia and death when he was six years old as well as his learning problems, created anxiety. He coped with it as many do—too much alcohol. Once he quit drinking, the anxiety flared and he dealt with it by switching addictions—this time to religion. (Could his exercising two hours a day be considered an addiction?) It's known that endorphins act on the same receptors as alcohol does, and that these endorphins can be released by ". . . deep expressions of religious faith," as Dr. Justin Frank wrote in *Bush on the Couch*.[77]

Bush's black-and-white thinking, ability to say one thing and do another ("I am a compassionate conservative"), and notorious lack of introspection (neither he nor other family members go for that "psychobabble") can also be symptoms of the untreated alcoholic personality.[78]

In the extremes, we can look at monsters like Hitler (raised by an abusive father who hated Jews) and Saddam Hussein (father beat and humiliated him constantly) who sometimes grow up to be monsters themselves. Most abused children don't become perpetrators, but too often, they don't deal with their broken hearts or wounded psyches.

Sadly, many people live with the struggle and addictions that result from trauma.

Trauma Makes Us More Vulnerable to Stress

Does America seem to be stuck in adolescence to you? From road rage to continual belief in the power of war to stop war, Americans sometimes act like kids who just have to have their way—*now*. Futurist Carl Sagan said it best when he coined the term "technological adolescence." He stated that perhaps there are no records of other civilizations more advanced than ours because, at this stage, we annihilate ourselves.

The effects of trauma go beyond the personal to the collective. In *The God Code*[79], Eric Hobsbawm called the period from 1900 to 1999 "... the most murderous century in recorded history." Advanced technology, without the wisdom of the mature and compassionate heart, not only promotes addiction but is dangerous to life.

It wasn't until after I started my own healing that I was able to grow up emotionally by learning to replace what was missing—the ability to tell myself the truth and go inside for safety, comfort, nurturance, and LOVE. Compare that with always running away from myself by going out with friends, or constant busy-ness or sucking on the ever present cigarette.

Trauma makes us more vulnerable to the ordinary stresses of life. When we're stressed and our biochemistry has been programmed with ups and downs, it causes us to seek other stimulants or chemical soothers to get through the day. The ordinary stresses of life in and of themselves lead us to seek relief, however our culture deems acceptable.

Trauma is painful because of its vast, far-reaching consequences that radiate out from the individual to society as a whole. Today, science is verifying what therapists have long known and worked for—that we can heal most of the effects of trauma with bodymind skills. However, we also need awareness and skills to stop preventable traumas such as child abuse from occurring in the first place.

While it takes effort to heal our hearts and our souls, the work pays off for us individually, for our families, and for the greater whole. The question to ask is: "If life takes a certain amount of work, do I want to just survive each day or put in the effort to feel better, be happier, and raise healthier children?"

It's been fascinating to watch my extended family become increasingly more functional as one by one almost all have quit abusing substances. With healthy self-examination or with therapy, we have released enough of the fear and stress of childhood to be happy and live consciously. In my observation of families for over 20 years, when one person in the family changes addictive behavior, it sets off a positive domino effect.

If you're wondering if you're a trauma survivor, take this assessment to find out.

TRAUMA SELF-QUIZ

If you're wondering whether some of the fear and stress you experience relates to trauma, here is a chance to check in with yourself. The first job of childhood is survival, so painful memories often get tucked away. If you're feeling emotionally vulnerable or unsafe, don't take the assessment until you have the support of a friend or therapist. You may want to go to Chapter 11 and do a Special Place Imagery exercise beforehand.

Answer these questions fully and honestly for yourself:

What's my first memory as a child? _____.

Did I experience physical, emotional, sexual abuse or rape as a child? Yes | No

Are there memories of childhood that are still painful or that I avoid? Yes | No

Did my caretakers have substance abuse problems? Yes | No

Have I been in a car accident or had other serious injuries? Yes | No

Do I use alcohol, drugs (legal or illegal—prescription or non), food, work, or other addictive activities to cope with stress or anxiety? Yes | No

Was name calling, yelling, or threatening part of my parents' style of communication when I grew up? Yes | No

Do I have anxiety or depression? Yes | No

Do I have flashbacks (intrusive memories) or nightmares? Yes | No

Do I have physical symptoms such as irritable bowel syndrome, migraine headaches, high blood pressure, fibromyalgia, or chronic aches and pains? Yes | No

Do I overreact emotionally to real or imagined slights from people close to me or people who have power such as a boss, partner, parent? Have I been told I'm over-sensitive by family members? Yes | No

" The root cause of
modern stress is the
discrepancy between TM (thinking mind)
consciousness and AM (ancestral mind)
consciousness, between modern
world and **ancestral** world.[8] "

~ Gregg D. Jacobs, Ph.D.

CHAPTER SIX

Chapter Six:

Chronic Stress and Addiction

MEET MARTHA. Martha is tired, very tired. She's also grumpy, overweight, has big bags under her eyes, and just wants to get through one more day. Martha is 40, married 16 years, has two teenagers and works as a personnel director for a large county office. Last summer her mother had a stroke. Martha is the only child living in the area and has been elected by her family to be there for mom. Before her mother's stroke, Martha knew the meaning of *stress*, but she kept it in check by walking three or four days a week. Now she just can't find the time. She's putting back on the 15 pounds she'd lost and every time she looks in the mirror she thinks, "Ugh, who is that woman?" Over the winter, she caught every flu or cold bug that came through the office. Her cholesterol is way up and she knows she's a wreck, but is so overwhelmed, all she can do is survive.

Martha, like lots of stressed folks, drinks a lot of coffee to get through her day. She stops at a Starbucks drive-thru on the way to work every morning and orders a Vente—20 ounces and 180 mg. of caffeine. At her morning break, she tops it off from the break room coffee—12 ounces and 210 mg. of caffeine. Lunchtime arrives and she has a large diet Coke—16 ounces and 65 mg. of caffeine. When her 3:00 PM slump hits she gets an afternoon Starbucks—8 ounces and 160 mg. of caffeine. That's a grand total of *615 mg. of caffeine* without her evening chocolate of 40 mg. she eats while watching TV. Martha thinks she's helping herself by keeping her energy up. But she has insomnia, stomach problems, heart palpitations, and anxiety. She's thinks she may need an anti-anxiety medication like the ones shown on TV ads. What calm, happy, beautiful people they are!

Martha, like so many of us, is unaware of the serious effects such high amounts of caffeine can have. After all, caffeine is a *drug* and caffeine intoxication is listed in the therapists' Diagnostic and Statistical Manual known as the DSM IV as a potentially serious problem at only 250 mg. I doubt the FDA would ever approve caffeine today.

I asked Martha to take the Caffeine Quiz (at the end of this chapter) and notice which symptoms she was experiencing. Here was our conversation after completing it.

"I can't believe my insomnia, heart palpitations and stomach aches are just because I drink coffee. I'm quitting today!" she said.

"Hang on, Martha. I suggest you wean yourself off caffeine gradually or you'll have big-time withdrawals like headache, fogginess, deep fatigue, nausea, even vomiting. Why don't you try cutting back a little at a time? Which of your coffee times would be easiest to let go of?"

"My mid-morning break coffee. I think I can get by until lunchtime."

"Do that for the next week, then pick another coffee time to let go of the following week."

Martha felt hopeful knowing that it was within her power to change how she felt. Over a six-week period, she reduced her caffeine down to her morning and an afternoon Starbucks. Her next goal is to go to half caffeine and half de-caf. After just two weeks, Martha noticed she was sleeping better and feeling far less anxious.

WHAT IS YOUR CAFFEINE INTAKE?

Start by first checking out how many cups of coffee you're drinking a day and what the caffeine content is. Then take the Caffeine Quiz at the end of this chapter to see if caffeine is a problem for you. Use this chart to add up the amounts. (Yes, Starbucks coffee does have more caffeine than most other coffees.)

Coffee, Anyone?

8 oz. brewed coffee	140 mg. caffeine
20 oz. brewed coffee	300 mg.
18 oz. brewed decaf	15 mg.
Starbucks	
8 oz. drip (Short)*	160-200 mg.
12 oz. (Tall)*	300 mg.
16 oz. (Grande)*	400 mg.
20 oz. (Vente)*	500 mg.
Starbucks Espresso (behind-the- bar drinks)	
8 & 12 oz. (1 shot espresso)*	90 mg.
16 & 20 oz. (2 shots espresso)*	180 mg.
Other Drinks	
8 oz. cup green tea**	40-50 mg.
6 oz. black tea**	70 mg.
12 oz. soda**	40-100 mg.
Red Bull	"One can of Red Bull® Energy Drink contains approximately the same amount of caffeine as a cup of coffee." (www.redbull.com)

* Starbucks info provided by customer service rep 11-17-04.

According to Stephen Cherniske, author of *Caffeine Blues*, anything over 600 mg. daily intake of caffeine leads to almost certain addiction. Symptoms of caffeine addiction include mood swings or periods of depression, headaches, fatigue, anxiety, insomnia, irritability, constipation, and muscle tension especially in the neck, shoulders, or stomach (a partial list). Isn't it interesting that what we use to fix the effects of stress makes us more stressed?[81]

Are we as a nation becoming more addicted to caffeine? Talking to a newspaper reporter, Starbucks spokesperson Nicole Millers said, "Starbucks will open 1,800 more units worldwide this year (in 2006)," making more than 11,000 stores worldwide and counting. Specialty Coffee Association of America notes that Americans spend about $10 billion annually at coffee outlets of all brands.[82]

I'm increasingly concerned about caffeine abuse. I see more teens blithely using caffeine to get through the day, needing their coffee before school, a Red Bull or two at break, and sodas later in the day. Davey, 16, complained bitterly about not being able to sleep at night. His parents dragged him in to see me because he was abusing alcohol to get to sleep. At the most extreme, abuse of caffeine has been reported to include nausea, vomiting, racing heart, hallucinations, panic attacks, and chest pains ending for a few in a stay at an intensive-care unit.

Everybody gets stressed occasionally and then we rebalance, right? In theory, yes. But what's happening in our culture is alarming. Rather than giving our bodies time to naturally replenish, we bump up our expectations and drive ourselves harder. Caffeine is the perfect stimulant for that. Unlike the ever-ready Eveready bunny, we can't just insert more batteries to keep performing, so we increase our caffeine intake. Like Martha, we know we *should* do something different, but being constantly on the go and stressed has become the norm. After all, isn't *everyone* stressed?

Toxic Stress: A Set-Up for Addiction

Pamela Peeke, M.D., who wrote the catchy-titled *Fight Fat After Forty*, researched chronic, or what she calls toxic stress and how it leads to weight gain and addictive acting out. Dr. Peeke says that stress becomes toxic when it starts to poison our body systems chronically "... and when it never allows the body to shut down the stress response." ... "When Toxic Stress is allowed to permeate your daily existence, it can result in self-destructive behaviors. These behaviors include anything perceived as an antidote to emotional pain such as inappropriate eating, excessive alcohol consumption and the use of tobacco and drugs."[83] Add chronic or toxic stress to the recipe for addiction. Stress increases vulnerability to grabbing whatever's handy, anything to get relief *now*. How does Martha spell R- E- L- I- E- F? Starbucks! For Bob, it's a few hours nightly with his free-cell computer game. Unfortunately, Bob ignored his family, didn't pay the bills, and isolated himself. His hobby became an addiction and a problem.

As noted by author Doc Childre in *Freeze Frame*, "Science has shown that we pay a serious price for our stress. A 20-year study conducted by the University of London School of Medicine has determined that unmanaged mental and emotional reactions to stress present a more dangerous risk factor for cancer and heart disease than cigarette smoking or eating high cholesterol foods."[84]

We're Even Competitive About Stress

Gina heard a bragging yet complaining martyr-ish tone from many of the guests at a Christmas party she attended. She had recently sold a company and now has plenty of money to retire. She spends her time buying, fixing up, and selling houses. Her past job smothered her in stress; now she was enjoying a more relaxed pace—"more precious than money" as she says.

Listening to all the busy professionals converse around her, Gina was struck by the high degree of stress being experienced. She heard statements like "Why, I've had to go to three parties so far this week and I have two more tomorrow. This is our busy time of year; I don't know how I'll get through the holidays." (Of course, one can choose not to go to a party or two.)

Some people wear stress like a badge of honor that measures value and worth. It's not just about how much money we're making, but how exhausted we are. This attitude of denial reminds me of the story about frogs in boiling water. If Americans 50 years ago were plunked into a typical lifestyle today, they would immediately leap out, aghast at the pace and the pressures. But we've been slowly warming to this pace for the last 40 years and have adjusted—sort of. One researcher has measured life as now 44% more difficult than in 1964[85]. We're altered to the point of not letting ourselves see how we're slowly cooking ourselves to death.

Younger workers have never known anything different. During the high-tech, high-demand years of the 1990s, people thrived on working 60, 80, even 100 hours a week. Of course they were exhausted with no time for relationships or self-care, but they were making tons of money. Thrilling and worth it, right? There's an old saying in addiction treatment circles: "The higher the high the more painful the crash."

Change: The Faster We Go, the Better?

In the early 1990s, I began noticing the speed of change around us and its stressful ripple effects. I taught "Moving

Through Change" seminars to raise awareness and counter the effects of stressful change on the bodymind. The Internet was beginning to ignite and cell phones had come available, though not yet widely used. Personal computers started showing up in our homes, not just our offices. This new exciting technology made people accessible 24/7, whether they wanted to be or not.

Andrew Wood, a communications professor at San Jose State University, calls the need for a constant barrage of electronic media and technology "omnitopia." He says people think they have the right to play their booming music but don't necessarily consider the rights of the people around them.[86]

My cousin Kim, a world-renowned polo player who practices daily balance, told me about Grant, who'd arrived for their date and barely said "Hi," then got on his cell phone for the next 20 minutes. He totally ignored her. And then he had a hard time understanding the problem when she said, "Grant, I turn off my cell phone when I'm on a date. I'd like it if you did the same." Since he didn't get her message, he didn't get to spend time with her.

What's up with (primarily) young people walking together down a street yet talking separately on their cell phones? Yes, relationships are changing as a result of technology. As Aunt Phyllis told me, "When I was young, we used to smoke while walking down the street. Cigarettes were our little friend. You don't see a lot of kids smoking anymore, maybe because they're on their cell phones."

A survey of 575 high school students found that the top third of cell phone users—students who used their phones more than 90 times a day—scored higher on depression and anxiety measures compared to students who used their phones only 70 times a day. (Study presented May 23, 2006 at a meeting of the American Psychiatric Association in Toronto)[87]–

Author Doc Childre states that the "mind-emotional reactions" caused by constant

". . . shifting from cell phones, email, voice mail, faxes, co-workers and family trying to get your attention means you're shifting your attention up to 150 times a day."[88] Attention deficit anyone? This constant shifting of attention adds stress and affects health and well-being.

PACE OF CHANGE

In 2001, information was reported to double every 12 to 18 months.

In 1995, information doubled every 30 to 36 months.

In 1954, information doubled every 20 years.

It took the planet several million years to reach 3 billion humans and only 50 years to add the next 3 billion.

WARNING: IMPENDING HEART ATTACK

John, 58, was recovering from a heart attack that almost ended his life. His doctor recommended counseling to lower stress and address his workaholic lifestyle.

"I'm lucky to be alive. The doctor says I need to cut back on my work, but my customers need me," said John, explaining that his tile company needed him and he loved working.

"Unfortunately, working is all I do. My family has never been too happy about it and I guess it hasn't been good for my health."

I introduced the idea of balance. We talked about how much total energy he had during the day and how much he was giving out to others. We also discussed possible ways to replenish his energy: rest, fun, and relaxation.

"What do you do for fun, John?" I asked.

"I work. That's fun for me."

"Okay, let me ask you something. What did you do for fun as a child?"

"I played cowboys and Indians and baseball and regular boy stuff."

"Of those, what was the most fun?"

"I haven't thought of this in a long time, but I had a stamp collection my uncle helped me start. I think I still have it somewhere."

"Hmm . . . tell me more."

John described a loving relationship with his uncle that made him feel normal in his "crazy family." During the summers, he'd visit his uncle and they'd spend time buying, selling, and booking stamps.

"I think I'm okay because of Uncle Stewart. I learned so much from him. We'd take off and go to stores all over Southern California looking for a particular stamp. When I'd go back home, I'd look at my stamp book almost every night. I knew Uncle Stewart cared about me."

John decided he wanted to see if he could find his old stamp book and check into stamp collecting. We also discussed balancing social time with family and friends. Over a few months, he made a genuine effort to redistribute his energy from "all work and no play" to something healthier. His progress was impressive.

Like John, most of us are so busy, we're not conscious of the negative, cumulative effects of stress. We run on a continual stress high. According to Doc Childre, ". . . the sheer volume of stressful reactions people face—many of which are automatic and unconscious—represents the most serious challenge to health, productivity and organizational coherence. It is nonstop."[89]

Self-Care: The Antidote to Stress

"Every state of mind is a state of our immune system."[90]

- Dr. Candace Pert

My friend Dewey, a bank executive took years of ribbing from his associates because, every day after lunch, he turned off his phone, closed his door, and napped for 20 minutes. I think he was more in tune with his needs than most people will let themselves be. He retired in good health and is thoroughly enjoying life after work. I admire him for having the courage to listen to his body's needs and attend to them.

We can't forget that our bodies aren't machines. We function best when we have balance between the demands of our lives and the needs of our bodies. Animals and young children live from their body wisdom. They nap when they're tired, eat when they're hungry, and cry when they need attention. Every waking dog or cat stretches its muscles. How much muscle tension would we let go of just by stretching throughout the day?

STRESS CHECK-IN

Without judgment, ask yourself how stressed you feel on a scale of 0-10 (10 most—0 least). Where in your body do you most experience the stress?

Try this right now: Reach up to the ceiling with both arms. Look up at the ceiling and push one arm toward the ceiling and then the other. Do that two or three times. Let your arms float back to your lap. Then take a full, deep breath into your abdomen, allowing it to fully expand with your inhale. As you exhale, imagine a balloon collapsing. Take three or four more breaths. Notice any places of tension on your body and breathe right into those.

Breathe in and imagine that your inhale is nurturing every part of you—your mind, your body, your emotions, and your spirit. Let your breath flow into your heart and stay there a moment. Exhale and release, release, release everything you don't need. Take at least ten breaths, then give your body your gentle attention. Notice what's different.

If you skipped over this, go back—please go back—and do it. In only a few minutes, you can give yourself a mini break. Your body, your mind, and your co-workers & family will thank you.

What is Self-Care?

"Psychological stress is the net effect of a condition you are resisting or wish to escape, but the condition does not have any power in itself."[91]

- David R. Hawkins, M.D., Ph.D.

* * *

At the third session of a Take Loving Charge*tm group, Connie checked in by saying how hard it was for her to give herself even ten minutes a day.

"I know I'm supposed to be practicing that daily Emotional Check-In, but every time I sit down to do it I feel so *guilty.*"

Other women in the group nodded. Jessica, 5-feet' 2

inches", dressed all in black, burst out, "Connie, I know just
what you mean. It's like I'm not worth the time to take care
of myself, yet all day long I'm taking care of others. I raid the
fridge after the kids go to bed—food will take care of me. I'm
so good at guilt I could scream."

"I'm just like my mom, giving, giving, giving and resenting
the hell out of it," Wendy said. "Mom would wear herself out
baking cookies for Girl Scouts, Boys Scouts, whatever, and
cleaning all day long. Of course, we couldn't sit down either.
We had lists and chores and not much play time. She died at
age 54 of a heart attack. I was in my 20s, had two babies, and
needed her more than ever."

Julie, with short brown spiky hair tipped with red,
tightened her mouth, "My mom took care of herself all day
long by smoking cigarettes and drinking beer. When I got
home from school, I made dinner and helped my brother
and sister with their homework. By that hour, she was gone,
ya know, drunk. Dad came home and helped me. He at least
appreciated all I did," Julie added.

"If I try to relax or take it easy, I'm scared I'll become
Mom. I don't drink, but I sure can eat."

Sheila, with flawless dewy skin, laughed, "You should see
the letter I got from my daughter-in-law. Last time I told you I
was going to say something about her complaining all the time
about how tired she is. She wrote me a letter and said she was
'. . . highly offended that (I said) the stress in my life is of my
own making.' Does she think the stress fairy is picking on her?"

"So, why do we have so much resistance to taking care of
ourselves?" I asked.

"What do you mean 'take care of ourselves'?"
Wendy asked.

"Well, I define self-care as the ability to be *aware of my
needs* for rest, replenishment, and balance, then *taking the*

necessary actions to meet those needs," I said.

"Sounds impossible and not much fun," said Joan, quiet until now.

"I'm forty-eight and I grew up being taught to take care of my brother and sister. I watched all the women in my family and my friends' families spend most of their time taking care of other people. It feels *sinful* and completely unnatural to take time for myself. I know we're supposed to practice this new stuff and it doesn't have to be comfortable, but this might be too hard."

"We all have been in the place where we do something we don't want to do because of guilt rather than because we really want to. I love what Dr. Mate, who wrote *When The Body Says No*[92] says about *guilt*. When he feels guilty, he sees it as choosing to do something for himself and is able to ride the guilt out. He says if the choice is between choosing for himself and resentment at the other person, he'll choose guilt every time.

"Everything in life comes down to choice. I've been working on balance for twenty years, so practice these new ideas a step at a time. Yes, doing anything that pushes our comfort zone is difficult. And I still feel guilty at times. But an hour lying out in the backyard with a book on a spring day with the sun warming my shoulders is fun for me. It refreshes me. I've learned it feels better than the alternative—being stressed and pissed off or depressed. We're *not* used to nurturing ourselves. Like you said, Wendy, we're afraid. But, believe me, we are worth the practice it takes. A few minutes a day has a big payoff."

In my groups, I teach people to *pay attention to their feelings and to what they need.* Self-care means listening to and taking ourselves seriously. Many women (and even more men) feel uncomfortable choosing to nurture themselves. It goes against all their training to be nice and pleasing—*for themselves*. They feel *bad* if they're not constantly keeping their antennae tuned to the needs of everyone else around them. Others push, push, push to stay on top of the game of life by out-competing everyone. Neither one reflects care and compassion for the self.

My group members resist giving themselves even a little time each day because it goes against their "take care of others" programming and drive to constantly be productive. They forget to do their homework or even lose their paperwork. They look blank when I ask how the last couple of weeks were emotionally. "Fine, okay, good." Both guilt and punishment they understand, but being kind and loving makes them feel even more guilty. In my experience, it takes a new group six months to a year to consistently practice self-care skills.

Some women are furious about being asked to consider self-care. After giving a talk on the subject to a group of Soroptimists, an irate woman came charging up to me practically spitting in my face. "How dare you tell me I'm responsible for my stress. It's not my fault. I am so insulted!" Her anger was so powerful, I took a step back. I knew she was more angry with herself than me. And I felt sad because nothing I said that moment would make any difference. This victim's attitude of "it's not my fault and I can't do anything about it" isn't uncommon. But if she's not in charge of her life, who is?

Prevention = Love and Gratitude

Are most babies stressed? Not usually. As infants, we're in love with ourselves. We're born with the fullest capacity and potentiality to love. We quickly learn it's okay to love or feel good about ourselves only if we please others, get good grades, make the team, and so on. We think, "It's not okay to love myself when I've done something wrong. I need to defend myself against making mistakes. I must be constantly vigilant and preferably perfect." This tension to "do" rather than "be" creates stress.

We learn to turn away from our internal awareness system, our emotions, and body wisdom; we rely on what others think. Of course, deep inside, this doesn't feel right either. Now we're struggling and ask, "Should I follow my heart and become a dancer or do what my mom wants and go to law school? She'll be so proud."

The thousands of tiny struggles within our mind (rational, critical, analytical) and heart (emotional, imaginal, spiritual) wear us down. The *struggle*—push or pull, right or wrong, good or bad, makes us prone to stress, illness, and coping with addictive behaviors.

Love, appreciation, and gratitude seem like foreign territory only because we've forgotten. We're taught to be well-behaved workers more than loving, lovable, and balanced human beings creating the lives we thrive in. But somewhere deep inside, the traces of wisdom remain. It takes re-educating our bodymind to live from love and gratitude rather than stress, chaos, drama, trauma—and addiction.

Self-care isn't just watching a football game or shopping with the girls. They're fine and fun, but I'm talking about honoring our true needs. When we're in touch with ourselves, we have a guidance system to rebalance the stresses and strains of modern living. We may not feel capable of changing the world, but we can begin to heal ourselves today.

The world won't quit making demands of us—but we can *choose* which ones we pay attention to. Like a divining rod seeking water, with time and practice, we develop the ability to find and honor the source within us. Struggle, pain, and suffering shift—even totally release—as we fill up with what truly nourishes and nurtures us.

LOVE AND ACCEPTANCE

"I remember when I came for the first meeting and you said your goal for us was not about losing weight, but about learning to love, appreciate, and accept ourselves. You said when that happened, the weight would come off. Lynn, I almost got up and walked out. What kind of a diet program is this?" Joan shared in one of our first group meetings. "It didn't make sense to me, either," Wendy added. "How can I possibly love and accept myself being fat? That would mean I'd given up on becoming skinny. I was sure I wasn't going to come back, but you were so gentle and we laughed a lot. So, I thought, what the heck, I'll try it again."

"Yeah, but then you started having us *notice* how we feel and what we need—what the hell is a *need*? I need to eat, I need to shop, and what else is there?" Sheila paused. "But you know, once in awhile, I can tell that I'm angry. So instead of answering my mother-in-law's calls, I pretend I don't hear the phone. Someday I'll be able to say no to her, but not yet."

"I actually did some stretching and breathing the other morning before work and I had a great day. Taking those five minutes for myself turned out to be easy. But afterwards, I felt uncomfortable and didn't do it the next day," said Wendy.

The Heart Knows the Way

Guided Imagery is like EFT in that it quickly (and effortlessly) demonstrates the benefits of relaxation and self-care. Guided Imagery has been studied with Viet Nam veterans and other trauma survivors. Along with EMDR (Eye Movement Desensitization and Reprocessing), EFT has become considered *the* treatment of choice for stress and trauma.

Guided Imagery is easier to practice than meditation yet produces the same results. It reduces anxiety, increases relaxation, improves mood, increases self-esteem, decreases emotional numbness, and improves cognition.[93] I'd say that's good medicine.

* * *

"Heart opening imagery increases feelings of love, gratitude, and connection with the larger world..." which increases our ability to be self-nurturing.[94]

* * *

Relaxation Response

Bodymind practices—like getting out into nature to garden, walking, camping, consciously breathing, doing yoga or meditation—have been effective in reducing the stress response and increasing the relaxation response.

The relaxation response phrase was coined by Herbert Benson in 1975 after researching the health benefits reported by practitioners of Transcendental Meditation or TM. These meditators had lowered their blood pressure, heart rates, breathing rates, and muscle tension. They also had less anxiety, less physical pain, and improved sleep patterns. Notice that all of these physical improvements are the exact opposite of what the stress response creates.[95] Dr. Gregg Jacobs, who wrote *The Ancestral Mind*, says that TM and other bodymind practices reduce the stress response because they relax the constant mental chatter of the thinking mind and activate the mammalian and reptilian brains, which are connected to sensory and emotional experience.[96] Experiencing the world through our senses and emotions is more pleasurable than using only the objective and distant thinking mind. And pleasurable emotions and body experiences increase relaxation. Because we feel nurtured from within the way nature meant for us to feel using our own natural senses and emotional experiences, anxiety is reduced. Consequently, the need for addictive coping to escape or falsely comfort ourselves diminishes.

In the Take Loving Charge groups, we practice both EFT and imagery because it takes the participant *within*. Through breathing, body sensing, feeling appreciation, and right-brain creativity begins reconnecting us to our inner selves.

How? Guided Imagery bypasses the so-called left-brain where judgment, analyzing, and over-thinking take place. For optimal fulfillment, we want a high-functioning left brain *in balance* with the right brain and with emotional and physical awareness.

If all this seems foreign to you, you're in good company. If you don't know how to speak Spanish, when someone begins telling you how to make burritos in Espanol, you won't get it. But if the cook shows you the ingredients and walks you through the cooking process, then the language barrier melts away.

IMAGERY TO RELAX YOUR BODY

If you have soft music to play in the background, put some on to help connect your heart with your right brain.

Allow yourself to get comfortable, either sitting with your feet on the ground and ankles uncrossed or lying down. Begin to become aware of your breath without changing it . . . just allowing your breath to gently move in and out of your body. Now imagine there is a balloon in your lower abdomen and as you inhale, your breath expands that balloon. As you exhale, the balloon collapses. Take a few slow, deep breaths, focusing on your breath expanding and collapsing that balloon.

Imagine a golden ball of light or energy above your head. This beautiful "lite" light is swirling and moving slowly and then breaks open like an egg. It pours its gentle energy over and through and around you . . . from the top of your head to the bottom of your feet . . . allowing relaxation to flow through you.

The golden light pours into the top of your head, flows down the sides and back of your head, and moves across your forehead. It swirls around your eyes, releasing tension there, and through your temples and ears . . . continuing to breathe consciously, that golden light allows your cheeks to let go and your mouth and jaw to release any tension . . . and that golden energy flows through your neck and into your shoulders where it deeply penetrates the muscles there and moves down your arms. . . all the way through your wrists and hands into your fingertips and right out the ends . . . pulling what you don't need with it. The golden light moves through your upper, middle, and lower back muscles and cells. As you breathe, your body keeps letting go of its burdens, its cares and worries. . . and that golden light wraps around your torso into your chest and especially the area around your heart . . . relaxing, relaxing, relaxing. . . and flowing into your solar plexus, abdomen, hips, and bottom . . . allowing a sense of connection with your body as the light flows down your legs and ankles and finally into your feet and out your toes.

As the golden light moves out your toes it pulls with it any remaining tensions or cares you'd like to release. Breathe into your abdomen and just be aware of your body. . . no judgment, just a gentle noticing of any sensations, tingling, places of comfort. . . and when you're ready, you can allow your attention to come fully back into the room. . . bringing with you whatever you need.

"Everyone needs
emotional recovery. **"**

- Young patient at end of a 30-day treatment program

CHAPTER SEVEN

Chapter Seven:

Emotional Wisdom Defined

MOST PEOPLE who enter in-patient or—out-patient treatment don't do so willingly. The court, an employer, spouse, or other family member is fed up with the behavior of the addict and shouts in frustration, "Go to treatment, or else."

When I was a counseling intern in 1985 at a large in-patient facility in Sacramento, California, I witnessed the "blessing" of being forced into treatment. A young man in his 20s (I'll call him Jeff) had reached the end of a 30-day recovery program. He "graduated" amidst congratulations from the staff and his family.

Jeff, nervous and clutching his coffee cup, stood before us at the ceremony. "I've learned so much in the last few weeks. I just wish everyone could get treatment. I don't mean only addicts and alcoholics, I mean *everyone*. We *all* need recovery— to know how to deal with our feelings." We counselors looked at each other and nodded, immediately grasping his point—that we live in an addictive society largely caused by our lack of emotional education. As a result, *everyone* could benefit from emotional recovery programs. In some ways, those in treatment are lucky; they're shown the path that leads not to the Emerald City in the Wizard of Oz, but to their own hearts.

Like a shiny red apple that you bite into and find the rotten spot within, society has taught us to package ourselves so we look good from the outside. But when the emotional core gets pricked, what happens? Fear, confusion, pain, stress, and emptiness emerge. We try hard to appear normal, plod along, keep making a living. But how many of us know how (or want to take time to learn) to go inside for healthier solutions?

"OH, HELL, ANOTHER DAY"

Before you freak out and say, "I'm not like *them*—those people in treatment," hang on. If you're reading this book, you're right— you're probably not as far along the continuum as those who end up in treatment. Yet, is the quality of your life right now *really* what you want it to be? Are you as happy, balanced, peaceful, energetic, and full of vitality as you'd like? Or perhaps you wake up already stressed on Monday morning saying "Oh, hell. Another day." Do you use fast food, shopping, or Internet browsing (or all of these) to distract yourself from how unhappy you feel? No matter how many cups of coffee you drink or shoes you buy, does anything change inside?

The difference between the addicts in treatment programs and those outside is this: The addicts—at the far end of the addiction continuum—have let their lives career out of control. However, millions upon millions of others who'd never call themselves addicted struggle with similar emotional challenges. (Are you included?) Their days fill with problems and moods—and they shrug if off, saying "that's life."

However, you can learn skills that will put you more in charge. Thank goodness.

Addictions are driven by emotions, particularly fear, which I lump together with all the so-called negative emotions of anger, resentment, sadness, guilt, and shame. These aren't really negative emotions, but they're the ones we resist and avoid because they don't feel as good as the happy ones.

Of course, judging ourselves for having "bad" feelings makes us feel even worse. We come to believe we should get rid of those feelings in any way possible because then, we hope, we'll feel better. And, we do—temporarily.

A BRIEF HERSTORY OF EMOTIONAL REPRESSION

In 1973, Billie Jean King defeated the gleefully sexist Bobby Riggs in the man vs. woman tennis match of the century. At the time I lived in Boise, Idaho, with my first husband Marty, his younger brother Steven, and my younger sister Lane. There was a lot at stake on the outcome of the match in our household. If Bobby had defeated Billie Jean, Lane and I would never have heard the end of it. But with Billie Jean winning, the balance of power in our household tipped. We were jubilant. Imagine, mere women could be fully capable, strong, and smart—just like Billie Jean King.

What changed for us? After this match, Lane and I didn't have to tolerate as much overt machismo as before. We felt more comfortable asking for and demanding equal participation with household chores, making dinner, and going to the market. Not that the guys always complied, but Lane and I— and women everywhere—felt energized by this victory. Billie Jean's win became a victory for all of us.

Prodigal Daughter Needs to Come Home

Over the last 30 years, much has changed for women in America and western society. Today, women have an increased number of opportunities and increased amounts of stress to go with them. We work outside the home, raise our families, and manage our households. Increasingly, we expect more of ourselves and our relationships. Yet with the greater number of opportunities for women, the so-called feminine qualities of love, compassion, and the heart haven't advanced much in our society.

I call these qualities "emotional wisdom" and view it as the prodigal daughter who needs to be welcomed home from her long banishment. In some ways, the advantages of the women's movement have dampened appreciation of feminine emotions. In the corporate world, for example, many women find themselves forced to be "like the guys" to compete for plum jobs and be taken seriously. Recently, millions of working mothers have been escaping corporate confines to run their own businesses so they can stay home and care for their children. Attorneys in particular seem to be fleeing the mainstream rapidly. Could it be because the legal profession is the most analytical and least feeling-oriented one around?

Feminist historians such as Elizabeth Gould Davis[97] or Riane Eisler[98] wrote that in early history, feminine values like nurturing and creativity were equal to or even valued higher than male traits like aggression. The plentiful artwork left behind on cave walls portrayed women's revered, full-bodied status. Amazingly, it did not depict war and weapons, but relationships, mystery, and beauty.

However, at least since the time of early Christianity, there's been a split between the valuing of intellect and emotions, head and heart, male and female. It's essential that we heal this split because the over-valuing of intellect— reflected by the thinking brain discussed in Chapter 1— leads to imbalance. In turn, that imbalance leads to addictive behaviors in order to cope with the disconnection.

In the last decade, the importance of emotions has been gaining recognition. Published in 1995, Daniel Goleman's *Emotional Intelligence* received a lot of attention because of studies indicating the value of emotional IQ—not only in understanding and knowing individual health, but in preventing social problems. Dr. Goleman states that self-awareness is about recognizing a feeling as it happens, as he wrote, "Socrates's injunction: 'Know thyself' speaks to this keystone of emotional intelligence: awareness of one's own feelings as they occur."[99]

Getting to Know Ourselves Inside

In the 2001 movie *What Planet Are You From?* actor Gary Shandling plays an alien from a planet of men who experience no emotion. While accomplishing his mission of impregnating Earthwomen to replenish his planet, he begins to *feel*—something he's never experienced. When he goes back to his planet to teach the next batch of Earth-bound men what to expect and how to act on earth, he tells them that emotions are the way we go inside ourselves. Unless we can go inside, we can't know who we are.

For living in such a me-oriented culture, we are often woefully ignorant of what goes on inside us. We've learned to override our built-in tuning system of emotional and body awareness. As Baby Boomers reach mid-life by the millions looking for deeper meaning and greater fulfillment, a hard-to-ignore awareness has emerged that the perfect house and car and career are only a superficial solution. But who are we really?

"Only the Shadow Knows." This tagline from a 1940's radio show hints that the roles we accumulate—employee, mother, father, executive, single woman, son, daughter—act like layers of sediment covering a kernel of truth deep inside. An authentic self waits inside for us to discover—beyond our "somebody-ness" as Ram Dass notes in his book about his spiritual journey, *Be Here Now*.[100] (Ram Dass, previously known as Richard Alpert, experimented with psychedelics, as did many of us in the 1960s.)

In an undergraduate class I took, the professor asked this question: "Who are you, really?" I raised my hand and started spouting off my roles and accomplishments. He kept asking me the same question. I kept getting uncomfortable and soon stopped talking. The good student in me couldn't figure out the "right" answer. I felt embarrassed. Now I know I was answering from the "surface me."

EXPERIMENT: Tap into your emotional wisdom to answer the question "who am I?" How? By noticing your feelings and body sensations. What is your experiential truth of this moment? How are you feeling? Where are those feelings happening in your body? What are they telling you about what you need—attention, nurturing, adventure, rest, what else?

Take the few precious moments required to slow down and answer this vital question.

Bump Up Against Avoidance

Sally, a client who had a serious history of trauma, called to tell me she's getting married. We talked two minutes about her wedding and 20 minutes about all the illnesses plaguing her. That's not to say Sally's illnesses aren't a problem, but when I asked her if she was seeing a counselor to deal with them, she said no. It's clear to me that Sally is attached to what Eckhart Tolle calls her "pain body." He says that "... if you don't bring the light of your consciousness into the pain, you will be forced to relive it again and again."[101] I recommended Sally seek a therapist who works with EFT or EMDR. (You'll learn about EFT in Chapter 10.) Why? Because without learning to tell her own emotional truth, she runs the risk of becoming addicted to her illnesses and avoiding the deeper work of who she is. Marriage won't fix that.

To further explain the idea of "pain-body," in *The Power of Now*, Tolle states that we are addicted to our suffering, our pain-body. "The pain-body consists of trapped life-energy that has split off from your total energy field and has temporarily become autonomous through the unnatural process of mind identification. It has turned in on itself and become anti-life, like an animal trying to devour its own tail."[102] How does this addiction to suffering occur? It happens when children get confused about what's valuable and what isn't. Plus, we see addiction to suffering modeled by our parents when they cope with dissatisfactions, stresses, or constant busyness. It's like my mother used to say, "Children are like monkeys—monkey see, monkey do."

Lying to Avoid Pain

Commonly, children learn to lie about how they feel. Sally, for example, avoids her pain by lying—that is, social lying based on keeping her perceived image of being okay in place. "I'm okay, I'm getting married." Most of us take lying for granted, denying we ourselves are liars—such an unpleasant term. *We've come to believe it's unsafe to show or even feel our hurt, pain, or even our bliss.*

Now we didn't pop into this world lying; we acquired it from the people we most look up to—our parents, teachers, and clergy. They teach us through the small "white" lies they tell to make them look good or leave a particular impression. We learn through the large lies (such as sexual abuse in families or homosexuality hidden by the Catholic Church), too. Again, we get the message that how we *look* to the outside world is more important than how we *feel* inside.

White lies become hurtful in a my-parents-aren't-perfect sort of way. Could these white lies be your parents' cheating on their taxes or bragging about how much they paid for the pool their cousin put in for cheap? We vividly remember the first time we caught our parents lying in a big way. Didn't it feel like the wind had knocked us down? For me, it was when I realized that most of the drunken fights my parents had centered on Mom's infidelity and Dad's inability to forgive her.

Lies often become secrets. Our families (and that larger model, our government) attempt to keep the lid on them, yet children know anyway. When a parent realizes a child has overheard a grown-up's secret, that child is told, "Don't tell the neighbors. It's no one's business but our own." No matter how hard we try to control these secrets, they leak out.

Lies and secrets wound families, sometimes irreparably. In the neighborhood I grew up in was a bully named Leonard who scared the hell out of us kids. We all knew Leonard got beat up by his drunken father every Saturday night and we tried to stay out of the way of his anger. Leonard later became a cocaine addict and was killed in a car accident.

In the "good" Catholic family across the street—the family that didn't eat meat on Fridays and went to mass all the time— the dad was an alcoholic. In our family, our big secrets were the miscarriages caused by drunken brawls and the fact that Dad sometimes looked at us girls in a way that made us want to disappear.

Probably the greatest consequence of lying is that we learn to lie to ourselves. In addiction terms, we call this denial. My son Rich was forced into therapy by his father and me when he was a teen. He hated it and took great pride in not talking to the therapist. He even lied to the therapist. I told Rich it didn't matter so much that he was lying to the therapist; it mattered more that he was lying to himself. The therapist came up with a creative idea that I questioned at first but finally agreed to. He bargained with Rich and said he'd pay him ten bucks a session if he talked about something truthful and meaningful. Their agreement worked! In therapist terms, we call this "meeting the clients where they're at!"

Lies and secrets add up to a fear that others will find out that we're flawed. In truth, we're all flawed. Every time

I conduct a workshop or a weekend retreat, everyone shows up displaying their best, most polite selves. As we start talking about what's real, our flaws float to the surface and we discover we're normal. Flaws are part of life. Whenever people feel safe enough to reveal who they really are, I'm touched by how quickly the façade of politeness slips away.

The years have taught us to cloak who we are behind expressions like "I'm normal, I go to church, I have a good job, I'm married, and have two wonderful children. I look good to the outside world because I work hard at it." Yet all the hiding takes a lot of energy. It often results in addictive acting out to cope with stress and illness when our bodies can't take the abuse anymore.

What do we do about it? We learn to tell the truth *to* and *about* ourselves by paying attention to our bodies—like we did when we were children. As we peel off the layers of emotional debris, we learn that who we really are turns out to be much better than we believed.

"Aristotle put emotional intelligence this way: being able to 'be angry with the right person, to the right degree, at the right time, for the right purpose, and in the right way.'"[103]

The Nature of Emotions

Emotions are the navigational system to self-awareness and self-knowledge. Without knowing how to navigate them, we resemble ships bouncing on top of the ocean with no rudder. Some of us figure out by trial and error what to do but others either shut down and live in an emotional greyness, chaotically zooming up and down to find the next adrenaline high.

Once we learn and practice the necessary skills, we can put down the rudder, change direction, and head for emotional balance quickly and almost effortlessly. This keeps us feeling in charge and able to handle our challenges.

Little children are great examples of how emotions naturally flow. One minute my granddaughter Gracie is happily playing with her grandfather until he moves her toy car the "wrong" way. She gets mad, frowns, and says sternly, "Poppa, that's not the right way." Next minute, all is well.

MANDY AND ICE CREAM BINGING

Mandy, in one of my Take Loving Charge groups, had also been seeing me privately for about a year. One day, she walked into my office with a big smile on her face and said, "You know, Lynn, I am finally getting how Touch, Accept, Release, Action and Emotional Freedom Technique work together. Remember how I used to binge on a quart of ice cream every night and that wasn't enough? The first step was getting ice cream out of the house and that was hard. I'd let myself go to Baskin-Robbins once a week for a treat. Of course, I cheated once in a while. Well, it's been a whole month and I haven't gone to Baskin-Robbins at all. I don't feel that crazy 'gotta have it, gotta have it.' If I get a craving, I ask myself how I'm feeling and write it down, then I tap it out using TARA and EFT." (Go to Chapters 9 and 10 for details on these techniques.)

"Mandy, I'm so happy for you. And I can tell you like feeling more in charge."

"Not only that, but it's been really intense at work. Now when I'm angry, I stop and check in with how I'm feeling before I blast my partner like I used to. I breathe and tell myself 'it's okay to be mad and it's not okay to yell at her.' Then I wait until the right time to say what I need to say."

Yes, emotions are neutral energy until we wrap our judgments around them. When we let them move through us without attachments, no residues collect in our bodymind. But early on, we learn to stop the flow of this neutral energy because of criticism, shame, or dismissal of our feelings expressed by others around us.

The dictionary defines emotion as "an affective state of consciousness in which joy, sorrow, fear, hate, or the like, is experienced as distinguished from cognitive and volitional states and usually accompanied by certain physiological changes, as increased heartbeat, respiration, and often over manifestation, as crying, shaking or laughing."[104] The original meaning of the word "emotion" derives from *emotere*, the Latin word for "to move out."[105] While people once believed that thought was all-powerful, today we know that emotions are behind every action we take—the driving force of thought. Let's face it. Without our feelings, we'd sit dormant like an unplugged computer.

When we judge or suppress our "bad emotions" as children, we also suppress our joy and aliveness. It's the price we pay. Said my friend Marianne Peck, "When you bury your demons, you bury your angels." Many adults put their mouths in a permanent frown and wrinkle their eyes due to sadness and disappointment. They're victims of an old belief that "you're born, you suffer, you die." Hope, joy, and possibilities have been tromped out of these folks. How old were they when they gave up—at age three when they'd been called a brat a zillion times? What traumas have broken their emotional backbones throughout their childhoods?

We certainly don't want to get rid of feelings; we want to tune in, learn what we need from them, and let them move through us. If we avoid feeling the challenging emotions of fear, anger, guilt, or shame, we also limit our ability to experience the upper ranges of joy, even bliss.

Emotions show up on our faces when we frown or reveal joy when we're happy. *Feelings* are what we're aware of consciously. When driving the freeway, we might acknowledge that "I'm angry that guy won't get off my bumper." *Moods* last longer than feelings and it's harder to determine a specific trigger for them than for feelings. We make statements like, "I'm in a bad mood for no good reason" or "I constantly have anxiety in my stomach."

ADVANCED EMOTIONAL WISDOM

You know how you feel on a really good day when your spirits sing and you face the dreariest of chores with lightheartedness. What if you had more of these blessed days to make your life a joy rather than drudgery? Is it possible to *manufacture those days on demand?*

Here's the great news. By practicing emotional management skills like TARA and EFT (see Chapters 9 and 10) along with negative thought management (see in Chapter 12), you'll not only increase your available energy, vitality, happiness—your joy. You *will master your destiny.*

" We must recognize that
emotions, conscious or not, have
enormous influence
over our behavior: emotions are
motivations. Addictions are external
means of regulating **emotions**...[106] "

- Richard O'Connor, Ph.D.

CHAPTER EIGHT

Chapter Eight:

The Power of Emotional Wisdom

DURING THE 1980s, a shift toward less judgmental treatment of people with alcohol and drug addictions rippled into the mainstream. Treatment professionals stopped blaming the addict and started examining the origins of addiction—a quest to really understand what drives people to become addicted. A kind of consensus emerged: *Underneath all addiction is a disconnection between head and heart, between self and soul.*

Addicts gasp with relief when food not only fills their bellies but soothes their souls. When that first drink creates an "ah, finally I feel like myself," they feel better in the moment, believing they're "home" although it's a false home. (If you're saying, "But, I'm not an addict. I don't let alcohol or drugs get the better of me!" read on. "Lite" addicts also benefit from knowing about the origins of addiction.)

Many of my clients who have addictions say to me, "I just want to be *normal.*" Sometimes I laugh and respond with irony, saying, "I think it's normal to wonder if we're normal." But I know what they mean by "normal." They want to know they fit in, that they're okay. They want to know how to "quit beating the crap out of myself with judgment and perfectionism." As they get better, many even wonder what it would be like to be happier and more at peace. I call that sense of peace Emotional Wisdom.

If you're wondering what emotional wisdom consists of you're not alone. To get you started, look at the following list reflecting different characteristics of Emotional Wisdom. Pay attention to how you feel as you read each statement. Then go back and read through the list a second time and put a checkmark next to the characteristics of emotional wisdom that already exist in your life.

This list is not meant to "fix" or "perfect" you, but to acknowledge where you are and guide you where you want to go.

Emotional Wisdom to Increase JOY and Reduce Stress, Fear and Addictive Coping

- Enjoy your favorite ice cream without resorting to a binge and without guilt.
- Pop yourself back into balance or peace when your mood is low or your buttons get pushed.
- Sing your favorite melody in the car or dance through the house, just for the joy of it.
- Accept the full chorus of feelings—anger, sadness, fear, guilt, shame, joy, peace, even bliss—accepting the emotion is often enough to let it go.
- Access intuition—don't let buried emotions block it
- Walk your talk—be honest more than not.
- Heal your inner cynic by creating new eyes with which to see people—basically good, yet flawed—in other words, "normal."
- Have trusted friends you feel safe to be with—share your vulnerabilities, insecurities, doubts, and accomplishments.

- Care for others but don't over-care. If your 30-year-old son still lives at home rent-free and you're washing his clothes and cooking his food, you're over-caring.

- Practice radical stress management—pay attention to how you feel and what you really need: a new job, a relationship, no relationship, exercise, meditation, prayer, saying *no*, a nap, a night out, zoning out with your favorite TV show.

- Create loving self-care rituals—a healthy breakfast for enough energy until lunch, moderate exercise, getting enough sleep, taking time for replenishment (at least a two-week vacation once a year).

- Evaluate life satisfaction at least twice a year—appreciate where you are or make changes.

- Practice gratitude a few minutes each day—especially on the crappiest days.

- Have enthusiasm for life—a sense of aliveness and vibrancy that comes by accepting yourself, others, and the gift that life is.

- *Be* present—take time to *breathe* and ask, "Is my attention in this moment or on my never-ending to-do list?" While you're "doing" take a moment for "being" by noticing the sunset, the smile of a child at the supermarket, your neighbor's hello.

- Access connection with Spirit or Source—listen to your internal guidance.

- Take up a hobby for pleasure—whatever brings you joy. Find a way to engage with life creatively—sew, cook, work on your car, ride horses, paint, play baseball, garden, write a short story. As Auntie Mame said in Leo Buscaglia's *Living, Loving & Learning*, "Life is a banquet and most of us poor bastards are starving to death."[107]

- Be aware and accepting of a full gamut of emotions—yes, even resentment, shame, guilt.
- Appropriately express emotions—know the difference between accepting your feelings and telling others how you feel.
- Pop back into emotional balance when your buttons are pushed—take responsibility for staying in a "mood" and learning how to shift out of one.
- Be honest—not just saying it, but doing it.
- Be appropriately emotionally available/vulnerable with others.
- Live with integrity—if you say you will do something, others know you will follow through.
- Know and value your strengths—accept imperfections.
- Accept the loving nature of self and others—behave the opposite of "cynical."
- Be aware of your body's messages—emotions, sensations, needs.
- Feel alive, enthusiastic, energetic, vital, joyful—wake up happy to enjoy another day with a sense of excitement or peace.
- Use your emotional energy as a well-spring for creativity in the form of gardening, sewing, memory books, cooking, playing sports, writing, playing music, painting, drawing, singing, dancing, and more.
- Show gratitude—take a few minutes each day saying thank you for people and things in your life.
- Be able to create abundance or/and be happy with what you have—recognize that it's okay to have stuff, but stuff alone isn't the route to joyfulness.
- Know what you want out of life and have the energy to go after it—if you're stuck living life below the line in drama/

trauma/victim, you're focused on what's *not* working.

- Cope with stress and problems in healthy ways—breathing, nature, meditation, prayer, Yoga, Tai Chi, exercise, imagery, TARA, and EFT (explained in this book).
- Be present in this moment—breathe deeply and often.

After going through the list, select and circle the three statements that represent behaviors or feelings you want *more* of in your life. What specific actions are you willing to do today, tomorrow, and this week to experience them? Next, write down the specific actions, share them with a friend, or post them somewhere that you'll see regularly.

For example, let's say you want to feel more alive. What three actions might you take this week to bump up your feelings of being alive? Put on your favorite music and dance, take a brisk walk outside no matter what the weather is, tell people how much you appreciate them and why, or do a round of Touch, Accept, Release, Action (TARA). (See next chapter)

Be aware of your feet on the ground, your belly, your heart, your head. Now breathe. How are you feeling? Mad, sad, afraid, guilty, ashamed, numb, happy? Don't judge, just notice what's going on with your feelings, body sensations, and thoughts.

How Emotional Pain Drives Behavior

Consider the following situations that happen to people every day.

George couldn't understand why his wife wants to leave him because he sits in front of the TV every night and doesn't talk. Susan, whose grown daughter isn't going to college and living the life her mom wanted, can't figure out why her daughter is furious with her. Jeff denies hating himself; it's others he hates and says he could be homicidal. This same young man had two abusive and alcoholic stepfathers, no relationship with his biological father, and is troubled in his own marriage. Janet, an overweight woman, blames herself for the mother who shamed her for being fat and the husband who won't have sex with her for the same reason.

George, Susan, Jeff, and Janet are all in different layers of denial about the reservoirs of pain they carry. But with willingness, patience, and support, they will find that once they look the dragon in the face that it's no longer 20 feet tall. They can watch the dragon transform from tormentor to teacher to friend.

At age 25, even though I was unaware of all the emotional pain held in my body, it drove my daily behavior. My defensive outbursts and short fuse demonstrated more than my self-assured appearance ever could about what was really going on inside. I repeatedly showed up late at the best-paying job I'd ever had and finally got fired. I would "forget" to pick up my son from some event and then feel horribly guilty. I couldn't get out of bed once a month because of depression. I thought I drank to have fun, but in reality, it was to escape.

Later, in therapy, I reported my "happy" childhood of drinking parents, being molested at age 7, pregnant at 15 and 17, and estranged from my parents. I spent two years in therapy looking at what really happened growing up, then feeling and releasing the emotional baggage attached. As I did, the rages stopped and the depression that had felt "normal as breathing" began to lift.

When Buttons Get Pushed

"Our parents install our emotional buttons and those closest to us know exactly how to push them."

- Unknown

CONNECTING THE DOTS

Samantha's husband was hurrying the family to get to church on time, she walked out of the house and burst into tears, then went back in and collapsed on the couch. Samantha cried for two hours. She felt better but didn't understand why she needed to cry in the first place. In our session as we talked about her overreaction, Samantha recalled being molested for years by an uncle. I asked her when she first remembered this. "I'd recently been watching a TV show about a young girl being molested by a neighbor. All of a sudden, I flashed to my uncle's visits and what he did to me in his car when he'd drive me to the store for an ice cream." Until the movie triggered her memories, Samantha hadn't "connected the dots" of her uncontrollable outburst.

The emotional overreactions and self-defeating defenses that occur when a person's buttons get pushed are attempts by the unconscious to get attention—to wake up and heal. If this information is avoided or ignored, the unconscious can "up the ante" with more stress, struggle, pain, or physical symptoms. Bill Harris of The Holosync Meditation Program says all stress and struggle is about resistance. Psychiatrists starting with Freud have had similar opinions about resistance. I simply believe it's human nature to want to avoid pain.

What drives overreactions is often trauma that's lodged in the unconscious and in the cells and muscles of the body and brain. Emotional Freedom Technique (EFT) is based on releasing the emotions caused by current events that resemble (consciously or not) the original traumas. For example, at one time, if anyone criticized me, I'd become extremely defensive or angry. I wasn't aware of where those feelings came from or even of this pattern until my husband would say, "You're so defensive." Eventually, I caught on that I really did feel defensive. Later in therapy, I understood why. That is, if situation A happens, critical statements are made, sparking response B, an overreaction.

When I remembered my childhood and my relationship with my father, this formula of an automatic reaction pattern made sense. As researcher Bessel A. Van Der Kolk noted, "Traumatized individuals may blow up in response to minor provocations, freeze when frustrated, or become helpless in the face of trivial challenges. Without a historical context to understand the somatic and behavioral residues from the past, their emotions appear out of place and their actions bizarre." Van Der Kolk, Bessel A. *Psychological Trauma*. American Psychiatric Pub Group, Washington, D.C. 1996. [108] Today, I'm often able to say thank you when someone pushes my buttons. Not usually in the moment but after I calm down and go through the TARA and EFT processes. (Notice how TARA and EFT are big factors in helping people. To learn more, go to Chapters 9 and 10.)

The Iceberg Theory

It's not unusual to be clueless about the emotional baggage we're carting around because, as the iceberg theory states, we're only aware of about 10 percent of our thoughts and feelings and behaviors.

Picture an iceberg floating in the ocean. Just a small part of the iceberg is above the surface of the ocean; about 90 percent is under the water and invisible to the naked eye. This is happened to the ocean liner Titanic when it went down in 1912. *What we don't know that we don't know can get us in trouble.*

Lacking awareness doesn't mean we're good or bad. On the scale of priorities, first we have to survive, then we have the luxury of growth. It's human to be in denial, to avoid rather than to pay attention. We're afraid that if we look too closely at ourselves, we might discover we're crazy or bad or have a strange desire to run naked down the freeway.

The truth is, most of us believe we're unlovable, so it becomes a habit *not* to pay attention to the messages of our bodies and our emotions. Unfortunately, that doesn't change anything.

TRAUMA FOLLOWS GENERATIONS

When you have an overreaction to your partner's jab, your child's behavior, or your boss's request, you can bet it's the unconscious mind that's driving it. This story tells about the power of the unconscious and how it travels from one generation to the next.

My grandfather on my paternal side was a successful insurance man with his own business. Then the depression hit and he lost everything. My grandmother cleaned houses to feed the family because my grandfather had a nervous breakdown from which he never recovered.

After a stint in the U.S. Army and a year of college, my dad, who was a bright man, worked as a bookkeeper for StarKist Tuna in southern California. The company wanted him to become a CPA, something my dad could easily have done. He wouldn't do it. They wanted to promote him anyway and send him to Peru where they had operations. After a two-month trial period in Peru, he refused the promotion and they let him go within the year. I rarely heard my dad say anything about growing up, but one thing I do remember is this, "I'll never push myself like my dad did." I think what he meant was, "I'm afraid that if I go after my dreams, they'll be taken away from me and I'll go crazy like my dad did."

In August 2006, I met with Gilbert Renaud, a naturopath from Canada. He lectures and conducts private healing sessions based on Total Biology, a healing process created by Dr. Hammer from Germany and refined by Dr. Sabbah. (See Resources section for more information.)

I reported a sciatica problem in my left hip to Gilbert and he asked me, "When have your dreams been taken away?" I was startled and shook my head and frowned. The first thing that came to mind was being a happy little girl in love with horses when I was molested by the pony photographer. Gilbert asked me what was going on in my life today and I told him about my excitement and fears about looking for an agent for this book. "I've been going back and forth, not just now, but my whole adult life. I create big dreams and take action to a certain degree, but then I back off and sabotage myself. I wrote my first book *The Greatest Change of All* and after about a year and a half of marketing it, I just dropped it."

"What was happening when you were 27?" he asked. (His technique called Total Biology looks at patterns that tend to get repeated at regular age intervals and says that the psychological conflicts of the parents become the biological conflicts of the child.)

"Funny you should ask," I said. "I was studying for and failing my real estate exam. It took me three or four times to pass the test and it shouldn't have. My husband couldn't understand why I kept failing it. I couldn't either."

"How is this related to my hip?" I asked.

Gilbert looked at me through his glasses with a benign expression on his face and asked, "This was your dream at the time, yes?" (He has a charming French accent, which is his first language.)

"Yeah, but why would I . . . " I stopped, feeling confused.

"When you were seven years old and you went after your dream of being with the pony, you were hurt. Afterwards, your unconscious said dreams were dangerous. So at age twenty-seven, your conscious mind wanted to sell real estate, which was your dream at the time. But your unconscious mind said, 'If you pass your test, your dream will be taken away, just like the pony man took your childhood from you.'"

"Ah . . . this is making sense."

"What happened at age fourteen?" he asked.

"I really wanted my dad to take the job he was offered in Peru. I thought it would be exciting to go to a foreign country and practice my Spanish. I also thought it'd be good for our family. When he said no to the job, I could see Mom was really disappointed. Their marriage fell apart shortly after that and they divorced. Her drinking escalated at that point."

I thought about my son Rich who has had a sciatic problem the last few months and told Gilbert about it. "Rich is your second-born, yes? Your dad is a second-born. In Total Biology, the fourth generation works out the issues of the first. Is your son having trouble accomplishing his dreams?"

"Not on the surface. He's a many-times world champion paint

ball player. He and his wife own a successful business. But I see there's a level of financial success he hasn't reached yet and he's frustrated. It seems Rich is acting out the financial challenges of my father and me. This is fascinating."

Total Biology believes that gaining awareness of the story's beginning and how it's played out in our lives is enough to heal the issues. I'm not so sure it's that simple. But since this session with Gilbert, I've had no more sciatica pain.

Addictions "Sort of" Work

"I believe that, if deprived of their drugs (alcohol, tranquilizers, antidepressants, illegal drugs), a large part of the population would become a danger to themselves and others." [109]

- Eckhart Tolle

It may seem strange, but our habits and addictive behaviors "sort of" work, don't they? At the end of a demanding, stressful day, zoning out in front of the TV does provide relief. If we're depressed or irritable, a glass of wine or a hit off a joint can bump our mood a notch. When our anxieties become too overwhelming, we want relief and we often go for the quickest fix. The problem isn't in using these activities moderately; it's when we overuse and over rely on them to make us feel better. Our addictive coping slots us somewhere between "not too alive" and "not too dead." We feel less anxiety because we feel less of everything. Sometimes we just feel numb.

We start the morning out with our usual extra-large coffee, have 32 ounces of soda at lunch, and go shopping after work even though we don't need a thing. We wrap up the day with gorging on super-size hamburgers and another soda, and we finally make it home to be entertained by the TV. If these behaviors "sort of" work, why would we want to change? Because when we practice awareness of our emotions and listen to the sensations of our bodies, we add back the zest our bodies can give us. The super-charged bliss I had from a cocaine high felt terrific for a few hours but I couldn't call the next day anything close to terrific.

A young methamphetamine user told me he used meth at work out of boredom. As long as he was using it, he wasn't bored. When his wife and parents found out, they set a firm line—either quit using it or they would disinherit him. He was glad for this clarity; he admitted this agreement was the only thing keeping him from using meth for good. Now in recovery, David has to deal with his boredom in other ways. He's taken up running again and started reading in the evenings. Beneath the boredom he felt, what were David's needs? He wanted uncertainty, excitement, more intellectual stimulation. When he met those needs more consistently, his recovery went smoothly.

Similarly, I started running when I was 24. In the process, I discovered that the depression that'd always been in the background became easier to manage. We now know that aerobic exercise increases the same neurotransmitters that many drugs do—without the negative side effects.

EXPERIMENT: The following checklist can help you become more aware of the feelings and behaviors that drive addictive coping. These behaviors or substances don't create problems when used occasionally, but if you're having financial, relational, or health-related consequences because of addictive coping, it can become a huge problem. Then it's critical to look at the *motivation* for using certain substances.

Granted, it's no big deal if you're stressed and drink a beer to unwind once in a while. But when that becomes the only coping method and it's creating problems with work, relationships or health, heed the warning signs. So without judging yourself, pinpoint the challenges in your life on the list below. I call them warning lights that represent symptoms of being out of emotional balance.

Check all the feelings and behaviors you currently experience. Rate how concerned you are or how intense the feeling or behavior is for each checked item on a scale of 1-10 (1 = no concern, 10 = very concerned). If you checked stress, for example, on an average day, how high is the stress level? (If you have trouble identifying your own behaviors, ask a trusted friend. Others are often able to see your blind spots when you can't.)

Emotional Warning Lights Checklist

- **Stress** (that goes on and on)
- **Anger, irritability** (touchy at every little thing)
- **Depressed** (for more than two weeks)
- **Anxious** (more than two weeks)
- **Panic attacks**
- **Numb**—don't feel much of anything
- **Constantly fighting with loved ones—**
  If "they" would just change, I'd be okay
- **Negative**—Cup half empty, cynical, judgmental, blaming
- **Cope with feelings or stress with any,**
  or a combination of:
  - alcohol
  - drugs—legal includes prescription
  - anti-depressants
  - gambling
  - sex—your primary or only way to "unwind"
- **Eating problems**

- anorexia
- bulimia
- compulsive overeating

- **Smoking cigarettes**
- **Cope with feelings** or stress with "lite" addictions like:
  - shopping—do you get a "buzz" from the anticipation buying?
  - TV watching
  - Internet
  - Internet porn (a "lite" addiction if you only spend a couple of hours a week and are having no relationship problems—a "hard" addiction if spending hours and hours a week or your wife/girlfriend/boyfriend complains, or you're having other consequences like money problems)
  - coffee—how many cups a day?
  - sodas - how many ounces a day? (Are you having trouble sleeping, feeling tired the next day and using caffeine to get yourself going?)
- **Switch addictions**: stop shopping, start over-eating, stop smoking, binge on sweets, collect everything (pack rat) then switch to cleaning compulsively, stop alcohol, start Internet porn
- **Psychosomatic illnesses** such as high blood pressure, irritable bowel disease, headaches, stomach aches, tight, tense shoulders
- **Excessive busyness** that includes:
  - Over-thinking
  - Over-caring—being overly involved in others' lives

You know how a stoplight works—yellow means warning and red means stop. If you checked only one or two of the above items, you're mildly to moderately out of emotional balance. If the symptoms last less than two weeks in duration or are at an intensity of 5 to 7 (on a scale of 1-10 with 10 high), you have a yellow light warning. (In that case, go to Chapter 9 for more about Touch, Accept, Release, Action, and Chapter 10 for Emotional Freedom Technique. You might also enjoy the imagery practice for relaxation called "Creating Your Special Place" in Chapter 11. With practice, doing these three skills will greatly improve your ability to stay above the line in emotional balance.)

If these behaviors or feelings have been going on longer than two weeks or the intensity approached a 10 on a 1 to 10 scale. Beware. It's a red light. It's time to go to a therapist or sign up for a 12-step treatment program. There's no shame in needing help. It's sad and self-defeating to keep suffering in the same old ways, inflicting harm on ourselves and those we love.

I can't say enough about having the right therapist as a guide and support. I've had four therapists at different "growth" periods in my life. I would not be the healthy, loving person I am today without their skill and guidance. I thank each one of them for their compassionate, insightful support.

To interview a potential therapist you would work with, come up with a few questions about what type of therapy they practice, length in business, and education. Though I have a bias about selecting a therapist with a background in addiction, most important is seeing if you can connect with this person. Your goal of therapy is to heal the past so you can live in the present, adopt better skills so you feel better about yourself, improve your relationships, and get more of what you want out of life.

What's an Authentic Person?

Life for many is increasingly stressful and, well, busy. With so many demands, it's hard to remember there's an authentic person or "self" waiting for us to notice. If only we made the time to locate this self. An authentic person is the opposite of a liar. Picture someone who isn't afraid to tell the truth about who she is—an authentic person we'll call Nancy.

Nancy is able to be vulnerable with those closest to her. When her job is on the line, she lets her husband or friends know how frightened she is, rather than holding it in and blowing up over a side issue like the dishes not being put away. Nancy's comfort with herself assures her she is safe, even when she doesn't know how things will turn out. When new people meet her there is a sense of integrity that emanates from her and they think: "That's someone I'd like to get to know better."

Nancy doesn't hide or dwell on her struggles. One day, she finds her two-year-old daughter Marie coloring on the newly painted wall for the third time that week. Gritting her teeth, Nancy grabs her and asks, "Marie, where are you supposed to be coloring?" The toddler looks at her mother with a blank expression that turns to tears. Nancy's anger melts. Later she tells her girlfriend, "I was so mad, it took everything I had not to hit her. But that's what my mom did, and not on the butt. I won't react that way."

Nancy knows her strengths as well as her weaknesses. She accepts that she's not a "finished product" but a "glorious work in progress." In touch with her eternal core of goodness and lovability, she believes that if she stopped resisting the pain and joy of being human, she'd stop resisting life. She wants to embrace the mysteries of life. So for Nancy, sometimes emotions are like a colorful, out-of-the-lines painting, definitely messy and juicy. Other times, feelings bubble up from deep within and soar like hot air rising on a windswept plain.

Nancy has learned to embrace her feelings, knowing that trying to control them is like trying to control the ocean. She'd prefer to get out the surfboard and ride the wave in.

Applying Emotional Wisdom in Everyday Living

Do you know anyone who is emotionally wise? Many of our emotional role models have bounced between overreacting or shutting down with nothing in between. What are the benefits of learning how to be emotionally wise? What's in it for you?

Read the following stories and learn that it's possible to overcome unbearable tragedy, to forgive, to connect more deeply with yourself, others, and the divine. Also know that with emotional wisdom comes greater awareness leading to deeper consciousness and a sense of purpose.

1. **Emotional Wisdom supports us to connect with and know ourselves.**

Helen came to see me for weight issues. Here's how our discussion went:

"Lynn, I can't stay on a diet. My doctor wants me to lose a hundred pounds because I'm almost fifty and have high blood pressure. I don't know why I eat like I do."

Helen has short, red-highlighted hair, striking green, cat-shaped eyes, and a pixie smile. Like many women with weight concerns, she was out of touch with herself emotionally. Most times when I asked her to notice how she was feeling, she'd say "I don't know." I introduced Helen to the Touch, Accept, Release, Action (TARA) exercise (in Chapter 9) and asked her to do it anytime she headed for food when she wasn't really hungry.

After a few months, Helen became curious about what was driving her eating. At one session, she told me about her breakthrough. "I was walking around the house at night waiting for my husband to come home. Feeling anxious and bored, I started snacking. I wasn't paying any attention to what or how much I was eating. I shouldn't feel this way, but I'm mad that he works so late. Then I realized that, instead of pacing while I'm waiting for him, I could take the dog for a walk. I don't know why I've never thought of that before." Helen smiled and nodded her head in satisfied pride.

As Helen became aware of her feelings and how they were influencing her food choices, she began to feel more in charge. She could now go out to lunch with friends and feel pleased at her ability to eat small portions.

2. **Emotional Wisdom supports us to connect with others, express empathy, and feel part of humanity.**

Sometimes tragedy is the door through which we step to find ourselves. Mary had been seeing me off and on for a few years when her brother died from AIDS. She was devastated. After a year or so, when she could see the light at the end of the tunnel, her father and youngest brother were killed in a plane crash.

At that point, Mary stopped therapy and retreated from the world for about a year. When she began seeing me again, she raged at God and the airplane manufacturer. She blamed herself and felt guilty for not being a better daughter or sister. She was terribly lonely for her father and brother. It took another few years to allow the pain to move through her after writing letters to them and doing many EFT sessions. She desperately wanted to know *why*.

More time passed before she began to realize there wasn't an answer to the "why" that she believed had been so essential to answer. "I have to let it go and accept they're never coming back," she concluded.

Over the next five years, Mary was more at peace. As she worked through her grief, she developed more empathy for her mother and surviving brother who had alternatively clung to her or ignored her in their grieving. She wanted to do something to help others. About this time, Mary attended a conference led by Joan Borysenko, Ph.D. who was developing a training program called Interspiritual Mentor Training. Helen signed up.

At our session following her training, Mary looked radiant as she told me about it. She sat forward on the couch, her dark brown hair curling lightly around her pretty face. "I'm so excited about the possibility of becoming a mentor and being able to learn more spiritually and support others through difficult times. I really want this."

A few weeks later, Mary emailed me that she was one of a hundred selected for the program. I have no doubt that she will help many others because she's learned to forgive and let go of the past and to connect more completely with her own heart.

3.   **Emotional Wisdom supports us to get our needs met**.

If we don't know how we feel, how do we get our needs met? Since women are trained to focus on others' needs, I always encourage clients to begin a session by checking in with how they're feeling using the TARA exercise (explained in Chapter 9).

In the first example of Emotional Wisdom with Helen, it took her becoming aware she was anxious, bored, and angry to know she needed to do something other than just wait around for her husband to come home. By identifying her feelings she came up with a plan to exercise at night, which accomplished three things. The exercise worked off the feelings, burned calories, and kept her from eating—all contributing to feeling better about herself.

4.   **Emotional Wisdom supports us to rebalance**.

Most of the time I'm emotionally balanced and by that I mean I'm happy and peaceful. This doesn't mean I don't face challenges—that's life. But I really pay attention when my equilibrium tilts. When I'm mad at somebody or my buttons get pushed, I check and notice if a new action is necessary. My goal is to learn from how I'm feeling and, as effortlessly as possible, move back to peace.

My husband and I were approaching the date of our 25th anniversary. I was disappointed we weren't making more of a fuss than just a weekend away from home. I was also hurt that Dave hadn't bought me a present, though I hadn't purchased one for him. "That's not the point," I thought. "I've been putting in effort to make him feel special in the last few months. I bought him two pairs of those new shoes as a surprise and I've been giving him backrubs because he's so stressed." Notice the whiny tone. That's how I felt. My thinking Dave "should" buy me a necklace because I'd done so much for him is classic "getting" behavior as defined by Dr. Greg Baer, author of *Real Love*.[110] I'm not proud of it, but there it is. I did the Touch, Accept, Release, Action exercise, writing out all the mad, sad, scared, and guilty feelings and then tapped. I felt immediately better. "Ah, back to peace."

I needed to tell Dave how I felt, though, and asked him when a good time would be. Later that evening, I said, "Dave, I'm disappointed we didn't take the time to make more of a big deal about our twenty-fifth anniversary and I'm hurt you didn't buy me something special. I've been saying I'd like a gold necklace for a couple of years now." We talked it out and it took less than 24 hours to re-balance what could have made misery out of a beautiful weekend. By the way, he surprised me with a pretty jade necklace he picked out and a promise to search for a gold one. The challenge for me in receiving a gift after I've used "getting" behavior is that the present doesn't feel as special as when it's given freely. Lesson learned.

5.   **Emotional Wisdom supports us to make decisions**.

Daniel Goleman, author of *Emotional Intelligence*, wrote,

"All emotions are, in essence, impulses to act."[III] In our mentally focused world where mind is valued over heart, we don't give enough credit to how much our feelings impact what we do and who we are. But consider any major decisions you've made. If you track it all the way through, emotion is always at the root.

Say you've decided to relocate to another part of the country because "the company tells me to go." But what feelings are connected to the decision? "I'd better buck up and find a way to be okay with this move because I don't want to lose my job. I've got to be able to feed my family, pay my bills."

6.   Emotional Wisdom supports us to have boundaries.

Feelings help us know what our boundaries are. Here are two scenarios.

Let's say your boss has asked you to do a special report. You've spent hours of extra time completing the assignment, only to see him take credit for it at the big meeting. It's appropriate to feel angry because your boss has just stepped on your toes, big time. First, breathe, which gives you time to think. Then consider your boundaries and decide how to respond.

In the second scenario, your husband comes home from work and announces he's moving out to live with his new boyfriend. You're going to have lots of feelings about that, like anger that arises due to the betrayal of trust.

If we don't know how we feel, we let people take advantage of us or we don't pay attention to the signals someone gives us. In my 20s, I had a girlfriend who taught me a big boundary lesson. This professed friend asked if she could temporarily move in with Dave and me. While there, she decided it would be a good idea to plant marijuana in little containers and set them in the living room window. Well, I liked to party back then, but pot wasn't my drug of choice and I had a son at home. I knew it wasn't a good idea to wave the red pot flag to our neighbors so I asked that she put them in the kitchen on the floor where they couldn't be seen. *It never occurred to me to say 'no' you can't have pot in the house.* After she moved the plants to the kitchen window, my very Christian neighbor called the police. Many thousands of dollars later, the matter was taken care of and in the process I realized this was no friend of mine. She never took responsibility and skated on the money owed us. It's still hard for me to believe I was so naïve and that some "friends" have bad intentions. In retrospect I think she planned the whole thing because she was jealous I was happy. Some friend. If I'd known how to listen to my gut's "uh, oh" feelings I would have said no and thrown those plants out.

7.   **Emotional Wisdom supports us to be "in flow."**

I attended a retreat called "Meditate with the Monks and the Monarchs" in Pismo Beach, California, a few years ago. The monk was Phra Ajahn from Thailand. (Phra Ajahn is to Thailand what the Dalai Lama is to Tibet.)

He arrived with his entourage amid much laughter at the home where the retreat was held. His energy was very childlike, sweet, and light. He laughed often, spoke quietly, and like a crystal glass that sends off a vibration, he pulled up our energies to resonate with his own.

As adults we experience flow when things are going well, we're at peace, feeling present and moving easily from one event to another. By practicing emotional balance, we can access this state more and more.

8.   **Emotional Wisdom supports us to deepen our spirituality.**

The focus of our days and of the world is external—usually searching "out there" for the quick fix to make us feel better. Emotional wisdom allows us to go inside ourselves and connect with our inner thoughts and feelings as well as the greater consciousness many call God.

Sometimes events happen that we don't understand. For example, in 1989, as a marriage and family intern, I searched for the right supervisor and thought I'd found her, but she happened to be working in a group of Christian counselors. I say this because at the time I had some baggage about "Christians." I overrode those concerns as Sharon told me she would be leaving the group soon and I planned on going with her.

Well, 13 years later I'm still with this group and I have let go of my judgments. I love these people because they embody the best of Christian principles without being rigid in their beliefs or their lives. In the beginning they graciously embraced me as the token "non-Christian." Now, we have a more eclectic group, a few Christians, a follower of Hindu, a Buddhist, a pagan, and me. Once a month we get together and catch up about our worldly and spiritual lives. We meditate and pray together. We occasionally go on retreats and currently we're supporting one of our group members who is moving through the experience of cancer. We have made a commitment to meditate each morning from 7:00 to 7:15. What a great way to start the day.

9.   **Emotional Wisdom expands creativity**.

Wrote Eckhart Tolle, "Because we live in such a mind-dominated culture, most modern art, architecture, music, and literature are devoid of beauty, of inner essence, with very few exceptions."[112] Creativity is the realm of artists, yet it belongs to all of us. Artists know that emotion is the deep place from which their art emerges.

Little children are naturally creative—they'll play with anything and use their imagination to make up playmates, tell stories, and entertain themselves. As a child I was horse crazy and my sister and cousins and I used to gallop along with strings for reins "giddyuping" madly all over the yard. You couldn't tell us we weren't riding a black stallion or palomino mare. We didn't need television to entertain us with stories— we were our own stories.

Somewhere along the path to adult responsibility many of us lose our open-hearted connection to imagination's guidance. I could never have written a book twenty years ago, though I talked about wanting to. Why? Because I didn't know myself. I was disconnected from who I really was. The pain I'd shelved and didn't want to re-experience kept a lid on my happiness as well. It took time to wade through the layers of built-up sediment and peel them back to regain entrance to my Self. As I've come to feel, express, and accept my emotional self, I've been able to re-engage my creativity and put it on the page.

10. Emotional Wisdom supports us to be conscious.

Consciousness is awareness. Emotional awareness leads us to more full and complete personal awareness by paying attention to the inner machinery of our thoughts and feelings. Pretty simple in theory, and takes a lot of practice because we're so trained and conditioned by our habitual mind to keep our attention external rather than internal. Wrote Jack Canfield and Janet Switzer in their book *The Success Principles*, "Psychologists tell us up to 90% of our behavior is habitual."[113] Some habits are positive in that we don't have to think about brushing our teeth, driving a car, and so on. But the real *me* can get lost in the unconscious activities we do all day long.

Paying attention to how we feel about what happens creates a pause between the habitual mind and the conscious mind. This inner awareness leads to *mindfulness*. That is, when I'm conscious of my internal responses, I have more choice about how I respond to life's situations. I also have more responsibility because it's harder to blame others when we're really paying attention to our internal feelings and mental dialogue.

What do we want? To develop the ability to notice what we're feeling, acknowledge the anger or fear or sadness, avoid reacting as if it's life or death, and let go. We practice a witnessing attitude like, "I'm angry the contractor isn't finishing the job in the time he said he would" rather than saying with a fist in his face, "You son-of-a-bitch, I'm going to sue you if you don't get that kitchen finished." Expanded awareness—mindfulness—can lead to greater inner peace. It's up to us where we focus the energy.

Expanded awareness often leads to greater peace because we get picky about where to focus the energy we have available. For example, rather than analyzing and taking personally my niece's not coming to visit this summer as planned, I notice I'm disappointed, sad, take a breath, and let it go. If that's not enough to feel peaceful, I take the 20 minutes to do TARA and EFT. It's well worth it.

"Letting go of the emotions that trap you, painful memories, fears, depression, or anger, is the way to a longer and **healthier** life."[106]**"**

~ Deepak Chopra, MD

CHAPTER NINE

Chapter Nine:

Touch, Accept, Release, Action

N EARLIER CHAPTERS, we've mentioned TARA—the four steps in a technique called Touch, Accept, Release, Action. The purpose of TARA is to feel good quickly. When we work through the difficult feelings of anger, sadness, fear and guilt we go into and through suffering and back to peace, even joy.

In the first of the four TARA steps, we TOUCH or identify what we feel, where the feelings reside our bodies, and how intense they are. In the second step, we allow ourselves to ACCEPT that it's okay to have these feelings. Third, we listen to the lessons our emotions teach us and RELEASE them. Without releasing them, they tend to get repeated until we do. Our deepest self keeps gently pushing, prodding, and pointing the way to releasing what we don't need so we can truly and completely shine. The fourth step is ACTION—doing something positive about the new awareness we've gained. For example, until I became aware of the pain that drove my self-destructiveness, I kept doing harmful things to myself—smoking, drinking too much, or using drugs. With new awareness, I was able to stop. (Note: If you're having health, money or relationship consequences, wanting to stop and unable to you probably need professional assistance.)

A SIMPLE EXAMPLE OF TARA IN MOTION

It's okay for me to feel angry with my husband for watching so much TV and ignoring me. It's unloving to take my anger out on him or myself. I've learned to take care of myself (and bleed off the intensity of the emotion) by first going through the TARA process in writing. Then, if I need to express how I'm feeling to Dave, I ask him for a good time to talk about something important. At the scheduled time, I say to him, "I'm angry with you for paying more attention to the TV than to me. I'd appreciate having one evening together away from the house or with the TV off each week. Would Tuesdays work for you?" Of course, I have to be willing to accept that expressing my feelings and needs to Dave doesn't mean he'll do what I ask.

Next, I release the emotional energy from my body by breathing and riding the wave of emotion, knowing it will complete itself. Then it's time for new action, in this case, letting him know how I felt (angry and hurt) and asking for what I needed (time with him without the TV on). New action also meant that I watched less TV, which was fine with me.

TARA can be used for the everyday emotional experiences of anger, sadness, fear, and guilt. When I'm worried whether my sister Lane will survive her alcoholism, I use TARA and other techniques to rebalance the anger and worry so I feel either neutral or peaceful once again. Sometimes TARA seems like magic. For example, I anguished over yet another of Lane's suicide attempts but 20 minutes after it, I once again felt balanced and accepting. This technique did not change the circumstances. But by addressing my feelings rather than avoiding them, they dissipated, which left me free to be in the present rather than caught up with the past.

In the past, I didn't always want to give up my "suffering"—like wearing an old ratty bathrobe I love but never wanted my boyfriend to see me in—my worrying about my sister felt bad and good at the same time. At first I felt guilty about choosing to shift out of misery. Now I know my worrying does nothing to help either of us.

Besides the ups and downs of life, many of us have varying degrees of emotional trauma. The milder yet still painful traumas of childhood like being the third daughter when a boy is wanted find a place at one end of the continuum. The trauma of abuse or neglect resides at the other end. We don't have to clear every single past hurt, pain, or problem. Instead, if we pay attention to our emotional buttons, they will lead us to past issues that still create emotional problems. As we heal the big emotional upsets, a positive ripple effect happens in the brain that clears similar issues.

Before I was ready to search for my daughter, I avoided anything related to adoption or birth mothers. The issue was always there, waiting to flare up, but it was too painful to address. Soon after I learned these techniques to release the intense pain, which gave me the courage to begin searching for Suzann.

TARA—A Movement Psychology Technique

The name Touch, Accept, Release, Action comes from a Movement Psychology technique I learned in graduate school. TARA embodies a major principle in Movement Psychology— that is, with awareness comes acceptance and choice. (Movement Psychology is a body-oriented therapy that uses postures and movements to increase awareness of unconscious patterns. Read more about it in Chapter 13.)

EXAMPLE OF USING TARA

In this situation, I believe my writing instructor Bill likes Marianne better than me. Here's how I used the TARA technique.

1) TOUCH: Identify the feelings related to the situation.
ANGRY: *feeling unrecognized or unimportant*
 I feel angry that Bill criticizes my work and praises Marianne's.
 I feel angry because he likes her better.
 I feel angry that I don't please him like she does.
SAD: *experiencing loss or relationship changing or ending*
 I feel sad because this is the same button Dad pushed.
 I feel sad because I let it bother me.
 I feel sad that I want Bill's approval.
AFRAID: *experiencing threat to safety or well-being*
 I feel afraid that I will keep giving my power to him.
GUILTY: *out of integrity with self, or NOT people pleasing*
 I feel guilty that I want to pull away from Bill and am jealous of Marianne—like I was jealous of my brother as a child.
GLAD: *finding one (or more) positive things about this situation*
I'm glad that I'm being honest and taking a step to let go of needing approval so much.
ASK: Where in my body do I feel this? *Solar plexus, shoulders, jaw*
ASK: Intensity Scale (0 to 10, with 10 being the most intense): 8

2) ACCEPTANCE: Is it okay to feel this way?
When I sat down to write out my feelings, I didn't realize how intense they were. *That's the power of writing out this exercise.* Writing engages the subconscious mind and gives it permission to reveal more and more feelings connected to the immediate situation. While I'm writing out my feelings, my critical mind yells at me for being childish, but doing that stops the flow. Suddenly, I'm *judging* my feelings, which is a major reason we don't pay attention to our feelings or accept them. Our mind takes over and gets us to stop, be nice, or just shut up. My rationalizing came out with this comment: "Well, Bill likes some of your writing and everyone has favorites. You'd just like it to be you."

(3) RELEASE: Take 10 breaths through my nose and release through my mouth.

If the wave of emotion is still high, I take 10 more breaths. At this point, the intensity number drops from 8 to 6 so I keep breathing and it moves to a 4. Ten more breaths and it's down to a 2. (EFT works even more quickly than breathing.)

4) ACTION: What's my next step?
   Is there a specific action I need to take?
I decided to share my feelings with Marianne because I planned to read this part of my book out loud in class. What was my motivation in telling Marianne? I wanted to take care of both of us—I trusted she would understand that the feelings I was experiencing weren't about her but rather about me, yet didn't want to surprise her. I didn't feel the need to tell Bill ahead of time, probably because of his many years of New York City editing and writing experience. I think he's tougher.

In the example of my jealousy with Marianne, as I wrote out my feelings and tracked them back, I remembered feeling jealous of my brother receiving my dad's attention. Often doing TARA brings you back into balance but if it doesn't, use Emotional Freedom Technique to quickly and easily release any remaining feelings or beliefs.

Finding My Adopted Daughter

I was 15 when Suzann was born and I placed her for adoption. Until I met her 32 years later, I was totally unable to forgive myself.

Fast forward to October 21, 2001. I stood in front of the Marriott Hotel in Charlotte, North Carolina, waiting to see her for the first time. In the week leading up to meeting Suzann, I was nervous and excited, teary with gratitude one moment and worried she would hate me the next. And then there she was—a reflection of me, blue-eyed and slender with my no-nonsense marching stride. I ran up to Suzann and hugged her. She hugged me back and then eased away, checking to see how I was doing. When I told her I was emotional, she backed away a bit more. Her best friend Janet smiled at me and said to her in a soft southern drawl, "Suzann, *this is an emotional event.*"

Suzann and I spent the weekend getting to know each other. When she made a point in conversation, she smacked the palm of one hand with the back of her other hand—just like me. Although I'd quit smoking 20 years before, the pack of cigarettes on the table was Marlboro 100s, the same brand I'd smoked. Suzann also smoked like I did—not much during the day, but after 5:00 p.m. and especially when having a drink, she could smoke a pack during an evening. Now in her 30s, she was also determined to quit.

Observing the way she moved and talked was like looking into a slightly tilted mirror. During our whole weekend together, I felt a bittersweet gratitude that Suzann had been raised by loving, involved parents. When she and her parents told stories about her accomplishments, like her skateboard championship at age 11, I felt awed and proud. My guilt and insecurity told me that if I'd raised her, she wouldn't have had the same advantages.

In my mind, I drifted back to the time I gave birth. Placing Suzann up for adoption hadn't been my decision, though I know it was the right one. Protective of my fragile heart, I knew I couldn't look at her before leaving the hospital. I knew if I did it would be too hard to let her go.

After giving birth, I spent a couple of days with my grandmother. With loving support, she shared the secret of her own illegitimate birth.

Grandma was unkindly informed she was illegitimate at age 16 when a schoolmate yelled out that she was "a bastard." When she went home and asked her mother if that was true, she was told the real story about her birth. Her Finnish mother had waited ten years for her fiancé to send for her from the United States where he was working as an indentured farmer.

In America for only a short while, my great grandmother had two babies close together. One morning her husband was late coming in for breakfast and she went to the barn to get him. He lay on the floor, dead of a heart attack at age 31.

Speaking no English and having a farm mortgage and two babies, she went to the banker for help and he became her lover. When she became pregnant, he wanted to marry her, but by then she'd fallen in love with another man, whom she married and later had six more children. Until someone called her a bastard, my grandmother thought she was the daughter of the first husband.

I've always believed there really are no secrets in families. I think Grandma must have had an inkling about her real father because on every birthday and Christmas, gifts arrived only for her from a mystery person. Not long after being told about her banker father, my grandmother saw him on the trolley in town and felt too shy to speak to him. This was the only time their paths crossed.

Grandma cared for me the best she knew how when I stayed with her those few days after I gave birth. Then I went home and no one ever asked me about my daughter again. I was somehow supposed to go on with a regular teenaged life, yet I couldn't seem to pick up and go on by pretending normalcy.

HOW TARA COULD HAVE HELPED ME

I would have benefited so much from using a skill like TARA when I placed my daughter for adoption. Here's how I imagine my grandmother could have introduced it to me.

When I came home from the hospital, Grandma would have talked with me about feelings and how important they are. She would have told me to name the situation and then guided me to write down what was going on inside by using the five basic feelings—angry, sad, scared, guilty, and glad. (*feeling words and definitions adapted from Stephen Bavolik's Nurturing Parenting work115)

Let's revisit this scenario.

THE SITUATION: Placing my daughter for adoption.

1) TOUCH: Identify the feelings related to the situation.

ANGRY: *feeling unrecognized or unimportant*

"I'm angry I got pregnant. I'm angry I didn't know any better or have better guidance. I'm angry I couldn't tell my parents and hid it for 7 months. I'm angry they didn't notice anything was wrong with me."

SAD: *experiencing loss or a relationship changing or ending*

"I'm sad I'll never see or hold my daughter. I'm sad I won't get to know who she is. I'm sad I had to miss so much school."

SCARED: *when our safety or well-being is threatened*

"I'm scared because I don't know what to do now. I'm scared to go back to school because everyone knows."

GUILTY: *out of integrity with self, or NOT people pleasing*

"I feel guilty about getting pregnant and hiding it for so long. I feel guilty for hurting my parents."

GLAD: *One (or more) positive things about this situation*

"I'm glad my daughter will be raised by parents who will be able give her a good life and love her."

ASK: Where in my body do I experience the intensity of these feelings?

Solar plexus, shoulders

What sensations am I experiencing?

A tightness in my chest, quivering in my belly, my jaw tightening and fists clenching.

ASK: On a scale of 0 to 10 (10 being most intense) how intense are these feelings? 10

I become aware of my breath, taking breaths through my nose into my abdomen. I release the air by exhaling from my mouth. (Exhaling through the mouth is better for releasing energy/emotion than is exhaling through the nose.)

(2) ACCEPT: Is it okay to feel this way?

Acceptance comes with both the awareness that it's okay to have feelings and with identifying those feelings. It comes with letting go of an ideal about what "perfect" is. A big sigh of relief occurs when I can accept my anger or anguish. Acceptance also comes in stages. For example, when I saw my first therapist and told her the story of my childhood, I felt heard and understood. Her kindness and warmth helped me move to the first level of acceptance. Another level came ten years later when I was able to turn that kind eye on myself. Full acceptance came with the ACTION of searching for my birth daughter. Action moved me to completion. Even if I hadn't found her, and I'm thrilled I did, I could choose to let go because I'd had the courage to follow the journey to the end. Searching for her was the final step in healing a major wound I'd dragged around for so long I'd forgotten who I was without it.

I can relate to Howard Raphael Cushnir, author of *Unconditional Bliss*, who says that accepting rather than running from his pain was really difficult, but that as he "...yielded more fully, something surprising happened. For the first time in my life it felt good to feel bad. I experienced the solace of free-flowing emotion, that paradoxical sweetness of just letting feelings be."[116]

"What we resist persists" is a well-known therapy axiom. Resisting our feelings is like the four year old who's afraid of the monster under the bed. Many adults believe there's a still a monster, but it is no longer under the bed—it's inside us. Having a self-care skill like TARA provides the support to face any emotions no matter how big they seem.

3) RELEASE: Take 10 breaths through my nose and release through my mouth.

Release is not about getting rid of feelings but about allowing the energy of the emotion to move through us as feelings naturally do without judgments and resistances. I take ten breaths through my nose right into the places in my body where I'm holding the anger, sadness, fear, and guilt—my solar plexus and shoulders. I ride the wave of emotion, knowing it will crest and subside. I exhale from my mouth because doing so releases carbon dioxide and emotional energy. If I need to, I take an additional ten breaths or more.

(4) ACTION: Is there any action I need to take based on what I've learned by going through this process?

At 15, the action I needed to take was go back to school and get on with my life. At 45 the action I needed to take was to search for my daughter.

EXPERIMENT: Write a brief statement about a situation that's pushing your buttons. Consider areas of work, relationships, addictive activities, stress, or illness as possible topics.

Stay focused on one situation as you go through the exercise.

Write out each feeling using this framework:

1) TOUCH: Identify the feelings related to the situation.

I feel (angry, sad, afraid, guilty, glad) because _____

I feel angry (feel unrecognized or unimportant) because _____

List as many emotions as necessary.

ASK: Where in my body do I most experience the energy of the emotion such as a sensation or tightening in my head, throat, heart, belly, foot? _____ (If you can't tell where you feel a certain emotions, be patient, and keep asking and sensing. You'll develop more awareness over time.)

ASK: Rate the intensity on a scale of 0 to 10, with 10 being the most intense.

2) ACCEPT: Is it okay to have these feelings? Am I willing to accept them?

If it's not okay to feel angry, or sad, or guilty, be curious about why not.

(Remember, accepting how you feel doesn't mean you approve of someone's bad behavior. It doesn't happen all at once either.)

3) RELEASE: Take 10 breaths into the areas where you experience the emotions.

If it doesn't come easy, just breathe into your belly. You may notice that a wave of emotional energy builds and then recedes. If 10 breaths aren't enough to smooth out the anger or sadness, keep breathing deeply into the place in your body where the feelings are, or your abdomen. Often just identifying the feelings is enough to feel better. This exercise is designed to rebalance your emotional self and leave you less vulnerable to addictive behaviors when your emotions get out of balance. In fact, emotions drive the desire for two things: ever-greater pleasures or the need to seek escape.

4) ACTION: What specific action do you need to do and take care of yourself? Is there someone you need to talk with?

Remember to ask yourself what your motivation is in sharing. If it's just to tell someone off, get revenge, or make someone hurt like you do, think again. Would you appreciate someone sharing this information with you? Is there a way you can do it respectfully? Now I'm not saying it's not a good idea to say how we feel—it's often important for us (not necessarily them) to do so. Do so lovingly, with tact and forethought. Caution: I don't recommend sharing with your parents unless they've asked or it happens in a therapy session. Although sharing with parents can be incredibly healing when both parties are willing to take responsibility, it's delicate.

As you become more comfortable using TARA, ask advanced questions like these:

When else have I felt these kind of feelings with this type of situation?

What's the earliest time I can remember feeling this way?

More Tools for Resolving Pain

Martin Seligman teaches 10 year olds the skills of optimistic thinking and action. His work has helped them cut their rates of depression by half in puberty.[117] Knowing what I know now, I believe if I'd had some tools for resolving my pain, shame, and guilt, I wouldn't have gone through the next few years of self-destructive acting out. Indeed, I am grateful I made it. My journey has given me a lot of compassion and understanding for people in general and especially struggling teens. Now, I realize everything that happened has been weirdly perfect because it's helped me become the person I am today. Suffering does serve a purpose if it helps us learn. But it can get to be a habit where too many get lost with no way to get home again.

Carrying around all that self-judgment weighed me down, caused me to escape into alcohol and drugs, and later made me a self-help junkie. For years I would become inspired about going after my dreams because of a talk I'd attended or book I'd read. Then I'd go home and start working to make them come true. After a few weeks or months, I'd get sidetracked because the fear-based thoughts, feelings, and beliefs would reassert themselves. Boom—back to feeling bad, then depressed. "Oh, what the hell. This is never going to work."

I began to wonder *why* I kept getting pulled back to the "loser" image rather than being able to appreciate my growth and accomplishments. I realized there were three reasons:

1) a negative self-image had imprinted itself in my emotional memory from the early trauma of the molestation at seven, the constant criticism and from the teenaged acting out.

2) I needed to face, accept, and release the emotional past from my bodymind.

3) I needed to imbed new positive thoughts, feelings, and actions in my mind until they became a habit.

Life is challenging enough on a daily basis. When we have emotional baggage from the past banging around inside us, it's like quicksand pulling us back into unconscious or self-destructive behavior. By learning to identify, accept, and release past and present trauma, we free ourselves.

In the 20 years I've learned about emotional management, these three tools—Touch, Accept, Release, Action and Emotional

Freedom Technique and Integrative Imagery—have been the most successful in creating a more loving and congruent me. You'll gain a better understanding of Emotional Freedom Technique; and Integrative Imagery in the following chapters.

" Earlier life experiences, many of
which took place in **childhood**,
long before we had any choice, appear
clinically to be one of the primary
reasons for certain kinds of
depression, phobias, **anxiety**, stress,
low self-esteem, relationship diffculties,
and addictions."[118] **"**

~ Francine Shapiro, *EMDR*

CHAPTER TEN

Chapter Ten:

Emotional Freedom Technique

ALTHOUGH Emotional Freedom Technique (EFT) is not exactly a magic wand that makes your problems disappear, it's the next best thing for releasing troublesome emotions. Emotional Freedom Technique creates trust so that we no longer have to pretend "we're fine" as well as it gives us a skill we can whip out at work, home, on an airplane or anywhere else to release or greatly reduce troublesome emotions.

EFT is the second of the three-pack skill set and works alone or in combination with TARA. First, TARA helps us identify how we're feeling with the goal of restoring emotional balance. But long-held pain that's created emotional patterns often needs the big guns of EFT. I often combine the two because TARA helps you know what you're feeling and EFT releases the emotional charge.

I introduce EFT in this chapter and teach a short form of it but this skill is easier to learn by demonstration than in a book. I'll provide lots of examples of the power of EFT to give you the basics of EFT. Please go to Gary Craig's website www.emofree.com to learn more. (To learn EFT from a book, the best one I've found on *EFT is The Promise of Energy Psychology* by David Feinstein, Donna Eden, and Gary Craig.)

EFT can be regarded as psychological acupuncture. "Look

Ma, no needles!" Ancient Chinese medicine holds that there are meridians or energy circuits that run up and down the body. Acupuncture theory notes that it's the stimulation along a meridian that breaks up the coagulated or "stuck" energy.

EFT works on any emotional issue. It works on performance concerns such as test anxiety, addictive behaviors, phobias such as fear of heights or snakes, and past and present pain. It is noninvasive, reliable, predictable, and has no negative side effects. In fact, we can be extremely skeptical—EFT works whether we believe in it or not. I've used EFT for many years with myself and with hundreds of clients. It is *the* most useful, effective approach I've found for relieving emotional pain and addictive urges.

"MAYBE IT WORKED A LITTLE"

Dennis, a left-brained computer scientist, was having relationship problems. As he talked, I could see he was feeling something because his brow was knitted and he was frowning, but when I asked how he was feeling, he'd say "Fine. Well, maybe a little anxious." I introduced Dennis to EFT and asked him to rate the intensity of the anxiety about his relationship. To his surprise, he rated it an 8. By the end of the session, he rated the anxiety down to a 1 or 2. Yet, when I asked what he thought about EFT, he didn't think it had worked. When I reminded him about the reduced anxiety, he grudgingly admitted, "Maybe it worked a little." It took a few EFT sessions before he became a convert.

The relief that occurs in a session is almost always lasting. However, addictions are complex and usually require more continued attention because of the layered feelings, beliefs, and frequent triggers from the environment. Capital "T" traumas such as years of abuse also require a longer treatment time.

CLINT USES EFT TO TREAT
A DRUG PROBLEM

Clint was a young man referred by his parents for methamphetamine addiction. Clint was tall, looked athletic, and had recently married. He had a shy smile and a hard time talking about what was bothering him. I assessed him to determine if individual therapy would be appropriate or whether his meth addiction would require in-patient treatment. Because he'd maintained sobriety for three weeks on his own and he was being randomly drug tested at work I agreed to work with him. I also let him know that if he relapsed he'd need to consider AA/NA or outpatient treatment.

Clint maintained sobriety for quite a few months by paying attention to how he was feeling—depressed, angry and guilty—about causing his family so much trouble. He used tapping and an amino acid program developed by Julia Ross to curtail cravings. (Ross's book provides assessments and specific recommendations for which amino acids work to boost particular neurotransmitters. For example, the amino acid 5HTP supports the body's production of serotonin, which is important for the relief of anxiety or depression, and also helps sleep. Serotonin is what many antidepressants affect. (See Julia Ross's book *The Mood Cure* or visit **www.themoodcure.com** for details about how amino acids and diet help manage anxiety/depression and thereby help sobriety.)

Then Clint missed a couple of sessions. When he came back to see me he told me he'd relapsed. Together, we tracked how the relapse had happened. Clint said he started romancing the idea of using again because meth made him feel "motivated and not lazy." He admitted he'd stopped using the daily emotional check-ins of TARA and breathing. When he used meth again, he was disappointed because it didn't give him the feelings he was hoping for. When he came home late one Friday night, his wife demanded, "Either get sober or get out." He reluctantly agreed to go to NA, as per our agreement.

For the first few weeks, Clint did daily tapping on the sticky emotions of depression and lack of motivation, and on his cravings. The commitment to tap when he felt upset or was craving meth kept him in touch with himself and aware when the cravings were getting intense. With the support of NA, his family, and a commitment to sobriety, he was able to stay sober even though it was difficult and uncomfortable at times.

I've heard many a recovering person say they don't know how, they just ended up in the liquor aisle in the grocery store, or in the bar, or at their dealer's before they realized what was going on. They're lying to themselves. At some point they chose to "check out" and not pay attention to how they were feeling. If a relapse "just happens," the addict doesn't have to take responsibility. EFT doesn't change addiction; it supports choice, responsibility, and hope.

Once someone has practiced it well, it takes 20 to 30 minutes for both TARA and EFT to process a BIG issue and much less time for smaller problems. To put it into perspective, doing the two exercises takes about the same amount of time as a half-hour sitcom. Try it a few times, then compare how you feel after watching TV with how you feel after clearing out bothersome emotions.

Remember Brad from Chapter 3? He's the 25-year-old graduate student who called me and announced, "I'm addicted to fast food, internet porn, and shopping."

In the first few sessions, I taught him TARA and EFT. Using these, he was able to stop his addictive behaviors within a month. Brad said he still had urges, but by using these skills, he felt far less anxious and was able to make healthier choices more often. About six weeks into therapy, Brad asked what might happen in the future should he become stressed and find himself going through the fast food window more than once a week. I said, "If that happens, ask when you stopped checking in with how you're feeling or when you lost awareness of what's going on inside? If you stay conscious and aware of how you feel and what you really need like rest, attention, connection, or comfort, then you'll be able to get back on track much more easily."

After that, Brad's relationship with his girlfriend improved dramatically, his focus on school became crystal clear, and he trusted that his addictive behaviors were in his past as long as he remained aware of his feelings.

The purpose of TARA and EFT are to manage feelings that occur daily and clear out past pain that fuels addictive behaviors. We also create more joy and energy for doing what we want as we clear the heavier emotions of fear, anger, resentment, guilt, and shame. By staying aware, we are more able to live in the moment because we have less static in our nervous system. Turning to these skills is like having a trusted friend who's always available. TARA and EFT don't *prevent* feelings from emerging. Rather, they allow emotions to move through us so we regain balance and peace.

How Emotional Freedom Technique Works

Emotional Freedom Technique is an energy-based therapy. Gary Craig's website (www.emofree.com) quotes Albert Einstein, who in the 1920s, said that everything is composed of energy. To that, Gary added, "The cause of all negative emotions is a disruption in the body's energy system." This disruption creates emotional disharmony in the nervous system. When an emotional event or trauma such as a car accident, parents constantly fighting, or stress from abuse or neglect occurs, these intense or repeated negative feelings cause a blockage in the natural flow of emotional energy. I think of this block as a kink in our emotional flow, similar to a twisted water hose.

The TARA example about my jealousy around Bill liking Marianne more than me in Chapter 9 helped me identify how I was really feeling. To release those emotions with EFT, here's what to do in four steps.

1. CURRENT FEELING: How do I feel? Identify the situation and the feeling, then rate your feelings on a scale of 0 to 10, with 10 being the most intense using the SUDS scale (SUDS means Subjective Units of Distress Scale)

Situation/Feeling: "This jealousy that Bill likes Marianne more than me."

SUDS rating: 8

2. BODY: Where in my body do I most sense the feelings?

Solar plexus, abdomen

3. PREFERRED FEELING: How would I like to feel instead of jealous?

Peaceful, neutral

4. CORRECTING FOR PSYCHOLOGICAL REVERSAL: Psychological reversal is the "Yes, but" we tend to have about change or letting go. There's a push-pull between "I want to be free of this" and "I don't want to be uncomfortable"— particularly when applied to addiction. Part of us wants to get better, part of us doesn't. Fortunately, EFT assumes the presence of psychological reversal and corrects for it.

To release my feelings of jealousy of Marianne, I tap on the karate chop point on the side of one of my hands. (It doesn't matter which hand I tap on.) Then I repeat this phrase out loud three times: "Even though I feel jealous about Bill liking Marianne more than me, I choose to love and accept myself." I breathe and notice how I feel.

When they reach this point in the EFT process, clients often close their eyes and go into their own world for a few breaths or a few minutes. Sometimes tears of relief come when someone gives themselves permission to acknowledge they're having feelings they "shouldn't have," such as anger or jealousy.

Once I've corrected for psychological reversal (a term Dr. Callahan coined referring to an unconscious part that wants to get better, yet at the same time resists getting better), I'll tap on the designated meridian points under one of my eyebrows, under my eye, on the outside of my little finger, and then back under my eyebrow. I tap approximately six to ten times as I'm saying the key phrase three times out loud: "This jealousy that Bill likes Marianne more than me." It's important to include the emotion because that's the energy I want to let go of. As I go through the tapping sequence I may feel a wave of emotion. If the emotion gets intense, I keep tapping because I know the wave will recede. If there's a surge of feeling on a particular point, I tap another six to ten times on that point while stating the feeling and situation, and then I keep going.

Let me continue to use the example of my jealousy about my writing instructor Bill liking Marianne more than me. Note how EFT follows the TARA emotions of anger, sadness, fear, and guilt.

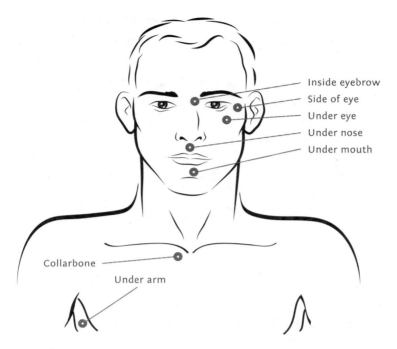

Inside eyebrow
Side of eye
Under eye
Under nose
Under mouth

Collarbone
Under arm

Where to Tap The sequence of tapping points are as follows

- -

EB ~ inside eyebrow, beginning of the eyebrow, next to the nose

SE ~ outside of eye, on the bone outside the eye socket

UE ~ under eye

UN ~ under nose

CB ~ collarbone, 1" over from the sternum on the lower side of the CB

UA ~ under arm, about 4" below the armpit

KC ~ fleshy part of the outside of the hand, the part you might use to give a karate chop, in the middle between the heel of the hand and the base of the little finger

OLF ~ outside edge of little finger near nail

outside little finger ——— Karate chop point

FIRST ROUND:

ANGER. I use the index and middle finger of one hand to tap on the outside of the little finger of the other hand. I say this phrase three times out loud: "I now release any and all angers from any and all roots and the deepest cause of this jealousy" (or you can just say of this issue).

SADNESS. With the first two fingers of one hand, I tap under one of my eyebrows right above the bridge of my nose and say this statement three times out loud: "I now release any and all sadness from any and all roots and the deepest cause of this jealousy" (or whatever the issue).

FEAR. With the first two fingers of one hand, I tap under my eye and say this three times out loud: "I now release any and all fears from any and all roots and the deepest cause of this jealousy" (or whatever the issue).

GUILT. With the first two fingers of one hand, I tap under my nose and say this three times out loud: "I now release any and all guilt from any and all roots and the deepest cause of this jealousy" (or whatever the issue).

EMOTIONAL TRAUMA. With the first two fingers of one hand, I tap under one of my eyebrows again and say this three times out loud: "I now release any and all emotional trauma from any and all roots and the deepest cause of this jealousy" (or whatever the issue).

NOTICING. After the first round of tapping, I sit and breathe. Then I ask: "Did I notice any thoughts, feelings, images, or body sensations as I was tapping?" If I didn't, fine. If I did, I jot them down to remember them. I notice that sometimes "tentacles" of emotion from other situations pop up as we're tapping on a situation. (For example, I had images and jealous feelings of my younger brother receiving lots of positive attention from my dad who'd waited through having two daughters until he got for a son.) Most of the time the images or feelings mean I'm releasing or processing the emotions I'm tapping on.

SECOND ROUND:

I think about the situation and use the SUDS scale to re-rate the level of intensity remaining. After one round, my SUDS rating was a 4. I repeated the tapping sequence in the same way starting with the psychological reversal statement. Sometimes our emotions, as rated by the SUDS scale, lower faster than other times. The goal is always to lower the SUDS to a 0 or 1. The more specific the statement is, the more quickly the emotion releases. Next, I re-rate the level of intensity remaining as I think more about the situation. After the second round of tapping, the intensity of the emotion was down to a 1.

FINAL RELEASE. When the SUDS rating is down to a 0 or 1, it's time to tap one time on each meridian point (side of little finger, under eyebrow, under eye, back to under eyebrow) while using this statement: "I now release and eliminate any and all remaining emotional roots and the deepest cause of this issue."

WHAT I WANT. Instead of feeling jealous I want to feel peaceful or neutral. To imprint the positive emotions, I tap one time on each of the four points and say out loud: "I now completely embrace and accept feeling peaceful or neutral about this situation." (Your subconscious knows what the situation is, no need to repeat it here.)

THE LEARNING. Afterward, I write any new thoughts or awarenesses that came as I tapped. For example, I could see why my buttons sometimes get pushed when others receive more attention and tapping made me remember my brother's favored status in our family. Before tapping on this issue, the attention Lee received from Dad was under the surface and I was unaware of how it affected me. Though unaware of why I would often still react, as I did with Marianne and Bill.

THE NEXT STEP. I ask: "Is there any specific ACTION I need to take? Do I need to write a letter, journal, tell a friend, or just be extra nurturing with myself?" For me, the action step was to stay present with any feelings that might come up in my writing group and to take care of myself around those feelings by journaling and by talking with Marianne.

How Traditional Therapy Compares with EFT

Traditional therapy has helped millions of people. I practice it in combination with TARA and EFT. I wish I'd learned these energy therapy techniques 20 years ago as a counseling intern because they speed up the healing process. Years of traditional talking therapy made me realize I wasn't crazy, which was a good thing. Non-traditional therapy, like pounding on pillows and breathing until I was dizzy, gave me a sense of my body, and, yes, I was angry. My study of Movement Psychology (see Chapter 13) made me aware of and more compassionate about my inner control freak. After a while, I felt done with these.

My life was good, yet certain old familiar buttons continued to flair up, especially around my daughter's birthday in January of each year. As the cold, dreary days of January rang in, I'd get more depressed and grumpy. I stared at the TV more and complained about Dave. I'd think, I've worked on my grief about my daughter, why do I still feel so bad every January? I also thought, "I should be over this." But I wasn't. I couldn't accept that "depressed and grumpy" was as good as I could feel. Then I learned Emotional Freedom Technique. EFT is an offshoot of the first energy therapy developed by Roger Callahan called Thought Field Therapy.[119]

THOUGHT FIELD THERAPY

Before I learned EFT, I'd read a short article in one of my therapy magazines about the parent form of EFT, Thought Field Therapy, developed by Dr. Roger Callahan. I was fascinated as he wrote about the story of a water-phobic patient who couldn't bathe or shower because of her fears. His office was in the back of his home and each time she came for an appointment, he had to close the blinds of the office so she couldn't see his pool.

A year of therapy had only slightly improved her condition. Frustrated, Dr. Callahan began researching alternative energy techniques such as chiropractic and acupuncture. In one session, he asked his client if it would be okay if he held an acupuncture point under her eyebrow while she thought about her fear of water and breathed. She agreed and within a minute told Dr. Callahan she could put her finger in the pool in his backyard. He didn't know why this approach had worked, but he was intrigued. Eventually, he developed a brand new type of therapy.

More Benefits of EFT

One Size Fits All: Emotional Freedom Technique, based on Thought Field Therapy, is a one-size-fits-all approach developed by Gary Craig. He reworked Dr. Callahan's approach and refined it from Callahan's many different tapping algorithms. EFT is more accessible because, once learned, it's not therapist-driven. EFT can be used anywhere, anytime, for anything from phobias, to stress, to trauma, to physical pain, and, as I'll demonstrate here, for emotional management of addictions or stress.

EFT Cuts Time and Cost: With managed care and time constraints, people don't have the time or money to spend years in therapy. EFT is a power therapy that drastically cuts the time necessary for most healing. One of the quickest EFT successes I've seen was Anna, a tall and stately woman in her 70s who hadn't driven over a bridge in 15 years. She'd heard about this "weird" technique from one of my clients and wanted to see if it could work for her. After only one session, she was able to drive over the Bay Bridge to go shopping in San Francisco. After the second session, she felt comfortable enough to use EFT on her own. I later heard through the grapevine she was happily driving everywhere she wanted.

Different situations require more or less time to heal. A simple phobia like Anna's usually takes one to a few sessions. Complex addictions like alcohol or eating disorders take longer than "lite" addictions such as zoning out with the TV for hours, constant email checking, or workaholism. Note that EFT doesn't *cure* addiction; it creates the equivalent of a pause button because it releases feelings. Uncomfortable feelings drive addictive behaviors. As the emotions are released, the obsessive thinking, ("I've gotta have it, gotta have it) and the compulsive behaviors become less intense.

Here's an example. Mary, a compulsive eater, comes home from work upset because her supervisor gave her a poor review. She starts to think about the cookies in the cupboard. Sure, she knows she shouldn't eat them because she's decided to lose weight. She tries to distract herself, but the more she attempts to *not* think about the cookies, the more she thinks about them and anticipates how good they'll taste. Eventually, she gives in. She grabs the bag and heads for the couch. When it's empty, she feels guilty and starts looking around for something else to eat. Once Mary has learned TARA and EFT, she's able to *identify* how she's feeling and release the emotions that would have driven her to binge on the cookies.

In general, EFT cuts the time it takes to feel better when compared with straight talk therapy. EFT empowers the client to trust they can handle daily emotional challenges because they have a skill that is readily available. I like that once the technique is learned and the clients are comfortable with their ability, the therapist is no longer needed.

Taking Care of Yourself

You may be wondering how you can find the time to take care of yourself and use EFT. It's amazing how creative we can be when we know experiencing relief is only moments away. Clients have reported going into a bathroom stall at work to tap on anger over a boss's reprimand. One woman told me she held each meridian point and quietly breathed when she became afraid because of her mother's criticism at a family event. I've used tapping to cope with my fear of heights while riding in the Palm Springs Tram. The attendant asked me if I was okay. I said, "Yeah, as long as I keep tapping."

Feel in Charge: Not only do people feel more relaxed and peaceful after tapping but they also feel more in charge. Ruth, who was seeing me for depression, reported with surprise that she felt happy after tapping, which wasn't a feeling she was used to. We then tapped on not feeling comfortable being happy so she wouldn't unconsciously sabotage herself.

Create a Safe Place: Good therapy does more than treat pain or teach skills. It creates a safe place for someone to get to know and trust someone else and themselves. EFT provides a simple, focused, and safe approach that, once learned, is easy to use. Unlike some therapies, it doesn't re-traumatize someone who has experienced abuse by forcing them to talk in detail about an event. The newest trauma research shows that one of the errors of traditional therapy occurs when clients feel overwhelming emotions every time they talk about an abusive event. As you'll see with EFT, it's only necessary to come up with a simple phrase that encapsulates the situation and the primary feeling, such as "this anxiety about driving" or "this anger that I can't quit eating at night." It's not that clients don't feel anger or sadness or fear as they're tapping, but the wave builds and recedes within a contained format. I recommend that individuals with childhood trauma learn EFT from a skilled professional.

Resolve Emotional Issues: EFT gives us the ability to resolve any emotional burdens or self-sabotaging beliefs. Unresolved pain collects like reservoirs in the nervous system. Unconscious emotions yearn for conscious awareness. It's almost like they look for ways to get our attention. When we avoid or deny our feelings, they find outlets in whatever we use to distract ourselves.

EFT is Safe: In general, EFT is a very safe approach. In the years I've been teaching it, only on one occasion did I feel concern after teaching it to a new client. This was when Maggie, whom you met earlier about her weight issues, came in to see me. Maggie wasn't used to showing her feelings, period, so the feelings that came up in our session frightened her. We didn't have enough rapport built up for her to feel safe. For this situation, I take responsibility. I hadn't taken the time that day to assess her level of safety and familiarity with her emotions. One reason I endorse EFT is the emotion that surfaces isn't often extremely intense. From the experience with Maggie, I learned that it's important for clients to have some level of comfort identifying and being aware of their feelings. This allows them to feel safe if their feelings spike when tapping. I often do a brief "safe place" guided imagery called Creating a Special Place (see Chapter 11) before using EFT for the first time. I also prefer that clients have learned TARA first so they are more aware of and in touch with their feelings.

WHO CAN USE EFT?

If you have a known background of childhood trauma and have never been in therapy, be sure to consult a therapist with EFT training or an experienced EFT professional. If you can't find someone with EFT training, then consult a professional trained in Eye Movement Desensitization & Reprocessing (EMDR). The early stages of healing trauma require the guidance and support of a skilled professional. EMDR and EFT are similar and work equally well. I prefer EFT simply because clients can use it readily.

I also encourage professional support if you're in recovery from hard addictions and have less than one year of sobriety. Once you've learned the technique and feel like you can manage your emotions comfortably, EFT greatly supports recovery. I believe we'd see much less relapse and true healthy, non-smoking, less caffeinated recovery with more therapies like EFT.

Trauma and EFT

EFT works on emotions and belief systems, and here's what I believe happens.

Let's say that in childhood, a big emotional event happens one time, or less intense events occur many times. As an example of a big "T" trauma, when my niece Sarah was four, her mother, who'd been drinking, was killed instantly when her car hit a tree. Sarah and her divorced mother had been living with Sarah's grandparents in Vermont. She hadn't seen her father since her parents divorced when she was nine months old. Lee, Sarah's dad, attended his ex-wife's funeral and brought Sarah home to California with him. Losing one's mother, meeting a stranger named "Dad," and joining a family where the stepmother was none too happy to have a new daughter was traumatic. She told me she kept waiting to go home.

Thankfully most of us don't lose a parent when we're young. However, repeated small "t" traumas can create pain that we ignore because it's not big enough to seem important. However, everything that happens gets stored in the brain (and the body) so some traumas can get triggered when similar events happen in the present. A seemingly minor event like your older brother getting more attention from your parents than you may not register when you're an adult—until your wife pays more attention to your son than to your daughter. Or, perhaps a sister blackmailed you to do her chores and beat you up if you didn't. Today, when your wife asks you to take out the garbage, you go into a rage and don't understand why.

Follow this progression. First, the original event or situation occurs—your brother gets praised for his behavior and you feel anger, sadness, fear, or guilt. Second, you tell yourself a story to make sense of the feelings or the situation. From that, you create a belief, which could be, "My parents love my brother more than me. I'm not as lovable as my brother. I'm not as worthy of love." Usually this story we tell ourselves is planted in the unconscious when we're children and the forgotten. So we're not aware that when we find ourselves at the refrigerator at 2 a.m., night after night, it's the hurt child wanting to be loved, or comforted.

In many ways it's easier to know we need help if we're aware of big "T" traumas because they show themselves so visibly. Charlene saw my ad in the yellow pages listed under Holistic Weight Management. She'd just had a lap band procedure for weight loss and said she was an "emotional wreck" because she could no longer eat to deal with her feelings. She'd been in therapy as a teen because her childhood had been less than perfect. At age eight, her parents had divorced and her mother started a string of relationships that left her ignored and lonely. She managed to cope by eating. I taught her to use TARA and, a few sessions later, EFT. Both helped her tremendously in the adjustment period from over-eater to healthy eater.

Addiction and EFT

Because most addictions are driven by emotions, particularly anxiety, EFT is a perfect fit for managing not only feelings and moods, but cravings as well.

James, at five-foot-seven, dressed in shorts and flip-flops, was referred by his doctor for health issues stemming from anger. When I showed him into my office, he chose to sit on the leather chair (90 percent of men pick the chair while 99 percent of women pick the couch) and told me about his constant irritation.

After listening awhile, I asked, "Are you anxious?"

"Well, maybe a little."

I suspected that he wasn't addicted to a substance, he was addicted to an emotional state—anxiety. So I asked, "Would you like to take a brief anxiety assessment? It'll tell us how much anxiety you're experiencing." Right in my office, James answered the 15-question assessment in *From Panic to Power* developed by Lucinda Bassett.[120] He was surprised that his anxiety scored in the highest range. This good information let him pinpoint a reason for his irritation and anger, which was tied to his unidentified anxiety.

On the conscious level, James knew his angry behavior was pushing his family away and he wanted to change. We talked about his dad dying when he was 12 and his having to work for his uncle, who managed the family heavy equipment business that James had been told he'd inherit at age 25. That didn't happen, yet at age 40, he continued to work the business. Every day, he was angry at his uncle, but believed he shouldn't be. All the grief and frustration and unfairness he carried around fueled his anxiety, which fueled his anger. He felt totally stuck in this vicious circle.

First I taught James to breathe and do progressive body relaxation each night to break the hold of tension and anxiety.

Next I taught him TARA to help him identify his feelings and triggers. He realized that staying conscious about how he was feeling reduced both his anxiety and anger. Then I introduced EFT to him. Once James experienced the relief that came with the tapping, he was immediately open to it. By staying aware through breathing, TARA, and EFT, James managed his anxiety and released the long-held pain of losing his father. He also released a sense of being out of control that had been perpetuated by working for his uncle.

Some who have addictions are driven by the desire for pleasure and others to avoid pain, but whichever one it is, at the root is anxiety. The cocaine addict says he's just going for the "high," but when he's sober and we talk, he reveals a lot of pain he's never looked at. The food addict thinks she eats because she has no will or is "weak," but she's never paid attention to the anxiety humming under the surface that says, "I'm not loved, I'm not enough, and I've got to run from these feelings any way I can."

When I use EFT with clients dealing with addictions, I focus on the primary emotions of anger, sadness, fear, and guilt, and negative or self-defeating beliefs. We usually start with the current emotional event, such as anxiety about being sober to a fight with a spouse. Then we determine where the current situation and feelings hook into the past, such as my feeling overlooked by my writing instructor Bill. I was jealous of the attention Marianne got because of the attention my brother got from our dad. When my button got pushed, it was like Dad was sitting in Bill's chair and I was the hurt little girl. If this situation had happened in my 20s, I would have denied or repressed the feelings and later gotten rid of the tension by drinking or partying. Today, I know that running away from feelings feeds anxiety. By going through the feelings, I'll come out the other side to peace or neutrality, maybe even happiness.

Clearing the original pain is particularly freeing because when emotional blockage gets cleared, there's nothing for the mind to attach to in a negative way. The emotional kink in the hose has been released and the instinctual emotional brain can re-balance. Relaxation and peace result. After using EFT, I could think about being criticized by either Dad or Bill without reacting. My response was neutral. That's *freedom!*

"Imagination is
more important
than **knowledge**. **"**

~ Albert Einstein

CHAPTER ELEVEN

Chapter Eleven:

Imagery

IMAGERY IS the third of the three mindbody skills that lead to joy by reducing the symptoms of stress and trauma that often result in addictive coping. Imagery is pictures in the mind often associated with feelings in the body. It speaks to our hearts and souls through symbols, metaphors, our senses of taste, touch and smell, and of course our emotions. We use imagery every day as we think of a fun time we've had, a warm-hearted childhood memory, or someone you love.

Imagery communicates through word-pictures because it engages the right side of the brain. Hearing "the lemon is on the table" evokes a bland image compared with "the red-headed boy bit into the yellow lemon and its juices squirted across the room." Both sentences produce images, but the second makes your mouth pucker, doesn't it? Powerful.

One day, I walked into the waiting room where I work and a large woman with short red hair and wild eyes asked me, "Are you Lynn?"

"Yes," I replied.

She immediately launched into "My name's Elizabeth and I'm going to have gastric bypass surgery next week. I'd like to see you after I'm feeling better." Then she looked at me expectantly. I said sure and we chatted a few minutes without setting an appointment. I wished her well with the surgery and wondered if I would ever see her again.

A couple of months later, Elizabeth called in a hysterical panic. "I had the surgery, I've lost fifty pounds and now I can't eat. I'm afraid I'm dying." So I made an appointment and when we met, she told me, "I don't know who I am without the weight. I've always been big. I'm terrified."

"Take a breath," I said. "You're bumping up against big questions here, so no wonder you're afraid. *Who are you now* if the person you see in the mirror looks completely different? How do you adjust to not using food to numb or escape your feelings? How do you become comfortable with the 'new you' and all that means?"

Elizabeth nodded. "Okay, what now?"

I could tell she needed a sense of safety fast. And Imagery would be perfect. It's a beautiful way of working with inner images, body sensations, and feelings to access the deeper self.

After I described Imagery to her she asked, "How do I know if I can get images?"

"I think what you're asking is how will you know if what you're getting are images or not," I said. "Try this experiment. Close your eyes and let an image form, however it does, of a circle, a square, and a triangle. Now, describe what you're seeing or sensing."

"There's a dark background and a bright red triangle, a pink circle and a purple square with yellow polka dots," Elizabeth laughed. "Okay, I get it. I just let my mind draw pictures for me."

"We all access images in different ways," I told her. "Some of us don't get pictures at all. Some of us have more of a feeling or sense or body sensations. Others get colors without form. There isn't any right or wrong. We just allow the images to come and present themselves and after a while, it's as easy and fun as turning on a TV set—and much more interesting."

Next I took Elizabeth through a "Creating a Special Place" imagery piece, similar to the one following this example. She quickly relaxed and began to describe her special place. "It's very green and lush. There are lots of tall pine trees. It smells heavenly. Oh, there's a waterfall in the back and it's very private. No one else is around. I like it here," she smiled.

I encouraged Elizabeth to just breathe and be in her place with the lush trees and the smell of pine. Next, I asked her to invite in an image of a wise person who could help her with her current situation. Almost immediately she reported, "There's an old lady here. She has long grey hair with white streaks and she's looking at me with such compassion." Tears slid down her face. "The old lady says she's here to help me let go of all the years of being responsible for everything. She's telling me I'll be happier as I'm lighter in weight and she's says I'm really strong. She's also telling me I need to relax and calm down, that everything is okay. Somehow I believe her."

"Okay," I said. "Go ahead and thank this image and say goodbye for now, knowing you can bring it back whenever you choose. Notice your special place again and slowly bring your attention back into the room as you feel your body and take a some deep breaths." I yawned as I usually do when I'm leading an Imagery session or teaching EFT. Like Pavlov's dogs, my body knows when it's time to relax.

I asked Elizabeth what her next step was. "It's to take care of myself by following the directions of the doctors—to eat, exercise, and take my vitamins. I feel so relaxed and hopeful. I'm not scared right now."

I saw Elizabeth for only a few sessions because she made such rapid progress with self-care and adjusting to her new thinner identity.

SPECIAL PLACE IMAGERY

(Here's an example of a guided imagery I use with clients. If you can, find someone to read this to you because it's easier to relax when you don't have to guide yourself. Or, you could record it and then listen to the recording of your own voice.)

Become aware of your breath and take a couple of breaths without changing the way you're breathing. Completely exhale all the air from your lungs by gently squeezing your abdominal muscles. Now, take a deep, full breath through your nose. Notice how much more space you've created in your lungs by fully exhaling first. Scan your body for any places of tension, tightness, or soreness. Breathe right into these places . . . . Continue breathing in through your nose, and breathe out through your nose . . . relax . . . relax . . . relax . . . .

Allow an image to form of a place that's special to you. This might be a place in nature you've actually been to, a comfortable spot in your own home, a childhood memory of a comfortable, cozy place, or a place you make up. Just allow an image to form that seems right to you. There is no right or wrong way for images to form. Some of us get clear, visual pictures in our mind's eye. Others get colors, a sense, or feelings.

Just notice the way you access images. Once you have an image in mind, allow yourself to explore your special place. Look around and notice the colors. Are they bright or soft? Which colors most draw your attention?

Notice the sounds... birds singing...waves crashing...the wind through the trees or water bubbling in a brook.

What smells catch your attention? Fresh pine trees...or the salty smell of the ocean...or the dry sage-like aroma of the desert?

Pay attention to how you feel in your special place. Also notice your body in your special place. Are you sitting, lying down, or walking? Breathe and let yourself enjoy this special place that's just for you. This is your place only and no one may come into this place unless you invite them. Go ahead and breathe and let yourself be for a few moments...

When you're ready, allow your attention to come back to physical reality. Take a deep breath, feel your feet on the floor, your legs, and the rest of your body. Know that this is a place you can come back to anytime you choose, just by going within and giving yourself a few moments of renewal.

Imagery Takes Us Within

In its simplest terms, Imagery affirms for us that all of our answers lie inside. Belleruth Naparstek, psychotherapist and creator of the bestselling *Health Journeys* series of imagery audio programs used in more than 1,500 hospitals and clinics, calls guided imagery a user-friendly form of meditation and a purposeful use of the imagination. It uses relaxation, breath, words and phrases, fantasy, and memory to create receptivity in the mind.[121]

Guided Imagery targets the right hemisphere of the brain where perception, sensation, emotion, and movement reside. The left hemisphere is the analyzing, verbalizing, and synthesizing part of the brain. We need the balance of both to feel our best and get the most out of life.[122]

Imagery is "... a natural thought process using one or more of the five senses and usually associated with emotion. Imagery is a bridge between the conscious and subconscious mind."[123] Guided imagery usually uses scripted exercises that are read or recorded and listened to. (See the examples in this chapter called *A Special Place* and *Freeze Frame*.)

Another type of Imagery is called Integrative Imagery, developed by Terry Reed and Sue Ezra of Beyond Ordinary Nursing. I studied with Terry and Sue and became certified in their program in 2003. Integrative Imagery dialogues with the person's own images, as Elizabeth did in my session with her. Dialoging engages the left part of the brain. Because Imagery naturally engages the right and left brain, Integrative Imagery is a more whole-brain experience than is simple scripted Imagery.[124]

Terry and Sue have used their unique brand of imagery to support the physical, mental, and emotional healing processes of illnesses. They conducted a research study at Mills-Peninsula Hospital in Mill Valley, California, in 2003 that compared elective hip and knee replacement patients who either received an individualized Imagery session and customized audiotape pre-operatively or did not. The outcomes showed a significant reduction in the amount of pain and use of pain medications, and a shorter length of recovery with those that had the Imagery sessions and tapes.

HOW DAVE USED IMAGERY TO HEAL

Years before I'd ever heard of guided Imagery, my husband Dave came up with his own version in response to a serious hang gliding accident. Dave started hang gliding in 1989. In his younger years, he'd raced dirt bikes and had always been a bit of an adrenaline junkie. A friend invited him to Lake McClure, California, in the foothills of the Sierra Nevadas, to watch friends hang glide. After the first weekend spent watching men leap off a 1,200-foot cliff and soar like birds, he was hooked.

Unfortunately, Dave learned how to hang glide like some learn to ski—by going down the hill with few or no lessons. His first (you heard first, right?) accident resulted in a bad break to his upper left arm in two places. The orthopedic surgeon wanted to put in metal plates to stabilize his bone. Dave had other ideas. After exploring more options, he went home with a hanging (appropriate term) cast. For the next six weeks, he slept sitting up with his arm dangling, first from a tree in the backyard, and later from a contraption he rigged up in the living room. The purpose of the hanging cast was to allow the bones in the arm to set themselves.

But Dave didn't just let his arm heal on its own. He looked carefully at the x-rays the surgeon had taken. Many times a day, and especially at night when he couldn't sleep, he visualized the bones growing back together perfectly and quickly. It paid off. At his six-week appointment, the surgeon was amazed at his progress. Within three months, his arm was completely healed and he's never had any residual lack of movement or pain. Dave proved that Imagery (and the focused mind) can be a powerful healing modality.

Teaching Imagery

A few years ago, my son Rich asked me to speak to his paintball team about teambuilding. I understood I'd have to find a way to get these young men to relate to Imagery on their terms.

None of the ten young men on the paintball team had ever heard of Imagery. But they had heard of Mark McGuire, who has used imagery (and probably steroids) since 1991 to improve his game. Other athletes that have excelled with performance-enhancing Imagery include Brock Marion, defensive back of the Dallas Cowboys and 1994 Super Bowl Champion, tennis champion Jimmy Connors, and about one-third of all professional golfers and many Olympic athletes. Once the paintball team got past the idea that Imagery was a "girl" thing, they dove in. I taught them to set goals for themselves and visualize the results as if they'd already happened.

Imagery is so effective because the brain can't tell the difference between imagining an event and performing in it. Here's a potent example of what I mean. Colonel George Hall was a Vietnam vet imprisoned for five and a half years in Vietnam. He spent most of his time in solitary confinement in an $8\frac{1}{2} \times 8\frac{1}{2}$ cell. He survived and kept his sanity by mentally playing golf every day at his favorite golf course. He'd had a 4 handicap when he went into the Service. After his release, he played with a group of friends and, although he was physically weak, he could still play with a 4 handicap.

How Imagery Can Heal Trauma

We know that there's a link between addictive coping and trauma. Trauma creates a physiological battleground in the body that disrupts biochemistry, lowers self-esteem, and can make day-to-day functioning a tremendous struggle.

Techniques such as EFT and Imagery work on the big "T" traumas such as rape, war, domestic violence, abuse, or car accidents and the small "t" (and often ignored) types such as constant criticism, neglect, or over-control. Imagery-based therapies go through the back door using metaphors, symbols, body awareness, breathing, and relaxation. These techniques create a sense of safety that words alone can't accomplish as well as engage the senses as participants imagine purposefully.

Imagery appears to actually raise the stress threshold that's trauma has impaired. Clinical trials over the last 20 years have demonstrated success rates with healing the psychological effects of trauma, improving immune system function, and managing chronic pain.[125] Physiologically, stress from trauma causes an overproduction of cortisol and adrenalin, which eventually turns into underproduction that's equally as harmful for the body. Trauma survivors with chronically low levels of cortisol often complain of numbness or boredom. A stressful event can spike coristol levels (more so than in someone who hasn't experienced trauma) and then plunge it back down again. Low levels of cortisol are especially found in immune system illnesses such as chronic fatigue syndrome.

In my 20s and 30s, I used to go into explosive rages or blue meltdowns. Today, I realize these states were fed by the stress of childhood trauma and a lack of self-care skills. I'm not perfect—I still have my tantrums like when I read my bank statement and think I've been charged for something I shouldn't have been charged for. But now I get over it in a few minutes rather than a few days—and I don't take my tantrum out on the people I love (or others either).

I have never used antidepressants or medication, and although I am not opposed to them, I prefer natural supplements over pharmaceuticals. I've found that the amino acids 5HTP and GABA naturally balance mood, promote relaxation, provide a buffer for stress, and produce more restful sleep than many of the antidepressants available today. Amino acids work effectively for mild to moderate depression while more severe depression requires stronger medication. The supplement 5HTP boosts serotonin, which is what most antidepressants regulate while GABA relaxes the muscles of the body. (If you're interested in this alternative form of treating stress, anxiety, and depression, please see Julia Ross's book *The Mood Cure* or visit www.themoodcure.com.

Freeze Frame Technique

An organization called HeartMath specializes in teaching quick, easy-to-use practices that manage emotions with Imagery and intention. I've used the following "Freeze Frame" practice over the years when I teach stress management workshops, adapted from the work of Doc Childre and Bruce Cryer.[126]

The purpose of Freeze Frame is to address negative feelings rather than avoid them, and to learn how to switch to more positive feelings by listening to your heart. As the body relaxes and attention gets refocused in the heart, new solutions and insights emerge, generating fresh action and buffering against stress.

EXPERIMENT: Follow these steps to "Freeze Frame" your experience.

1. Breathe. Pick a situation that's bothering you. Recognize any stressful feelings, and Freeze Frame them by stopping the action like you do with the pause button on a video camera.

2. Make a sincere effort to shift your focus away from a racing mind or upset emotions to the area around your

heart. Pretend you are breathing through your heart, and, if you'd like, place your hand on your heart to help your attention stay focused there. Breathe and keep your focus in your heart for ten seconds or more.

3. Recall a positive feeling or memory and attempt to re-experience it. (If there are sad or unhappy feelings that are also connected, pick another memory.) Amplify the positive feelings by allowing yourself to BE in the experience—smell the smells, hear the sounds, imagine touching your surroundings.

4. Now, using your intuition, common sense, and sincerity, ask your heart what would be a more efficient response to the situation, one that would minimize future stress.

5. Listen to what your heart says in answer to your question. What specific action or actions would be helpful?

Practicing Freeze Frame retrains your physiology. How? As Childres wrote, "Just as the amygdala in the brain has the power to conjure up negative emotional memories that can rob clear perception, you can generate positive feelings which restore balance physiologically."[127] As you practice shifting from automatically reacting to stressful situations to using the power of our mind through Imagery and positive intent, the effects of stress neutralize. Even if you're unable to find a positive emotion when you go to your heart, just shifting attention away from the upsetting emotions while breathing and staying focused in your heart can neutralize negative feelings. Neutral, according to Childre and Cryer, is a "state of quietude inside—not total silence or the total absence of thought, but a state of greater balance than usual, a dynamic peace."[128]

As you practice Freeze Frame, your mind and body will respond more frequently to the invitation to evoke positive feelings. The human body craves homeostasis, healing, and balance. Given the opportunity, it instinctively knows how to achieve it.

GIVE YOURSELF A TREAT

If you haven't experienced a guided session with a trained Imagery expert, I encourage you to give yourself this treat. Something magical happens when you give your unconscious, or higher self a chance to express itself. I've taken a problem into an Integrative Imagery session and received surprising answers that my left brain would never have generated.

To find an Imagery expert in a large city, look in the yellow pages of your phone book under Imagery or go to www. Integrativeimagery.com or www.Imageryinternational.org to locate someone in your area. Also, many massage therapists or yoga teachers practice Imagery so look there as well. Just be sure to treat yourself!

"Positive thoughts are a biological mandate for a happy, healthy life. In the words of **Mahatma Gandhi:**

Your beliefs become your thoughts,
Your **thoughts** become your words
Your words become your actions
Your actions **become** your habits
Your habits become your values
Your values become your destiny."[12] **"**

- Bruce Lipton

CHAPTER TWELVE

Chapter Twelve:

The Mind Thinks It Knows

A T AGE 29, I realized selling real estate was *not* my dream job. This occurred to me as I was speeding down the street, yelling at the idiotic drivers, and feeling miserable—negative, grumpy, and pissed off. (Sound familiar?) Ah. . . another wake-up moment. At this stage of awareness, I thought real estate wasn't the job for me because of other people in the business—especially title reps and loan officers who never got their paperwork done on time. Now I know different. It wasn't them, it was all about my negative slant on everything. Over the next few months, I quit real estate and went back to school.

These days, I visit my chiropractor, Dr. Harry Brown, about once a month for an adjustment. Besides being a cutting edge chiropractor, he also happens to be a magician who hires out for birthday parties and corporate events. While he was adjusting my back one day, he said, "I've been experimenting with some of my patients. I ask them what's good about their day. A few of them can't come up with one single positive thing."

"I've experienced the same thing with some of my clients," I said. "It's sad that we don't realize how our habitual thinking traps us. I sure didn't when I was younger. I think the mind tends to be negative because it's critical and analytical.

And, then there are our role models."

"Well, the brain is a problem-solving mechanism," Harry said.

"I do have to work at being positive," I responded. "Don't you, Harry?"

He nodded.

"I think we have to consciously train our mind away from negativity. I realized through studying *The Course in Miracles* and Buddhism that my mind would be thinking of something most of the time; fighting it was like trying to make the color blue, red. Impossible. What works better is to notice when I'm feeling bad and what thoughts are the cause. Then I use the phrase "cancel, cancel" that I learned from attending Betty Bethards lectures in Walnut Creek, California, during the late 80s.

It works like this: I notice I'm having judgmental thoughts about myself or someone else and that I am feeling bad. I say out loud, if at all possible, "CANCEL, CANCEL." Then I replace what I was thinking with a more positive thought.

If you have trouble coming up with a positive phrase, think of the opposite of what you were thinking. For example, say I wake up in the middle of the night and can't sleep because I'm worrying about finishing this book. I say, "Cancel, cancel." Then I ask, "What would I rather be thinking about?" I replace the negative worry with happy thoughts about Gracie, my granddaughter. Before long, I'm off to sleep.

At first, it takes a lot of work to become aware and then take the time to practice the new thinking. But after a while, a happy "Fido" response occurs. We clearly feel so much better when we switch from negative to positive thinking. It's like the brain begins to notice negative thoughts in anticipation of a new treat—feeling better.

In his book *The Success Principles,* Jack Canfield noted that the average person talks to himself 50,000 times a day, that most of this self-talk is about himself, and that 80% of it is negative.[130] Thoughts like "I shouldn't have done that; they don't like me; what's wrong with me" permeate our conscious and unconscious thoughts. Our bodies react to negative thoughts with stress symptoms such as high blood pressure, stomachaches, and headaches.

Here's an example in my life. I stopped visiting an elderly friend of mine because I felt so awful being with her. She never had anything good to say about anything or anyone. She'd lost both her adult children in bizarre accidents so I felt sorry for her. But one day, I burst into tears and told her I couldn't take her constant negativity anymore. Shocked, she was completely unaware of what constantly came out of her mouth.

We're Not Victims of Our Minds

The first self-help book that drove home the power of the mind and emotions was Dr. Wayne Dyer's 1970s bestseller *Your Erroneous Zones.*[131] Dave and I bought copies for our friends and relatives because he challenged readers to take responsibility for their thoughts and feelings and to stop victimizing themselves. Perfect timing. This book inspired me to change my mind (although it took many years to transform my thinking).

One part of my mental retraining came through my son Rich. Until he was a teenager, I raised him as I was raised—with high expectations and criticism, sprinkled with a dash of rage and humor doled out occasionally. Not surprisingly, he started acting out as I had done as a teen. By the time he was 14, he'd developed a drug and alcohol problem. In counseling at this time, I started paying attention to how much of what I told him was what I *didn't* want from him rather than what I *did* want. In retrospect, I wonder how he managed to have any self-esteem at all.

That's when I started catching and changing my automatic tendency to criticize and started asking for what I wanted. I'd say, "Rich, I'd really appreciate it if you would take the trash out before you go out with your friends" or "It's great you came home on time" or "I like it when you use a glass for milk instead of the carton." (Well, the milk one never did work.) This approach gradually made a big difference in our relationship.

Rich went through a time where he'd punch me on the arm—lightly but it still hurt— (he was 6' 2" tall and strong) and I didn't like it. I asked and yelled about it, but nothing changed. Finally, my sister suggested that next time he punched me, I give him a hug and tell him I loved him. I did and he immediately stopped punching me. Isn't it interesting how we can break habitual patterns – Rich seeking and receiving negative attention – by one person being willing to try a new dance step.

Try the following experiment.

EXPERIMENT: Pay attention to how often you say to yourself or to others what you DON'T WANT rather than what you want. Examples include "I hate it when people cut me off on the freeway." (Instead, say this: *"I appreciate that there are some considerate drivers."*) "It drives me crazy that you (husband or wife or partner) never write your checks in the register." (Instead, say this: *"I really appreciate it when you enter your checks"* or *"I like it when you enter the checks in the register weekly."*) See how often you can think of a positive, powerful statement from a negative one. Over time, you'll develop "automatic positive, powerful" thoughts that contribute to your joy and well-being.

Retrain the Mind –The Rest Will Follow

A Course in Miracles changed my life because it changed my thinking. Much like the military puts new service people through rigorous physical training in preparation for combat, *The Course* uses theory and practice to re-train fear-based thinking to love-based thinking.

At first, doing the exercises drove me crazy (that's a positive, powerful thought) because of confusing and seemingly nonsensical statements such as this: "You may believe that you are responsible for what you do, but not for what you think. The truth is that you are responsible for what you think, because it is only at this level that you can exercise choice."[132] Huh? Although I regard some of the theory as gobbledygook and the writing style difficult, I go back to its messages time and again. After a few months of doing the daily work, I felt a big shift in the anxiety that had been my constant companion since childhood.

A Course in Miracles suggests reading a page or two of text and following up by completing a practice sheet from the workbook. Practice consists of statements such as: "I will forgive and this _____ (fill in the blank with the most apt emotion: anger, pain, anxiety, guilt, etc.) will disappear." At first I thought, "What hooey." But I've found the process works whether you believe in it or not—as long as you do the practices.

While on vacation many years ago, I realized I didn't have to believe the theory for the practice to work. I ended up in the same car with my cousin April, who, like my brother, is five years younger than me. I felt uncomfortable because I'd taken advantage of her a few years before when I had her frequently baby-sit Rich while her mom and I partied. Understandably, she was angry with me and I still felt guilty. As we drove down the street, my gut knotted, I silently repeated this phrase over and over to myself: "I will forgive and this anxiety and guilt will disappear." A few minutes later, we were laughing—the tension totally forgotten. A shift had occurred without my ever saying anything to her. It felt like a miracle. Not surprising, *A Course of Miracles* defines a miracle as a shift in perception. Our reactions are based on the meaning we attribute to the events that trigger them. (To learn more, you can find *A Course in Miracles* through Unity Church Bookstores, do an online search, or order it at Amazon.com. In addition, Marianne Williams's *A Return to Love* is based on *A Course in Miracles* and provides an excellent introduction to its principles.)

Over-thinking Mind + Negative Mind = Stress

Because so much has been said about the power and dangers of negative thinking, I want to highlight the value of addressing negativity in reducing stress and increasing peace to create choice and even prevent addictive coping. The mind thinks it knows everything and likes to be in control. It pretends to be the general in charge, with our emotions, body, and spirit acting as foot soldiers and obeying its orders. But these "soldiers" have their ways of rebelling.

The Thinking (over-thinking) Mind defined by Dr. Gregg Jacobs sports these qualities: critical, analytical, not in the moment, self-absorbed, socially conditioned, separate from nature, past and future oriented, and controlling. Although these attributes might be practical in the business world, they don't necessarily bring happiness or peace. In fact, those qualities often keep us from the experience of life that comes through our senses and our relationships.[133]

I believe it's essential to have methods to reduce the stresses of modern life that are driven by the over-thinking mind. Dr. Jacobs recommends spending time in the Ancestral

Mind, which is defined this way: being in the moment, nonverbal, unconscious, intuitive, physically grounded, emotionally connected, and part of nature. If you've ever taken a yoga class, afterward you feel highly relaxed with a quiet mind. As the body relaxes, the mind must follow suit. This is why it's essential to have regular bodymind practices to balance us in a hectic, stressful, activity-filled day. After yoga, my body feels alive, almost pulsing. I access the non-thinking part of my mind; my practice places my awareness and attention on the sensations of my body, emotions, and spirit. By accessing these softer parts of myself, I smooth out the drive and control demanded by my over-thinking mind.

The Relaxation Response

Dr. Gregg Jacobs's *Ancestral Mind* research supports the early work of Dr. Herbert Benson, the first to explore the relationship of stress on the body. Dr. Benson coined the phrase "the relaxation response." The relaxation response slows brain wave patterns, quiets mental chatter, and reduces stress hormones. It also reduces heart rate, breathing rate, and sometimes even blood pressure. This is one reason meditation works, especially meditation involving a mantra or a repeated word or phrase, which shifts the mind away from everyday thoughts.[134]

EXPERIMENT: Check your stress level right now and assess it on the SUDS (Subjective Units of Distress) scale of 0 to 10. If you're not doing so already, sit down. Exhale all the air from your abdomen and lungs. Inhale through your nose and breathe deeply into your abdomen. Continue to breathe consciously. Repeat a word or phrase—for example, breathe in and repeat silently "love." Exhale out your nose and repeat. Continue this pattern for five to ten minutes. (One or two minutes are better than none at all.) Check your stress level again and note any reduction.

You'll find that doing a simple exercise like this daily will lower your stress response and increase your relaxation response. Stressful thoughts and feelings activate the fight-or-flight response. Likewise, relaxing, loving, calming, or peaceful thoughts reignite the relaxation response and begin to balance our nervous system. Do this breathing exercise in the car, at your desk, or in a meeting.

Be creative.

YOU CAN DO ANYTHING YOU SET YOUR MIND TO

Both of my grandmothers were moderately practicing Christian Scientists. My parents weren't, nor did they attend church, my mother vocally claiming it was nonsense. It's interesting, though, that one of my mother's favorite sayings was "you can do anything you set your mind to." I've heard versions of this phrase from others, but it speaks to a basic tenet of Christian Science—that the mind is all-powerful and has tremendous potential when we allow God (or our best self) to direct us rather than leaving that job only to the ego.

I have my own interpretation of my mother's saying, which is that when we combine the power of attention and intention to focus on what we want with action, almost anything is possible. For example, a few weeks I'd been playing with this affirmation from *The Wealthy Spirit*: "People love to give me money." [135] I say my affirmations out loud after I meditate each morning and sometimes at night before sleep. I've found that using EFT (tapping) while repeating affirmations adds juice and shortens the timeline for getting results.

One weekend, my cousin Kim flew in and we went to San Francisco for her birthday celebration. She unexpectedly offered to pay for the hotel for the weekend. ("People love to give me money.") A valet at the hotel backed into my car and the hotel compensated us with free parking and a night's stay (and of course paying for the damage). ("People love to give me money.") While shopping, I saw a gold necklace I fell in love with. Hesitating to buy it, I remembered that Dave had told me when I found the right necklace, he'd buy it to celebrate our 25th anniversary. I'd been looking a year and a half. It was fun, even coincidental, that I found the perfect one this weekend. ("People love to give me money!")

More significant examples of the power of focused attention (and action) include finding the perfect agent (Nancy Rosenfeld) for this book, deciding I'd like more clients and hearing the phone ring, needing a piece of information for this book and immediately discovering research or a book that led me to it, and my writing group, which came about when I said, "I need help writing this book."

My mom was right about the power of the mind, and I often thank her for this wisdom. It was her gift to her children.

Changing Negative Thoughts

I have found that positive thinking, or affirmations, aren't enough to change negative thoughts. What works best is a combination of approaches. I favor these three:

Touch, Accept, Release, Action (TARA) gets you in touch with how you're feeling.

Emotional Freedom Technique (EFT) clears or greatly reduces negative emotions.

Imagery, or using pictures with affirmations, makes the right-brain creation process fun and powerful.

Affirmations and images I've played include this: "I'm so happy and grateful *Intentional JOY* is complete." I could feel the weight of the pages in my lap as I held my finished book. I felt joy and success picturing the book's cover displaying the title *Intentional JOY* and my name with BEST SELLER emblazoned across the top. Doing affirmations and visualizations daily works! Try it now.

EXPERIMENT: The following is a powerhouse affirmation process. Use it only if you really want to create your heart's desire!

1. To build awareness of your less-than-conscious thoughts, buy a small notebook to keep in your purse or car. For the next week, write down every negative thought you become aware of. Become the observer or witness rather than the judge. You may have a tendency to say, "I'm not a negative person," but be careful. I didn't think I was particularly negative until I caught myself ranting in the car. When I did this journal exercise the first time, I was shocked to discover how much I beat myself up, how much of what I said about others was negative, and how angry I felt. Then do a reality check by asking people around you what they hear you say over and over. Ask, "Do you hear mainly negative or positive statements coming out of my mouth?" You may be surprised.

2. Use TARA (see Chapter 10 if you need a refresher) to identify feelings or beliefs that are feeding these negative thoughts. As you keep track of your thoughts in your notebook, let's say, for example, you notice you keep complaining about your boss taking advantage of you. Use TARA to identify your feelings about the negative statements in your journal. Write down your feelings. Don't hold back—write as many emotional statements as it takes to get them out.

3. "I feel angry about (or that) _____", "I feel sad about (or that), I feel afraid about (or that) _____", and "I feel guilty about (or that) _____." Notice where in your body you feel the emotions and rate the intensity level on a scale of 0 to 10, with 10 being the most intense.

4. Release the emotions or beliefs you identified using EFT. If you know EFT then use it to tap on the emotions of anger, sadness, fear, and guilt. Alternatively, take ten slow breaths through your nose into the place in your body where you most feel the sensations of your emotions. Exhale out your

mouth. If you can't tell where your body is holding the emotion, then breathe into your abdomen. If the intensity (using a SUDS scale) isn't much lower, take ten more breaths. (Once the emotions have been reduced to a 0 or 1, you don't need to repeat EFT. Only use it again if the negative feelings flare up.)

5. Develop an affirmation that represents what you *do* want rather than what you *don't* want. In the situation of having a demanding boss, for example, change your self-talk from "I don't like my boss because he pressures me to work late" to "I like checking in with myself first when the boss asks me to work late" or "Sometimes it's okay to say no to the boss."

6. As you repeat your affirmation, create a picture in your mind of asserting yourself with your boss as you check in about how it feels to be appropriately assertive. Practice, practice, practice!

Our Beliefs: The Lens Through Which We See the World

"If you want to know what you believe, look at what you're experiencing."

- Victoria Goldblatt, health consultant, singer, best friend

Eighteen-year-old Doug was dragged into counseling by his mother who told me when she made the appointment that she was afraid for his life because he was using meth. After the second session, I asked him not to use it the day he came into counseling and he agreed. He seemed to enjoy our conversations, asking good questions and listening intently. I decided to explain how we form beliefs. Doug slouched on the couch with his long legs stretched in front of him. Leaning forward, I looked into his eyes and said, "When we're kids, we have experiences and we have thoughts and feelings about those experiences. Most of these go into the unconscious or subconscious mind. We don't pay any more attention to them. But all these thoughts and feelings about how we're loved or not, valued or not, accepted or not, create a lens through which we see the world. This lens simplifies life because we can't pay attention to all the data and information that comes at us each day. However, it also limits us because once a belief is formed, we consider it to be the truth. This belief filters out new information that could be useful."

Doug said little but I knew he took it all in. In our third session, he told me his family history. He said he admired his dad's ability to quit drinking after 45 years of hard living but had no respect for his mom's workaholism or her extremely religious parents. Lots of pain and addictions in this family, I noted. His parents fought viciously when he was a child and his dad beat him severely. He made light of these beatings, declaring he was okay. "Then why do you think you're using meth?" I asked. He just stared at me.

Most addicts like Doug have one or a combination of these three beliefs operating under the surface—*I'm not enough, I'm unlovable,* or *I'm bad.* I could see all three running through Doug's drug abuse, his failure to move forward with his goal of getting into the armed forces, and the constant physical fights that he bragged about.

Doug wasn't game for EFT. Tapping on himself and repeating phrases out loud was too wacky for this tough young man and I respected that. But he loved guided imagery because it relaxed him. The Special Place Imagery gave him a safe place—perhaps the first internal one he'd ever experienced. We spent many months together and his drug use never stopped, but he reported using less and gaining weight. Then he stopped his sessions. After six months or so, his mother called again. In our next session, he came in weighing 30 pounds less than the last time I saw him. I felt sad seeing him look so bad and told him so. He agreed to in-patient treatment, and the center kicked him out after a few days. But he liked some of what he learned there. He disappeared again after a few more sessions. I thought of Doug from time to time and wondered what'd happened to him. Then, one day at the supermarket, I saw him and his father crossing the parking lot. I rolled down my window and called to him. He came over with a big smile on his face. "I'm sober," he announced proudly. "But I'm lonely. All my friends are still using meth." "I'm happy you're sober, Doug. You'll find new sober friends. It takes some time, but you'll find them," I reassured him. It made my day to see him, especially sober and with his dad. I hope he's able to push past his limiting childhood beliefs forever.

EXPERIMENT: Awareness is the first step in changing beliefs. Ask: "What beliefs have shaped my life? What pushes my buttons? What do I repeatedly overreact to? What am I experiencing that I don't like? What are my recurring patterns in relationships or repeating problems in my life?" See if any of these answers (beliefs) ring a bell for you: "I end up with men who hurt me or leave me or ignore me. I'll always be fat. If I were prettier, more handsome, smarter, thinner, whatever, my life would be easier. I try and try and I never get ahead. I'm not worthy to _____ (fill in the blank) have a loving relationship, have enough money, a great career, etc." These beliefs all seem to be the truth because, as Dr. Wayne Dyer has said, we collect evidence to support what we believe. Would you rather be right than change?

" As **I believe**, so I behave
As I behave, so I become
As I become, so becomes
my world. "

- Stuart Heller, Ph.D.

CHAPTER THIRTEEN

Chapter Thirteen:

The Body Really Knows

A FRIEND OF MINE, Janice, once called the body our "earth suit" because it's through the body and its senses that we experience the world. In *The Ancestral Mind,* Dr. Gregg Jacobs said that pre-civilized man was "one" with his environment, interacting with everything around him—the plants he ate, the animals he was dependent on for food, the materials he used for shelter, and the sun and the moon for inspiration or guidance. As the brain's neocortex evolved, humans gradually became self-conscious, objective, and more distant from our environment. Humans became "less being oriented and more thought oriented.[136]

For the modern developing child, thought becomes more pronounced as language develops—a process molded by our culture's mental focus. Although we're born with an awareness of our bodies, by adulthood we might act if we're walking heads—detached from our emotions. The price we often pay for this lopsided relationship is stress, negativity, and addictive coping.

EXPERIMENT: Next time you go shopping for groceries, notice if you feel connected with your body. Breathe and bring your attention inside while you're looking for the choicest tomato in the produce department. Take time to smell the tomato as you hold it and examine its color. Keep your attention on your sensory experience of the tomato rather than jumping ahead to what you have to buy next.

Body Wisdom

So many of us treat our bodies as if they belonged in a foreign country. We don't speak the language of our body's messages—aches, pains, twinges, pleasures, sensations—because we haven't been taught to do so. Unless it revolts from within, we don't listen to its style of communication that's driven by emotions and senses and sensations.

The first time I reconnected with my body as an adult (other than having sex) was at a movement psychology class at John F. Kennedy University in Orinda, California. Movement Psychology is a body-oriented therapy that uses movements and postures adapted from Tai Chi and other martial arts to expand awareness and create change. It was created by Stuart Heller and his student, Crystal Surrenda. One of the practices is called the Eight Directions. In class, the instructor would demonstrate a movement, class members would practice it individually, and then we'd pair up for observation and gentle feedback with our partners.

As I went through the movements of the Eight Directions—up, down, front, back, center, left and right, in and out—I questioned if I was doing the movement "right." (Instantly, I became aware of my always striving to do things "right.") The observers kindly noted that every time I finished a movement, my head popped up. Crystal said, "Exaggerate that movement and see what happens." As I complied, I felt aware of the need to stay in control. Over and over I went through the eight directions, paying attention to my habit of sticking my head up at the end. All of a sudden, it seemed like my mind popped open and I shifted back into my body. I felt a flood of energy with my heart beating, my lungs breathing, my blood and even my skin pulsing. I lost my controlling mind for only a few minutes and became deliciously aware of my whole being—totally IN my body. Like a butterfly floating with the breeze, sensing my body meant relaxing and going with the life force rather than resisting it. I became aware of my toes, legs, belly, arms, head, and face without analysis and fear. What a delicious yet odd feeling. Later when I was journaling, I wrote, "This must be how I felt when I was a child—alive and free."

I was so fascinated by Movement Psychology that I took a 12-month training program in addition to the nine months required in school. This forged in me a deep respect for the wisdom of our bodies and emotions. I learned that our minds may think they're in charge, but our bodies and our emotions tell another story.

Non-Verbal Communication

Because the body can't verbalize, it's easy to tune out its communication as if it's a "dumb animal." Yet people who love animals understand that, though they don't speak, they definitely let us know what they feel through their actions and body language. For example, there's no mistaking when my dog Maggie is hungry. She prances in front of me, lifts her eyebrows, and runs into the kitchen to deliver her "it's time to eat" message. I get it.

I've owned horses much of my life. My last horse, Black Mando, was a yearling when I got him. How joyful to watch him develop from a gawky adolescent to a muscled and magnificent stallion. On the ground or riding him, I was aware that, while he was trained to listen to my cues, first he had his own instinctual reaction patterns of flight. Should something frighten him, I'd best pay attention to his body language or I could end up on the ground.

Stuart and Crystal taught that the body is still an animal, no matter how the mind has attempted to convince us differently. Our bodies employ symptoms of stress to remind us of this fact. And unlike the thinking mind, the body can't lie. It speaks the truth—if we have ears to listen. In a positive sense, addiction, illness, and physical symptoms are alerts from the container of the unconscious—the body—to the conscious mind. Our bodies could be saying, "Listen up—I need you to pay attention to these symptoms. If you don't, I'll crank up the volume."

Because our minds have learned to override our emotions, we convince ourselves we're fine—but not if our minds and bodies are fighting each other. The mind says, "Hey, I'm doing great, I have a $60,000 a year job, I just got married, I have a new house and a mortgage I can afford. I'm working too much, but that's what it takes to get ahead." The body says, "Um, excuse me, I'm tired. Could we skip the gym tonight? How about taking a little nap on Saturday after the house is clean? And could ya lighten up on all the unhelpful criticism? By the way, I could be coming down with a cold."

We can become so skilled at ignoring feedback that we don't pay attention until something significant happens— migraines, upset stomach, irritable bowel, sleeping problems, bleeding ulcers, and so on. Then we ask a doctor for a quick fix and the doctor writes a prescription for antidepressants, sleep medication, or something to soothe our symptoms.

Do our bodies have to act in extremes for us to look at the deeper causes of illness? Do we even *consider* healing unfinished emotional business as a necessary step toward physical healing? What does the body know that the thinking mind doesn't? The thinking mind's orientation in the world is "abstract, self-absorbed, past and future oriented and controlling," according to Dr. Jacobs.[137] The thinking mind, known in psychological terms as the ego, will do almost anything to maintain control through denial, rationalizing, and minimizing to accomplish what it wants—safety and survival, pleasure, and the avoidance of pain.

Why pay attention to the body, the unconscious, in relation to addictive coping behaviors? Because emotions denied feed addictions. Our minds read our bodies and, through language, give meaning (or not) to these sensations. Our hearts register grief or loss, our throats close up when we can't express ourselves, our jaws clamp down, our fists ache when we're angry.

Awareness is the first step in healing because it allows us to have choice. Movement or other body-oriented practices switch on light bulbs of awareness. In fact, it's dangerous *not* to be aware. Applying awareness to addictive behaviors means that once the light bulbs turn on, we realize there are alternatives to feeling stressed, exhausted, hung over, bored, empty, if we're willing.

EXPERIMENT: Try this two-step process to become aware of how feelings shape your body. Because it's hard to read something and do it simultaneously, ask a friend to guide you through it and then switch. Just have fun and remember that there's no right or wrong way of experiencing it.

1. Stand up. Now, think of a time in the last few weeks when you've been angry. Allow your body to form a posture that represents this anger. You might notice your jaw tightening, shoulders or fists tensing, or something else. Next, exaggerate that posture and again, just notice. Now, shake your whole body and let both the anger and the posture go.

2. Think of a time when you've felt really happy. Allow your body to form a posture that represents this happiness. (For me, my arms naturally float up, a smile breaks across

my face, and my chest comes forward.) Exaggerate your
"happiness" posture. Hold it and don't let go, then TRY TO
BE ANGRY. Go ahead, get angry! Now, shake your whole
body and return to sitting. Notice any thoughts, feelings,
body sensations. Are you feeling slightly confused? If so,
that confusion is the mind saying something like, "Maybe
I'm not as much in control as I'd like to believe."

Do you see that you can become so used to tuning out
an awareness of your body that you don't realize what a
powerful teacher it is?

MOVEMENT PSYCHOLOGY INCREASES AWARENESS

In the Eight Directions exercise, there's a direction called "out."
While standing, I went through all the directions—up, down, front,
back, left, right, in, and out. (Bear with me, even if you don't quite
follow yet.) When I went "in," which you do by placing your hands
in front of your heart and then following your attention "inside," I
felt comfortable. After all, I was an introvert by nature. Doing the
movement of "out" felt extremely uncomfortable, as if I was on
stage giving a presentation. I felt in the spotlight, embarrassed—
exposed. I gently observed that while relating this feeling of
discomfort with being in crowds, at parties, and with large groups.
When I was younger, I used alcohol or drugs to help me get
through those uncomfortable feelings.

Movement Psychology is based on the principle that as we move
differently, we feel and think differently. As a result, we act
differently. So by becoming aware of this pattern and practicing
"out" over and over for months, my comfort with the practice
transferred into my life. Before this training, I had linked public
speaking with visions of torture. But practicing the "out" direction
allowed my bodymind to shift to a new behavior and today I often
do public speaking with ease, even JOY!

Clearly, to be fully alive, we need to feel our emotions and *be* in our bodies. Optimal functioning is whole-person functioning, which is mind, body, emotions, and spirit working together as harmoniously as possible. It's like ending my yoga class with the "corpse pose" and being led in guided imagery. I have had such an exquisite feeling of peace, it brings tears to my eyes. Fully in my body—barely any thoughts. Full relaxation. Body. Mind. Bodymind.

Remember the analogy of the blind men feeling the elephant? Each one names a different beast because they can't see the wholeness of the elephant before them. That's what happens when we leave behind the power and beauty and truth of the whole body to see the world through the lens of the intellect. Especially for people with addictive issues, we can reverse that by checking into our bodies and, through them, our unconscious.

Breath As A Power Tool

Do you unconsciously limit your breath and therefore limit the available energy supply to your mind and body? Consider the breath as a power tool that combats stress, helps cope with illness, moves emotional energy, and brings presence to each moment. Buddhists use the breath in meditation; programs such as Jon Kabat Zinn's Stress Reduction Clinic at the University of Massachusetts Medical Center use breath for stress reduction and pain management. (Please go to www.umassmed.edu.cfm/srp/index.aspx for more details.)

EXPERIMENT: Picture a baby having his diaper changed. The baby's belly, and if you watch closely, his whole body, rises and falls with his breath. He breathes naturally. Notice, without judgment, how you're breathing right now. Don't change anything. Just notice. Do you breathe mostly in your upper chest? Does your chest move much as you breathe? Is your abdomen involved in breathing at all? Or is it frozen from years of constricted breathing?

For people who've spent years habitually drawing small, tight breaths, it feels strange to include the abdomen. In reality, breathing often feels restricted, closed, and tight like a rusty hinge that's been unused for too long.

BREATHING AND DRIVING

I do the previous breathing exercise frequently in the car and a few years ago, on my way to an early-morning class, I was driving on the freeway when someone honked at me--a young man I was seeing as a client with his father, also in the car. I waved at them and carried on with my breathing. The next week, I saw him in a session and mentioned the freeway encounter. He looked at me with an odd expression on his face. I laughed guessing what was on his mind. I told him I was doing a breathing exercise to wake myself up and asked him, "Did you think I was picking my nose?" He laughed with relief and said yes. (This exercise has the added benefit of helping you not care what other people might think of you.)

As you begin breathing more deeply and fully through the nose and into the abdomen, you might feel lightheaded (that's increased oxygen), or notice body sensations you're not usually aware of, or experience emotions you don't normally pay attention to. These are all indicators of the aliveness available by being in tune with the body. With regular breathing practice, you'll connect with a revitalized energy flowing through your body.

EXPERIMENT: Empty all the air from your abdomen by gently squeezing or contracting your abdominal muscles and then doing the same with the air in your chest. Next, inhale into your abdomen first, allowing your abdomen to push out (women love this freedom!) and then filling your chest. Exhale by gently squeezing the abdominal muscles and then emptying the air from your chest. Notice your stress level on a scale of 0 to 10 before you start. Close your eyes and breathe consciously six to eight times, gently noticing your body's sensations.

Breath is to the body as fuel is to a car. Don't run on fumes and expect your body to perform as if you're putting high octane gas in the engine. To get extra energy, breathe more fully and deeply, or more fully and quickly.

EXPERIMENT: If you're feeling tired or brain dead at the end of a long day, try this brain-balancing breath. Take your index finger and close off one nostril. Then, take a deep breath into your abdomen through the open nostril. Switch your index finger to the other nostril and exhale out your nose. Inhale through the same nostril and switch again. Do this for a few minutes. Notice how you feel.

" Oh God, **help me**
to believe the truth about myself,
No matter how **beautiful** it is. **"**

- Old Jewish Prayer

CHAPTER FOURTEEN

Chapter Fourteen:

There's No World Without Love

DO YOU REACT to the idea behind this Old Jewish Prayer with a sigh of relief or a cynical smirk? How you react shows how worthy of love you believe you are; it points to how much control the over-thinking mind exerts. Do you give lip service to loving yourself, but binge on burgers at lunch or drink your way through every weekend? What is a loving person anyway?

The late Leo Buscaglia, author of *Living, Loving & Learning*, was known as the love doctor of the 1980s. He said that to give love, first we have to have it, but that if the love we have is " . . . neurotic, possessive or sick, then all we can teach is neurotic, possessive or sick love."[138]

The Concept of Loving Ourselves

I think this whole concept of loving ourselves is complicated. If we truly love ourselves—that is, accept that we are loving and lovable right now—there's no struggle; we can just *be*. But how would we function without the ups and downs, the good and bad, the right and wrong of daily living? What would we do without conflict? Who would we like or dislike? Which political party would we align ourselves with?

Some think that if I love and accept myself as I am, I'll become a bum and watch TV all day. Maybe I'll drink champagne and charge up my credit cards. (That could be fun—for a while.) Perhaps if I love myself, I'd sit around looking in the mirror, becoming so enamored with myself I wouldn't get anything done. Worse yet, I wouldn't care. And I'd never do anything for others because I wouldn't care what they thought of me—not what my neighbors think (I'll never mow my lawn again), not my boss (so screw going to work). But then, what's the point of life?

I once asked my client Mary if she loved herself and she replied, "I don't know what you mean. What is love?" That's a question that confuses many. The Random House College Dictionary defines love as "a profoundly tender, passionate affection for a person of the opposite sex."[139] Another version stated, "love, affection, devotion all mean a deep and enduring emotional regard, usually for another person." But the concept of *self-love* isn't mentioned.

How in this crazy world can anyone truly love themselves? If we're able to love ourselves, will all our addictive behaviors melt away? Will we be suddenly be thin, wealthy, and on the cover of *Glamour*? Will love create the solution to world peace? Or at least will we be able to pay our bills?

The basic premise of *A Course in Miracles* is that there are only two emotions, fear and love, and that it's impossible to feel both at the same time. You get to choose either one. Do you consciously make that choice for yourself?

EXPERIMENT: Read the Old Jewish Prayer at the beginning of the chapter several times and ask: "What do I have to let go of to accept that I'm lovable today?" (e.g., guilt, anger, shame, judgment, righteousness, blame, etc.) Then, doing EFT, tap on any of the feelings or beliefs ("I'm bad, not worthy, this is stupid") that come up as you repeat the prayer. Next, replace any negative feelings with what you want—peace, joy, happiness, calmness, neutrality. If you don't know EFT, breathe and allow the possibility that you're already worthy and lovable right now, just as you are. Record your feelings and sensations.

But Isn't Loving Yourself Selfish?

I know there are gifts in organized religion, but it often comes with the guilt, the "shoulds," the putting self last. When I talk to some clients about their body-image issues and ask, "What if you were more loving toward yourself," they reply, "Oh, I can't; it's selfish." Yet babies are born knowing they're worthy, lovable, and loving. Why does that get forgotten? Why do we lose that deep, joyful love seen blooming in the face of any infant? Before long, we learn to *earn* love. We get into an either/or relationship with ourselves. We bargain and say, "If I get good grades, I'll be loved. If I'm a good boy or girl, I'll be praised. If I don't perform, I don't deserve love."

Intellectually, we know that material love isn't love. Rather, it's accepting all the parts of who we are: accomplishments, successes, challenges, and failures, self-doubts, insecurities, mistakes. Love is the ability to embrace the dark underside of our mistakes, greed, misdeeds, anger, and shame.

Like an old-fashioned record needle stuck in a groove, humanity is mired in the punishment model that believes that to correct misbehavior or mistakes we must spank or manipulate someone with guilt, or incarcerate them because then they'll self-correct. Our Puritan influence has taught that if we punish someone—especially ourselves—enough, we will learn the errors of our ways. From feeling bad, we'll know better next time.

Do you buy into that? If so, in your best Dr. Phil voice, ask, "How's that working?" My question is: If the punishment model were successful, why don't more people reach their full potential?

What Is Love, Anyway?

Westerners often confuse love with romance or material indulgence. If I buy myself those great new shoes, then I'm loving myself. Okay, shopping may be fun, but it isn't love. And it's not an act of self-care if I can't pay my bills because of shopping too much.

Leo Buscaglia said that his students thought he was referring to an ego trip when he said that " . . . a loving person is a person who loves himself." But he had something quite specific in mind—that we learn to love ourselves so we can give that love away. He wrote, "I'm about a person who loves himself as being someone who realizes that you can only give away what you have; . . . and the only reason you have anything is to give it away."[140] Eckhart Tolle said that to love is to recognize yourself in another and that the longing for love of every child is the longing to be recognized on the level of being, rather than performance.[141]

Of course, love comes in different forms.

There's romantic love, which is marked by an adrenaline rush and intensity of chemical attraction. Yeah for lust and sensual aliveness!

There's long-term-companion love. My in-laws, in their 80s, have been married for more than 50 years. One afternoon while I sat having a glass of wine with my mother-in-law, Jeanne, she told me about her dying friends and her resulting sadness. "It makes me grateful for every day Stan and I have." Then she smiled, winked, and confided, "He still chases me around, you know." While my husband and his sisters affectionately call Jeanne and Stan "the Bickersons," they genuinely enjoy each other.

There's parental love, which is the protective, nurturing, accepting connection between a parent and child.

Finally, there's agape or brotherly love, which is the type of love experienced for humanity in general. This impersonal love encompasses wanting what's best for everyone globally beyond our family, state, or nation.

The definition of love I prefer comes from Eckhart Tolle's book *A New Earth*. He wrote, "Jesus spoke of the 'I AM,' the Buddhists call it Buddha nature, and the Hindus, Atman. The common thread is the '. . . the indwelling God' . . . because when we are in touch with this within ourselves we are in our natural state—LOVE."[142]

Love implies a sweetness or a softening of the protective edges that many of us are uncomfortable with because we fear we'll be seen as weak and perhaps unable to protect ourselves. Being gentle and treating ourselves like a best friend seems to be hard; to love ourselves truly and purely may be our life's greatest challenge.

When Love is Missing

"People needing other people" is a line from a Barbra Streisand song my mother played over and over when it came out in the 1960s. The lyrics assert that we all need each other. It's reinforced by the attachment theory in psychology, which encompasses the inherent need children have for connection. It also shows how its absence can damage a developing brain and self-esteem.

According to Thomas Lewis, Fari Amini, and Richard Lannon, authors of *A General Theory of Love*, humanity is in trouble when both parents work outside the home because a greater potential for emotional neglect exists than if one parent stays home. Overworked, underpaid daycare workers can't substitute for an involved, caring mother or father—let's face it, especially the mother.

Total Biology, introduced in Chapter 8, is a healing approach that tracks the root of a physical or emotional illness to the childhood or ancestral root. Gilbert Renaud, a practitioner of Total Biology, said the mother/father importance split is 75/25 percent. Emotional neglect in early childhood causes billions of neurons in the limbic brain to die off. Because the limbic brain is the emotional brain, neglect creates a condition that sets us up to seek the relief of cheaper substitutes such as alcohol, drugs, or TV to attempt to replace the love that's missing. Xboxes or Gameboys, cell phones, and the Internet don't fill our hearts or love us back.

On the far side of the continuum, children who are emotionally neglected or isolated are more prone to becoming violent. They act as if they don't care because they haven't attached to anyone—why should they care? Without enough love, care, and attention these children's brains can't develop the emotional capacity to be in relationship and they can't emotionally self-regulate. On the other hand, children who receive enough loving attention build a resilience to the stresses and strains of everyday life. As noted in *A General Theory of Love*, "For those who attain it, the benefits of deep attachment are powerful—regulated people feel whole, centered, alive."[143]

Our relationships provide great opportunities to rise above petty differences and practice giving love, as Leo Buscaglia modeled so well. Loving ourselves doesn't mean not setting limits or taking care of ourselves. In fact, quite the opposite. Real self-love includes boundaries and healthy self-care as I learned to do with my sister Lane.

MY SISTER'S JOURNEY TO SELF-LOVE

My sister turned 50 in June, 2006. At her birthday party, she gave me a big hug, told me she loved me and thanked me for saving her life. My husband Dave was surprised that Lane acknowledged how desperate things had been in the last year and a half. I wasn't. When my sister is sober, she's one of the most open-hearted and honest people I know. When she's not, she's one of the most angry and difficult.

In 2005, Lane was near death, once again, from her alcoholism. A few years ago, she called me in the middle of the night as the ambulance was arriving. She told me she'd slit her throat. All kinds of horrible pictures went through my head as I rushed to the hospital. Fortunately, the disposable razor she used made a fairly superficial cut.

This time, my sister's threatening death was slow due to starvation and pneumonia from her daily drinking and smoking. I felt so depressed whenever I saw her and rarely visited. Besides, she was in her "I hate Lynn" mode—typical when she drank heavily. I'd get to hear about what an awful person I am—always fun for me. When a neighbor called to tell me she was in bad shape, my usual anger flared up. I used EFT to bleed off enough of it so I could drive safely and be present with her.

In 2005, when I picked Lane up to go to the doctor, she clutched her cigarette defiantly in her hand. "God, she looks like Mom," I thought. I wondered how long she could survive. A part of me felt resigned. At the doctor's, she surprised me by asking for medication to ease her withdrawal from alcohol. When I dropped her off at her place, I gave her a hug and held my breath, partly because of how she smelled and partly because I was afraid I'd never see her alive again. I stayed in touch and learned that she began weaning herself off alcohol—and as of her birthday in June, 2007, she'd been sober a year and a half. My love for her wouldn't let me give up and kept me connected, though it was painful. I reminded myself that I didn't have to like her behavior, but I could still love the best in her. With as little judgment as possible, I held the door of hope open for both of us, though at times it felt like only a crack. She was finally able to step through into a better, happier place within herself.

Resisting Love

Children who receive adequate doses of love don't question their "enoughness"—that is, feelings they have about being good enough. Yet, the adult women in my Take Loving Charge groups start off defining themselves as flawed and unworthy, largely because they're overweight.

This chasm between the unquestioning self-acceptance of early childhood and the defeatism of adulthood has to do with the modeling of our parents, educators, and the media. As psychiatrist R.D. Laing wrote, "From the moment of birth you are programmed to become a human being, but always as defined by your culture and your parents and your educators."[144]

There are no neutral words for "fat" in this culture. Whoever came up with the labels "obese" and, even better, "morbidly obese" should go through a virtual reality experience of being fat like I did. One night I had a dream that I was in an auto garage trying to get my car fixed. The mechanics ignored me and I couldn't understand why until I looked down at my body and saw that I was fat. I felt ashamed, but my car needed work so I kept trying to get someone to pay attention—but not very hard, because I believed I deserved to be ignored. In the dream, I remember how heavy my body felt and how difficult it was to move. It was a powerful dream because, having been thin my whole life, I've never experienced the guilt and shame that seems to come with being overweight. (Lots of other guilt and shame, just not this one.) After this dream, I had a great deal of compassion for the women I work with who have weight concerns.

I ask this question of women in my groups and I'll ask it of you: What are you most afraid will happen if you really love and accept yourself? What if you let out the lovable person trapped inside or become the success you've always wanted to be? What would happen if you leapt into the fullness of your power rather than stepping back from it with self-destructive behaviors? I hear over and over from my clients, "If I love myself, I'll never lose weight." That's bass-ackwards. It's when we love and accept ourselves that we develop the guts to act in loving, kind, and *honest* ways.

WHAT IF I'M FABULOUS?

Danielle, a petite blonde college student, told me at her first appointment she had self-esteem issues. A few months later, she shared an "aha" with me. "I'm afraid of my fabulousness," she declared. "When everything's really good, I start sabotaging myself. I don't go to my classes because I get distracted by guys."

I held her eyes and asked, "What would happen if you let yourself be fabulous?" Danielle looked down. "I'd have to be more responsible and maintain it. It's terrifying."

"Danielle, if you let yourself be fabulous, it's not going to be comfortable for a while because it won't feel like you. It's like you're taking on a new skin, one that's a vibrational octave up from what you've practiced all your life. In a weird way, feeling uncomfortable is good. Eventually, like a snake, you'll grow a new skin that becomes comfortable."

Before long, Danielle became focused on school and getting As. She put her interest in boys in the footlights rather than the spotlights. And she's becoming ever more comfortable with her "fabulousness."

EXPERIMENT: This exercise is called "I AM ONLY LOVE" by Joy Migneault, Certified Massage Therapist, as shared with Maureen Minnehan-Jones, RN, author of *Body Stories: How Your Body's Messages Can Heal Disease*. This exercise takes only five to seven minutes (less time with practice).

To start, sit or stand quietly and breathe deeply for five or six breaths. (Do the TARA process from Chapter 9 and breathe in through your nose and out through your mouth to release the feelings or resistance.) Next, follow these steps.

1. Move your dominant hand in a clockwise circular fashion
    over your first energy center, located at the connecting
    point of your legs and torso. Repeat these phrases
    (preferably out loud): I <u>AM</u> ONLY LOVE, (YOUR NAME) <u>IS</u>
    ONLY LOVE, WE <u>ARE</u> ONLY LOVE. Speak slowly and allow
    a feeling of love to surface. Imagine a time you have felt
    loved or given love. Pretend there's a remote control in
    your hand and that you can push a button to magnify the
    feelings of love ten times and, if you're daring, even 100
    times.

2. At your navel, repeat the clockwise circular movement
    with your hand and these phrases: I <u>CREATE</u> ONLY LOVE,
    (YOUR NAME) <u>CREATES</u> ONLY LOVE, WE <u>CREATE</u> ONLY LOVE.

3. Repeat the clockwise circular movement and these phrases
    at your solar plexus: I <u>FEEL</u> ONLY LOVE, (YOUR NAME) <u>FEELS</u>
    ONLY LOVE, WE <u>FEEL</u> ONLY LOVE.

4. Move to the Heart Center, located in center of chest and
    repeat these phrases: I <u>EXPRESS</u> ONLY LOVE, (YOUR NAME)
    <u>EXPRESSES</u> ONLY LOVE, WE <u>EXPRESS</u> ONLY LOVE.

5. Next, go to the Throat Center and repeat these phrases: I
    <u>SPEAK</u> ONLY LOVE, (YOUR NAME) <u>SPEAKS</u> ONLY LOVE, WE
    <u>SPEAK</u> ONLY LOVE.

6. Now, go to the Third Eye, the space between your
    eyebrows and repeat these phrases: I <u>SEE AND HEAR</u> ONLY
    LOVE, (YOUR NAME) <u>SEES AND HEARS</u> ONLY LOVE, WE <u>SEE
    AND HEAR</u> ONLY LOVE.

7. Complete the exercise at the Crown Center—the top of
    your head—repeating these phrases: I <u>KNOW</u> ONLY LOVE,
    (YOUR NAME) <u>KNOWS</u> ONLY LOVE, WE <u>KNOW</u> ONLY LOVE.
    Take a few deep breaths.

Without judgment, notice how you feel. If you'd like,
tap on any mental chatter or emotions that were triggered.
Try this exercise faithfully for 30 days. I suspect you'll feel

more peaceful and accepting toward yourself when you do. Remember to use EFT (from Chapter 10) for any resistances or guilt that comes up.

Maureen Minnehan-Jones used this exercise as part of her treatment regimen for leukemia. It seems to have helped; she's in complete remission. Maureen uses it as a daily "clearing" while she's showering and suggests it could be done in front of a mirror, too.

I frequently do this "I AM ONLY LOVE" exercise to counter my negative mind and bombardment of negativity and fear from the media. I often change it to "WE ARE ONLY LOVE" I like to do this exercise while walking. When I'm silently saying it, I usually smile and then notice how people readily say hello and engage when I do! I also say this affirmation or prayer before bed, when I wake up and can't get back to sleep, when I feel grumpy, even when I drive in the car (without doing the hand movements).

The Scientific Side of Love

Our culture's primary orientation is intellectual, and the thinking mind values statistics and data that demonstrate the "truth" of the newest drug or medical cure. But is the power of love statistically provable? If we could scientifically prove the value of love, would we be willing to take more risks to open our hearts?

It's reassuring to know that research shows how love, care, and appreciation can counter stress. These qualities also improve or rebalance the thymus gland, which monitors and regulates energy flow. The health of the thymus is vital to a healthy immune system.[145]

In addition, researchers at HeartMath Institute have studied the effects of stress in the workplace and reports the following about IgA, an antibody in saliva related to the immune system health: "...the effects of anger versus care and compassion on average IgA levels (found) that one five-minute episode of mentally and emotionally recalling an experience of anger caused an immediate short-term rise in IgA, followed by a depletion that was so severe it took the body more than six hours to restore normal production of IgA. A single episode of . . . anger and frustration can depress your immune system for almost an entire day."[146]

The good news is that one five-minute experience "...of care and compassion caused a much larger, immediate rise in IgA, which then climbed above baseline over the next six hours. HeartMath goes on to state that other studies show that feelings of happiness and joy increase white blood cell counts needed for healing and defending against cancer and virus-infected cells."[147] (Freeze Frame is one of the books describing HeartMath Institute studies.)

The benefits of love can be measured scientifically, as HeartMath studies indicate. Stress (another form of fear) makes us more vulnerable to illness as measured by IgA levels. Even brief episodes of love marked by care and compassion feel better than stress and have the added benefit of improving our immune systems.

In 1994, two scientists began to collect data on 40 Harvard men who had participated in the original Harvard Mastery of Stress Study of the early 1950s. It had been conducted with 126 healthy male Harvard undergraduate students. In the results, love (specifically parental love) was linked to better adult health. For example, one segment of the Harvard study's original questionnaire rated the men's perceptions of their parents' love and caring. Drs. Gary Schwartz and Linda Russek analyzed and reviewed their answers and discovered that of the men who had rated both parents high in love and caring in college, 25% had developed physical diseases such as cancer, heart problems, and high blood pressure 35 years later. However, 87% of the men who rated both parents low in love and caring were diagnosed with a disease. "The higher (the men's) perception of parental love, the healthier their lives . . . independent of family and genetic history . . . divorce, history of parents, smoking, or marital histories of the men."[148]

Chemical Components of Love

When we're depressed, the relief of fresh neurotransmitters flooding the brain makes us feel better, even wonderful at times. Then their glimmering effects fade. Antidepressants might simulate the synthetic chemicals of "love" but they clearly don't model for us the healthy acts of a mother or father whose caring words or touch show us love.

Many of my clients taking antidepressants have the goal of resuming life without using the drug and experiencing its side effects. The body produces a natural love hormone called oxytocin. Researchers report that oxytocin levels are higher than usual when mothers are giving birth and right afterwards. It's interesting that prairie dogs, which are monogamous, jointly rear their young and both male and female have high levels of oxytocin. But the mountain variety of prairie dogs, which is not monogamous, show indifference to their young and have much lower levels of oxytocin. How long can it be before we see an advertisement for, perhaps "OxyCare"— "Just one every morning will make you feel more loved the whole day."[149]

Wonders occur as we dare to release self-hate and fear, and to believe in the beautiful truth about ourselves. Once we're aware we have a choice between love and fear, the responsibility falls on us to select. This ability to choose is both weighty and freeing. With awareness, we can no longer unconsciously blame and excuse ourselves for the misery or pain we create. This isn't to say making the choice for love, with its attributes of care, compassion, and kindness are easy. Life will always have its challenges.

THE DALAI LAMA AND JOE

Have you ever seen a photo of the Dalai Lama, the supreme head of Tibetan Buddhism? In his 70s, he appears vibrant and youthful. Yes, he has wrinkles, but it's his smile and the twinkle in his eye that draw warm attention. He works long hours, travels often, and lives in service to others.

Compare the Dalai Lama with Joe, who's 45 but looks at least ten years older. Joe works 60 hours a week, has ulcers, can't sleep, and fights with his wife because he constantly feels stressed. Depressed and angry, he avoids his feelings and overeats or zones out in front of the TV to cope. He feels stuck and says, "I've got a mortgage to pay, children to put through college. I couldn't quit if I wanted to."

Joe's doctor recommended Prozac and taking it seemed to help. Then he felt guilty because after a few months, he got depressed again. Isn't the Prozac supposed to make it all better?

Prozac may help reduce the symptoms of depression, but it can't address the cause. Prozac doesn't change the way Joe deals with his boss or the feelings he experiences but can't name. A pill can't manage the events in Joe's life or his reactions to them.

Joe must slowly learn to rebalance his life by acknowledging the value of his feelings and learn healthier ways to express them. When his head (what he tells himself he should do) and his heart (how he really feels) work together rather than fight each other, Joe will be in integrity with himself and have more energy and vitality.

Here's what I know from years of experience. Developing the courage to love and accept ourselves one step a time provides an inner resilience to the everyday stresses and strains of work, relationships, financial difficulty—even the process of saying goodbye to loved ones. Love simply *feels better* than stress and fear. And anything we practice, we get better at. My wish and heartfelt prayer for you is to practice love and allow its benefits to flow.

Even a serious eating disorder, one of the hardest addictions to treat, can be shifted with love. Annette from the example on page 250 has learned the skills of choosing love rather than fear. She shows the rest of us it's not only possible to stop addictive behavior but to live freely. This reflects an act of consciousness that comes with emotional wisdom.

Willingness to Go After Love

I'm not the same person today that you met on the first few pages of this book. First of all, 30 years have sped by. But most important is the shift that has occurred inside. I'm much more comfortable with myself today. Yes, I do love myself, still imperfectly, but better and better every day. Instead of cramming myself into an outfit that's too small and the wrong color and style (pretending it fits just fine), I've learned that blue and orange are great colors for my skin tone, that comfort wins out over style, and that lose-fitting waistlines are best.

A lot of comfort I experience today comes from my willingness to go after love and self-acceptance—and to keep going even through the toughest parts. Am I there yet? Well, I don't believe in a finish line, not even death. Do I live in peace or absolute bliss? Nice thought. I've heard of enlightened masters who actually do live in those states, which sounds fabulous, but I'm not sure how they'd manage even the slow version of the average American lifestyle.

I suppose that's the point. I used to say what's most important is love but I've found that love without skills isn't enough. I also need the emotional and bodymind skills to better manage my complicated life. I've worked with many courageous clients who climbed the mountain part way and made good progress, but few have gone the distance to a place of full love and acceptance. Annette is one such person whose journey hasn't been easy for either of us.

Annette, a tall blonde with a small, heart-shaped face, perched on the edge of the couch and licked her lips with nervousness. She barely made eye contact with me. Usually whatever clients need to say pours out of them. But with Annette, as with most anorexics, she seemed to have a stopper inside her blocking anything from going in or out.

Now in her 30s, Annette had been severely anorexic and bulimic since her teens. Like most people with eating disorders, Annette both wanted to get well and fought it like crazy. Over the course of our five years together, she attended in-patient treatment twice, was hospitalized twice, and kept every single appointment with me. Frankly, I almost gave up on her after the second hospitalization when the anorexia was dominating her, but she wouldn't let me.

"Annette, I think you're at a choice point here. It's time to decide whether you're willing to fight and make it to the other side with this illness or whether you're going to let it win."

"Are you firing me?" Annette asked in a small voice.

"I'm not sure I'm the right therapist for you. I'm wondering if someone different, with other skills, would work better for you. What I know is something's gotta change here. Because otherwise I don't know how you'll make it." I was frustrated and angry when I said those words—angry at her for failing to get well and angry at the anorexia that was killing her.

"I don't want to see someone else. I can't believe you're abandoning me." She paused for a moment and looked at the ground, then squeaked out, "I'm mad at you." (This was a good sign—she'd never expressed anger toward me before.) "Are you kicking me out if I don't get better?"

"I care about you. I want you to get through this and if I

can't help you to do that, maybe someone else can." We were both in tears. I felt confused—what was I doing booting her out of therapy? Yet I also felt determined that something needed to change. After much discussion, I agreed that we'd continue. I wouldn't give up on her but she had to decide what she really wanted.

This difficult time became the turning point for Annette. In the synchronistic way that occurs when we're ready, Annette found a nurse and Reiki healer through a friend who'd healed herself from anorexia. After three or four sessions with Ruth, Annette told me, "Okay, I'm starting to want to get well. I've always felt so empty and Ruth helped me find my spirit again. She said it's the part of me that left when I was two or three."

For the next year and a half we worked together to fine-tune her recovery. She anxiously began eating consistently and focusing not on the weight gain (too terrifying), but on staying in touch with her "spirit"—the loving essence of her best self.

At one of our last meetings, Annette radiated with excitement. She decided to leave her job as a teacher's aide for emotionally disturbed children because it exhausted her. "It's not the kids that make me want to leave; it's what the teachers expect. They want the kids to be on task, to prepare them for the world. I want them to know it's okay to be kind, and creative, and have fun. I love the kids until they understand better and can start to love themselves."

"What you said about the kids reminds me of what you've said about your family," I said. "You just want everyone to be happy and loving."

"Yeah, that's right," she laughed. "The kids call me the 'peace and love' teacher. You know what? In the last couple of weeks, I've even stopped smoking and drinking diet soda."

"That's huge Annette. You're a powerful example of what

I want for everyone—to forgive our wounds and imperfections, which are the blocks to our own loving nature. You are incredible."

"If I can love myself, anyone can. Lynn, *you* know how much it's taken, but it's like all of a sudden, all the work paid off at once. I now understand what you've been saying for years—that as we love ourselves, the rest works out. I truly don't crave cigarettes and sodas anymore because I have *me*."

Annette's courage came through—courage to fight the lie of her childhood, to reclaim her loving heart, to feel joy and trust in herself. Her recovery supports what I've come to know—that as we fill up with our own loving essence (for some, it includes a relationship with God or spirit), a desire to fill up with external replacements falls away.

LOVE IS THE BRIDGE

As Thornton Wilder said, "There is a land of the living and a land of the dead, and the bridge is love, the only survival, the only meaning."

The process of choice from fear to love is one that pushes us through the eye of the needle. First comes the awareness that choice exists. This choice places us onto the high dive platform and we begin walking toward its edge. Some of us will halt along the way, too afraid to continue. "Our lives are better," we say. "That's enough." Many of us will walk back and forth, uncertain, confused, bumping up against our inner barriers of guilt about how "beautiful" we might really be.

In the years to come, more and more people will have the courage to leap off the edge into the choice for love. Just as the Olympic diver uses years of training and skills to jackknife with barely a splash into the water, *so too will you*—using the skills learned in this book to develop the stamina and resilience to break through bonds of fear, stress, and addiction.

" We need to understand . . .
that **heaven** is not a
location but refers to the inner
realm of **consciousness**. "

~ Eckhart Tolle

CHAPTER FIFTEEN

Chapter Fifteen:

Love's Leap into Higher Consciousness

A T THE DAWN of the 20th century, people were forced to develop new ways of thinking and different skills that matched the demands of the Industrial Age. Today, according to Daniel Pink, author of *A Whole New Mind*, it's time to leap again. The Information Age, populated by knowledge workers, is soon to evolve into the Conceptual Age, driven by creators and empathizers.[150] This time, however, the jump will be *into* the self rather than *out* into the world.

We know that humanity made a monumental shift in the physical world with the Industrial Age. Today's evolution in consciousness is equally as profound. A hundred years ago, automobiles replaced horses and factories took over small farms, people had to stretch beyond their comfort zones to adjust to a change of this magnitude. To excel in these times, we are faced with a decision—live in a state of love and consciousness or drift along, restricted by fear and unconsciousness.

Although opportunities are boundless, few people reach even close to their fullest potential and end up unhappy, ill, or broke. I believe this tragedy occurs often because we're suffering from the effects of trauma, fear, and stress; we're either unaware or feel powerless to break out of the cycle.

Earl Nightingale, in *The Strangest Secret,* reminded us that of 100 people who are 25 years old, most feel hopeful about their lives. But by age 65, one will be rich, only one will be financially independent, 24 will still be working, and the rest will be broke.[151]

In the Information Age, knowledge is available to the masses as never before. Whether you want to become richer, happier, or healthier, have better relationships or spiritual bliss, information to do that abounds. But what needs to be present to take advantage of the opportunities? First, you have to have enough of your emotional baggage out of the way to feel as if you deserve all the good things in life. Second, you have to be aware that these possibilities exist. Authors and speakers like Mark Victor Hanson and Jack Canfield of the *Chicken Soup* series, or Robert Kiyosaki, of the *Rich Dad, Poor Dad* series, are visionaries whose messages contain much more than becoming wealthy. They push the boundaries of potential, requiring us to become consciously aware of who we really are, what we really want, and what holds us back from falling fully in love with ourselves.

What Is Consciousness, Anyway?

Awareness. Being aware of the feedback system of our thoughts and feelings tells us whether we're on or off track regarding joy, vitality, and aliveness. Awareness becomes consciousness when we use our inner power to embody our experiences, to connect with our deeper selves. I can remember when I first realized I wasn't a victim unless I chose to be. This both pissed me off and felt freeing. I was not at the mercy of my childhood baggage, damn it. It's up to me whether I march on in struggle or somersault with joy into the future.

Eckhart Tolle wrote that " . . . at the heart of the new consciousness lies the transcendence of thought, the newfound ability of rising above thought, of realizing a dimension within yourself that is infinitely more vast than thought."[152] He continues that the age old question, "Who am I?" is more than just a "voice in the head." The one who asks "Who am I?" is the witness or observer—as Jesus was said to be—in the world, but not of it. "To 'become conscious' is to become aware of something that had previously been unknown," wrote Kathleen Brehony, Ph.D., in *Awakening at Midlife*. Dr. Brehony tells us that "Consciousness includes all the things that we are aware of and know, but even more, includes an understanding of 'knowing that we know'...which implies self-awareness."[153] My first book, *The Greatest Change of All*, speaks of change as the instrument of consciousness and the desire we all have within us to connect with our best and most loving self.

Consciousness and Addiction Like Oil and Water

How did we go from addiction to consciousness? It's hard to act out addictively if you're being mindful of your thoughts, feelings, and body sensations. Doing the TARA process and writing out how you're feeling, where these feelings are in your body, and breathing into them creates a pause.

In the beginning, that pause may be short, but at least while you're doing it, you're not eating or obsessing about eating. With practice, the pauses create mindfulness and a healthier connection with yourself. The new neural connections forged by the improved habits of emotional awareness begin to feel so good, you don't want to go back to the old addictive escapes. Isn't it ironically sad that the good feelings we've been searching for outside ourselves have been inside all along?

Awareness creates a conundrum for the addict voice
in your head that wants to convince you the third piece of
chocolate cake will make you feel good faster than doing
your "feeling" work. The addict voice demands, "Avoid anger,
unpleasantness, or stress by covering them up, numbing them,
or distracting yourself from them. Use anything possible to
accomplish this." The aware voice says, "I'm feeling angry and
it's okay. There's no need to do anything. Instead, I'll go within,
notice how I'm feeling, then move things along with a little
tapping or imagery, so I can get back to what I'm doing."
Like bears and hikers (or fear and love), addiction and
awareness don't mix well.

WATER, LOVE, AND CONSCIOUSNESS

Dr. Masaru Emoto, the Japanese scientist who discovered that
molecules of water are affected by our thoughts, words, and
feelings, stated that the physical world and human beings are
composed of 70% water. In his book *The Hidden Messages in Water*,
Emoto wrote, "Humans are the only creatures that have the
capacity to resonate with all other creatures and objects found in
nature." [154] Everything in the world vibrates, including our words
and emotions.

To demonstrate this, Dr. Emoto conducted experiments taking
distilled water and placed it in glass bottles. Then he wrote on
pieces of paper and attached them to the bottles so the words
faced into the container. On the papers he wrote "love" and "love
and gratitude" and "you make me sick, I want to kill you" and "you
fool." After leaving the bottles sit overnight, Dr. Emoto later froze
the water and photographed the ice crystals that had formed. The
"love" ice crystals were clear and beautifully formed; the "love and
gratitude" crystals even more so. The "fear" or "you fool" crystals
were unformed, cloudy, and yellowish. His book features many
beautiful pictures of ice crystals. Especially those with the words
love *and gratitude* form with a unique depth and refinement, a
diamond-like brilliance. [155]

The Principle of Opposites

Do you know about the technology to eliminate engine noise from cars, leaf blowers, lawn movers and other audio scourges? Japanese scientists have actually been able to erase a sound by broadcasting an opposite sound. Dr. Emoto wrote about parallels to this principle with emotion, suggesting ways to shift the vibration of negative emotions like fear rather than trying to eliminate them.

Because everything vibrates, positive or negative emotions have particular vibrational frequencies. Based on this principle, you can get free from negative emotions by emitting the opposite emotion. As Dr. Emoto noted, combining two opposite waves (of energy or emotion), the energy gets neutralized.[i] That's why when you feel afraid, you can effectively use EFT to tap out the fear and replace it with love vibrations or its many variations—care, appreciation, kindness, or joy.

EXPERIMENT: For the next month, every time you catch yourself in a fear response that triggers you to feel angry, resentful, judgmental, or guilty, use EFT on the fear and practice replacing with love, care, appreciation or peace. (Go to Chapter 10 for a refresher and/or order how-to videos at www.emofree.com.) Try this: Tap with two fingers on the fleshy side of your opposite hand at the karate chop point and say out loud three times: "Even though I'm angry and/or afraid, I choose to love and accept myself." Breathe. Keep tapping and breathing. Notice any shifts.

A Conscious Choice: Love or Fear

Love is allowing and accepting. Fear is judging and expecting.

- Jerold Jampolski, *Love is Letting Go of Fear*

We have a choice. We can live in stress and fear (and live with the resulting addictive coping behaviors) or we can live in love.

Love doesn't mean we're wimps; love means we're strong enough to be gentle, caring, and honest with ourselves and each other. In fact, research at Harvard University showed that those who feel loved have better, more enduring health than those who don't. And data from the HeartMath Institute[ii] has shown that increasing feelings of care and compassion (love) decrease stress and make the work environment much more harmonious and productive. It's because a shift of consciousness occurs within us as love expands. David R. Hawkins, M.D., Ph.D., has studied the energetic or vibrational qualities of emotions as a barometer of consciousness for more than 25 years. The emotions of love, joy, and peace are at the top of the energetic frequency scale he has constructed.[iii] TARA, EFT, and Imagery give us the tools to shift out of the low-level energy of fear and climb the vibrational scale of love. When we use them, self-destructive cravings have a much better chance of becoming loving, self-caring behaviors. Bill Harris, creator of Centerpointe Research Institute and producer of Holosync audio technology, a CD meditation program, helps more than 100,000 Holosync students in 172 countries use his meditation technology to overcome addictions. He said, "By becoming consciously aware (of oneself), addictions simply begin to fall away." [iv] And love is one of the best parts of becoming more conscious. (For more information Holosync 6 CD series, go to Resources in back of book.)

Humanity is in the process of moving from a fear-based to a love-based world. Will everyone make this choice? No. But it's important to know there's a choice to be made. This shift includes letting go of the old paradigm of power over others based on fear and control that results in stress, illness, and addictive coping and replacing it with an inner-directed, heart-focused power based on love.

As we heal ourselves, we heal the world. You'll find that as you become more loving, you become more conscious and vice versa. Like the crystal glass that vibrates, your love creates a resonance that affects everyone around you. Love not only feels good, but it heals you and those around you.

Author's Final Note

The change from fear to love represents a shift of consciousness that occurs as a natural result of regularly practicing love rather than stress and fear. Joy is a natural by-product of a conscious life. Conscious living doesn't mean there's no more pain. But, we come to understand that suffering is more about holding on to pain and the past. Freedom comes with the willingness to embrace and move through the parts of life that are difficult and celebrate and appreciate the good times.

I've spent the last 20 years learning how to go inward using the bodymind skills presented in this book. These skills have rebalanced my over-thinking mind (still busy, but mostly positive) to guide my heart and soul to living with a joy I never could have imagined as a wounded teen and young adult.

Today, my life is rounded, colorful, rich, and my mind, body, heart, and soul move harmoniously in concert rather than fighting each other. I realize you likely don't have the inclination to spend the next 20 years struggling to feel better. Fortunately, you don't need to—if you take to heart the knowledge and the skills found in this book.

- Lynn Telford-Sahl

About the Author

At age 29, Lynn had a frightening flash of reality. She faced the fact that her own addiction to fear was driving her alcohol and cocaine abuse, and harming herself and her relationships. Pushing through denial, she knew she had to face the unconscious pain and deepest fears that were driving her self-destructive actions. Lynn spent the next 25 years searching for the truth about how to heal the driving force of addiction—fear, stress, and underlying trauma.

Retraining her fear-based thinking profoundly shifted her ability to care for herself lovingly. Lynn learned the skills of identifying how she really felt versus what she *pretended* she felt. Releasing the emotional baggage of childhood pain, though difficult, she experienced her own freedom. Practicing daily emotional management skills allowed her to correct her upset moods quickly and regain balance, peace, and joy.

The most meaningful result of her journey to freedom has been changing her fear-protection-control-based belief system to one bathed in the blessings of the loving values of care, compassion, courage, appreciation, and gratitude. She shares the skills she's learned and taught over the past two decades with heartfelt wisdom in *Intentional JOY*.

Lynn holds a master's degree in psychology with a holistic specialization from John F. Kennedy University, Orinda, California. She has earned a bachelor's degree in social work from Sacramento State University, Sacramento, California. A certified addiction counselor since 1989, she also became certified in integrative imagery in 2003. Before establishing a private practice in 1990, Lynn held positions as both an inpatient and outpatient counselor.

Lynn has presented and conducted dozens of workshops, trainings, and retreats, specializing in topics of stress, healing fear by choosing love, and emotional management. For four

years, she was a regular guest on the radio show "Addictions &
Answers" in Sonora, California. A columnist at *The Modesto Bee*
newspaper in Modesto, California, from 2006 – 2007, she wrote
primarily about addiction.

In 1999, Lynn published *The Greatest Change of All*, a
spiritual novel about women transforming their fear of change
through connection with their deepest self and with each
other. This book has inspired many. Most significantly, *The
Greatest Change* provided a catalyst to reconnect Lynn to her
birth daughter who had been placed for adoption when Lynn
was 15. At the end of *The Greatest Change*, Lynn included an
addendum stating her intention to locate her daughter. As
Lynn tells the story: "An 'adoption angel' called one day about
a year after the book came out asking if I'd found my daughter.
When I said no, she took me under her wing and led me to
Search Finders, an organization specializing in reconnecting
birth parents and children. Within a few months, they had
located Suzann in North Carolina.

"Not all reconnections turn out as happily as ours has. I'm
very grateful for Suzann's courage in opening her life to me
and for her parents' support."

Intentional JOY Resources

I have selected these key resources to take your journey into healing even deeper. Enjoy!

The Mood Cure with Julia Ross

(http://www.moodcure.com)

The Mood Cure: The 4 Step Program to Rebalance Your Emotional Chemistry and Rediscover Your Natural Sense of Well-Being, by Julia Ross, New York, 2002.

If you're looking for a natural alternative to anti-depressants or anti-anxiety medication, I suggest you read this book or attend a training with Ms. Ross. The Mood Cure is a natural approach that uses amino acids from high-protein food sources and supplements. I have used these supplements myself and have recommended them to clients in early recovery.

The following from page 10 of *The Mood Cure* explains how two of the four "mood transmitters" or neurotransmitters of the brain contribute to feeling emotionally balanced or not.

If you're high in serotonin – you're positive, confident, flexible, and easy-going.

If you're sinking in serotonin – (and this often happens around 3-4:00 pm and makes you vulnerable to grabbing something sweet or going for a caffeine fix) you'll tend to become negative, obsessive, worried, irritable, and sleepless.

If you're high in GABA – you're relaxed and stress-free.

If there's a gap in your GABA – you'll be wired, stressed, and overwhelmed.

LYNN TELFORD-SAHL 265

Total Biology with Gilbert Renaud, a naturopath in Canada
(http://www.totalbiology.ca)

Total Biology is a fascinating healing technique created by Dr. Hammer from Germany and refined by Dr. Sabbah. Gilbert Renaud, a student of Dr. Sabbah's, gives seminars about Total Biology in Canada, California, and on the east coast of the U.S. Once physical symptoms ranging from a tension in the neck and shoulders to cancer have been presented and various emotional events have been identified, the premise of Total Biology is that having awareness of the unconscious pain and knowing why it developed provides healing. Mr. Renaud presents many case histories in his lectures and on his website. I found this process to be revealing after two sessions with Gilbert. I used EFT to clear emotional energy and bring it to consciousness.

Emotional Freedom Technique with Gary Craig
(http://www.emofree.com)

Emotional Freedom Technique (EFT) is best learned in person, although this site features videotapes and DVDs for home study that are well done and easy to follow. EFT requires no special licensing although there's a comprehensive certification process for those who wish to become a Master EFT technician. Search on the site or on Google for workshops in your area.

Stress Reduction Clinic, University Massachusetts
(http://www.umassmed.edu.cfm/sfp/index.aspx)

Full Catastrophe Living: Using the Wisdom of Your Body and Mind to Face Stress, Pain, and Illness, by Jon Kabat-Zinn, New York, Delta, 1990.

If you want to go to the stress-master source, Kabat-Zinn was one of the first to bring the concept of mind-body stress healing practices to the public. Kabat-Zinn sent questionnaires to thousands who had completed his stress management program and learned that the ONE practice most found very helpful was the breathing techniques. This book explains effective breathing techniques used in his programs.

Holosync with Centerpointe Director Bill Harris
(http://www.centerpointe.com)

An accelerated meditation program, holosync uses a sophisticated form of neuro-audio technology. Its benefits (cited on the website) include reduction in stress and anxiety, improved mental, emotional and physical well-being, increased focus, memory, and learning. There are many benefits to meditation and it's important to find the approach for you. I used this program for three months and chose not to continue. I don't recommend it for those in the early stages of recovery as it brings up intense emotions and unconscious material that may be difficult to handle. However, excellent staff support is available if a participant experiences difficulties as a result of listening to the CDs.

Beyond Ordinary Nursing, Nurses Certificate Program in Imagery with Susan Ezra, R.N., HNC and Terry Reed, R.N., M.S., HNC, Foster City, California
(http://www.integrativeimagery.com)

Sue and Terry accept helping professionals as well as nurses into their imagery program. I loved the training experience with them and I became certified in 2003. I highly recommend it to those interested in learning imagery for themselves.

Imagery Products
(http://www.healthjourneys.com)

This website is the best resource I've found for imagery products, CDs, and classes. Everything is covered from stress to trauma and everything in between. Belleruth Naparstek's book *Invisible Heroes: Survivors of Trauma and How They Heal.* (Bantam Books, NYC. 2004) is available here along with many other authors.

Endnotes

[1] Bly, Robert. *A Little Book on the Human Shadow*. HarperSanFrancisco. 1988.

[2] Reich, Robert. *The Future of Success*. Knopf, 2000. p. 6.

[3] Tolle, Eckhart. *The Power of Now: A Guide to Spiritual Enlightenment*. New World Library, 1999. p. 35.

[4] Jacobs, Dr. Gregg. *The Ancestral Mind: Reclaim the Power*. Penguin, 2004. p. 4.

[5] *The Today Show*, NBC-TV, August 2006.

[6] Jacobs. p. 42.

[7] Ibid. pp. 29-32.

[8] Ibid. p. 15, 20, 21.

[9] Bly, Robert. *A Little Book on the Human Shadow*. HarperSanFrancisco. 1988.

[10] http://www.candacepert.com

[11] Lipton, Bruce H., M.D., *The Biology of Belief: Unleashing the Power of Consciousness, Matter and Miracles*. Mountain of Love/Elite Books. Santa Rosa. 2005.

[12] Levine, Peter. *Healing Trauma: A Pioneering Program for Restoring the Wisdom of Your Body*. Sounds True, 2005. p. 7, and Scaer, Robert C. *The Trauma Spectrum: Hidden Wounds and Human Resiliency*. W. W. Norton & Company, 2005. p. 2.

[13] Scaer, Robert C. "Trauma, The Freeze Response, and Its Clinical Syndromes." Lecture at Psychology of Health, Immunity and Disease Conference, Hilton Head, S. Carolina, December 8, 2006.

[14] Shapiro, Francine, Ph.D. *Eye Movement Desensitization and Reprocessing: Basic Principles, Protocols, and Procedures*. Guildford Press, 2001. p. 14.

[15] Scaer, Robert C. *The Trauma Spectrum: Hidden Wounds and Human Resiliency*. W. W. Norton & Company, 2005. p. 205.

[16] Ibid. p. 205.

[17] Glassner, Barry. *The Culture of Fear: Why Americans Are Afraid of the Wrong Things*. Basic Books, 2000. p.xi.

[18] Moore, Michael. *Bowling for Columbine*. 2002.

[19] Ibid.

[20] Bradshaw, John. *Homecoming: Reclaiming and Championing Your Inner Child*. Bantam, NYC. 1990.

[21] Manville, William H. *Cool, Hip, and Sober: 88 Ways to Beat Booze and Drugs*. Forge Books, NYC. 2003.

[22] Arntz, William, Betsy Chasse, and Mark Vicente. *What the Bleep Do We Know?* 2005.

[23] Peeke, Pamela M., M.D. *Fighting Fat After Forty: The Revolutionary Three-Pronged Approach That Will Break Your Stress-Fat Cycle and Make You Healthy, Fit, and Trim for Life*. Viking Penguin, NYC. 2000. p. 11.

[24] Mellan, Olivia. *Overcoming Overspending: A Winning Plan for Spenders and Their Partners*. Walker & Co., NYC. 1997. p. 18.

[25] Ibid. p. 18.

[26] Atcheson, John. "World Enslaved By Our Desire For Stuff." *Modesto Bee*. April 4, 2004.

[27] Buscaglia, Leo F. *Living, Loving & Learning.* Ballantine Books, NYC. 1985. p. 97.

[28] Winfrey, Oprah. "Women Who Are Living A Lie." *The Oprah Winfrey Show.* April 18, 2006.

[29] Tolle, Eckhart. *The Power of Now: A Guide to Spiritual Enlightenment.* New World Library, 1999. p. 155.

[30] Wright, Judith. *There Must Be More Than This: Finding More Life, Love and Meaning by Overcoming Your Soft Addictions.* Broadway Books, NYC. 2003.

[31] http://www.Myvesta.com

[32] Benson, April Lane. *I Shop, Therefore I Am: Compulsive Buying & the Search for Self.* Jason Aronson, 2000.

[33] Haddock , Vicki. "Lessons in human buy-ology." *San Francisco Chronicle.* Dec. 19, 2004.

[34] Perle, Liz. "Money, A Memoir: Women, Emotions and Cash." *Modesto Bee.* April 2006.

[35] Haddock, Vicki. "Lessons in Human Buy-ology." *San Francisco Chronicle.* Dec. 19, 2004.

[36] Mellan, Olivia. *Overcoming Overspending.* Walker Publishing Co, 1995, p. 31.

[37] http://www.sexualrecovery.com.

[38] Ibid.

[39] Interview with Patrick Carnes, Ph.D., sex addiction expert, *The Today Show,* March 2006.

[40] Hanus, Julie. "The Culture of Pornography is Shaping Our Lives, For Better and For Worse." *Utne,* Sept-Oct 2006. p. 60.

[41] Samples, John. "Gambling is the real scandal behind Abramoff." *Modesto Bee,* February 5, 2006.

[42] Schlosser, Eric. *Fast Food Nation.* Harper Perennial. 2002. p. 3.

[43] Humphrey-Jones, S. Hale and Melvin A. Slawik. *One More Time: The Gambler's Mantra.* Lang Mark Publishing. Austin, Texas. 2005. pp. 31-32.

[44] *Addiction Professional Magazine.* May/June 2007. Vol. 5, No. 3, p. 12.

[45] Humphrey-Jones, S. Hale and Melvin A. Slawik. *One More Time: The Gambler's Mantra.* Lang Mark Publishing. Austin, Texas. 2005. p. 32.

[46] Ibid. p. 26.

[47] Schlosser, Eric. *Fast Food Nation.* Harper Perennial, 2005. p. 4.

[48] Spurlock, Morgan. *Super Size Me.* 2004.

[49] Schlosser. p. 240.

[50] Hart, Dr. Cheryle and Mary Kay Grossman R.D. *The Insulin-Resistance Diet: How to Turn Off Your Body's Fat-Making Machine.* McGraw-Hill, 2001.

[51] Hirsch, J.M. "Diet soda makers drink in the wave of sales." *Modesto Bee.* Dec. 22, 2004.

[52] Brackett, Cori and JT Waldron. *Sweet Misery: A Poisoned World.* 2004.

[53] Pert, Candace, Ph.D. *Everything You Need to Know to Feel Go(o)d.* Hay House, 2006. pp. 71, 76.

[54] Wright, Judith. *There Must Be More Than This: Finding More Life, Love and Meaning by Overcoming Your Soft Addictions.* Broadway Books, 2003. p. 18.

[55] Robbins, Tony. *The Edge: The Power to Change Your Life Now.* Audio CD. 2005.

[56] Pert, Dr. Candace. *Molecules of Emotion: The Science Behind Mind-Body Medicine.* Scribner, NYC 1997. p. 273.

[57] Kasl, Charlotte Davis. *Women, Sex and Addiction: A Search for Love and Power.* Harper & Rowe. NYC, 1990. p. 25.

[58] Manville, Bill. *Addictions & Answers,* KVML AM 1450 Sonora, California. August 25, 2001.

[59] http://www.alcoholism.about.com   Carol Foundation News Release. 8-4-03.

[60] Schulz, Mona Lisa, M.D., Ph.D. *Awakening Intuition: Using Your Mind-Body Network for Insight and Healing.* Harmony Books, NYC. 1998.

[61] Melody, Pia. Stated at a conference in November of 2003. Pia founded The Meadows, an addiction treatment facility in Arizona.

[62] Dodes, Lance, M.D. *The Heart of Addiction: A New Approach to Understanding and Managing Alcoholism and Other Addictive Behaviors.* HarperCollins Paperbacks, NYC. 2002. pp. 4-5.

[63] Janov, Dr. Arthur. *The Biology of Love.* Prometheus Books, New York. 2000.

[64] O'Connor, Richard, Ph.D. *Undoing Perpetual Stress: The Missing Connection Between Depression, Anxiety and 21st Century Illness.* The Berkeley Publishing Group, NYC. 2005.

[65] Feinstein, David et al. *The Promise of Energy Psychologies: Revolutionary Tools for Dramatic Personal Change.* Tarcher, NYC. 2005.

[66] Naperstek, Belleruth. Asilomar Imagery Conference, October 2004.

[67] Pinksy, Drew, M.D. *When Painkillers Become Dangerous: What Everyone Needs to Know About OxyContin and Other Prescription Drugs.* Hazelden, Center City, MN. 2004. p. 10.

[68] Scarf, Maggie. *Secrets, Lies, Betrayals: The Body/Mind Connection.* Random House, NYC. 2004. p. xxx.

[69] Levine, Peter and Ann Frederick. *Waking The Tiger: Healing Trauma: The Innate Capacity to Transform Overwhelming Experiences.* North Atlantic Books, Berkeley, CA. 1997. p. 41.

[70] Ibid. p. 44.

[71] Shapiro, Francine and Margot Silk Forrest. *EMDR: The Breakthrough Eye Movement Therapy for Overcoming Anxiety, Stress and Trauma.* Basic Books, NYC. 2004.

[72] Scaer, Robert, M.D. *The Trauma Spectrum: Hidden Wounds and Human Resiliency.* W. W. Norton, NYC. 2005.

[73] Ibid. p. 89.

[74] Levine, Peter and Ann Frederick. *Waking the Tiger: Healing Trauma: The Innate Capacity to Transform Overwhelming Experiences.* North Atlantic Books. Berkeley, CA. p. 20.

[75] Harris, Bill. *Thresholds of the Mind.* Centerpointe Press, Beaverton, OR. 2002. p. 63.

[76] Dowd, Maureen. *Bush World.* G.P. Putnam's Sons, NYC, 2004.

[77] Frank, Justin A., M.D. *Bush on the Couch.* Regan Books, NYC. 2004. p. 3, 57.

[78] Ibid. p. xi, 1.

[79] Braden, Gregg. *The God Code.* Hay House, Carlsbad, CA. 2004.

[80] Jacobs, Gregg D., Ph.D. *The Ancestral Mind: Reclaim The Power.* Penguin Group, NYC, 2003. p. 60.

[81] Ibid, p. 36.

[82] Hirsch, Jerry. "Coffeehouse chain stirs up rivals." *Modesto Bee,* Modesto, CA. April 24, 2006.

[83] Peeke, Pamela M., M.D. *Fighting Fat After Forty: The Revolutionary Three-Pronged Approach That Will Break Your Stress-Fat Cycle and Make You Healthy, Fit, and Trim for Life.* Viking Penguin, NYC. 2000. p. 11.

[84] Childre, Doc. *Freeze Frame: Fast Action Stress Relief.* Planetary Publishers, Boulder Creek, CA,1994. p. xvi.

[85] Ibid. p. xv.

[86] http://www.sjsu.edu/faculty/wood

[87] "Depression linked to obsession with cell phone use." *Modesto Bee*, Modesto, CA. June 1, 2006.

[88] Childre, Doc. *From Chaos to Coherence.* Planetary Publishers, Boulder Creek, CA, 2000 p .63.

[89] Ibid. pp. 63–64.

[90] Lewis, Dennis. *The Tao of Natural Breathing.* Mountain Wind Publishing, San Francisco, 1996. p. 55.

[91] Hawkins, David R., M.D., Ph.D. *Power vs. Force: The Hidden Determinants of Human Behavior.* Hay House, Carlsbad, CA. 1995. p. 56.

[92] Mate, Gabor. *When the Body Says No: Understanding the Stress-Disease Connection.* John Wiley & Sons, Hoboken, NJ. 2003.

[93] Naperstek, Belleruth. Asilomar Imagery Conference, October 2004.

[94] Maperstek, B, and Scaer, R. *Invisible Heroes: Survivors of Trauma and How They Heal.* Bantam, NYC. 2004. p. 170.

[95] O'Connor, Richard, Ph.D. *Undoing Perpetual Stress: The Missing Connection Between Depression, Anxiety and 21st Century Illness.* Berkeley Publishing Group, NYC. 2005. p. 152–153.

[96] Jacobs, Gregg D., Ph.D. *The Ancestral Mind: Reclaim the Power.* Viking, NYC, 2003. p. 38–39.

[97] Davis, Elizabeth Gould. *The First Sex.* Penguin (Non-Ed), NYC. 1972.

[98] Eisler, Riane. *The Chalice and the Blade.* HarperCollins, San Francisco. 1988.

[99] Goleman, Daniel. *Emotional Intelligence: Why It Can Matter More Than IQ.* Bantam Books, NYC. 1995. pp. 43-46.

[100] Dass, Ram. *Be Here Now.* Lama Foundation, San Cristobol, NM. 1971.

[101] Tolle, Eckhart. *The Power of Now: A Guide to Spiritual Enlightenment.* New World Library, Novato, CA, 1999. p. 31.

[102] Ibid. p. 32.

[103] Goleman, Daniel. *Emotional Intelligence: Why It Can Matter More Than IQ.* Bantam Books, NYC. 1995. p. xiii.

[104] Urdang, Lawrence. *The Random House College Dictionary.* Random House, NYC. 1973.

[105] Bennett-Goleman, Tara. *Emotional Alchemy: How the Mind Can Heal the Heart.* Harmony Books, NYC. 2001. p. 99.

[106] O'Connor, Richard, Ph.D. *Undoing Perpetual Stress: The Missing Connection Between Depression, Anxiety and 21st Century Illness.* The Berkeley Publishing Group, NYC. 2005. pp. 114-115.

[107] Buscaglia, Leo, Ph.D. and Steven Short. *Living, Loving & Learning.* C.B. Slack, Thorofare, N. J. 1982. p. 6.

[108] Van Der Kolk, Bessel A. *Psychological Trauma.* American Psychiatric Pub Group, Washington, D.C. 1996.

[109] Tolle, Eckhart. *The Power of Now: A Guide to Spiritual Enlightenment.* New World Library, Novato, CA. 1999. p. 84.

[110] Baer, Greg, M.D. *Real Love*. Gotham, New York. 2003. p. 24.

[111] Goleman, Daniel. *Emotional Intelligence: Why It Can Matter More Than IQ*. Bantam Books, NYC. 1995. p.6.

[112] Tolle, Eckhart *The Power of Now: A Guide to Spiritual Enlightenment*. New World Library, 1999. p. 81.

[113] Canfield, J. and Switzer, J. *The Success Principles: How to Get From Where You Are to Where You Want to Be*. HarperCollins. NYC. 2005. p. 247.

[114] Gallo, Fred and Vicenezi Harry. *Energy Tapping*. New Harbinger. Oakland, CA. 2000. p. 15.

[115] Bavolek, Stephen J., Ph.D. "Nurturing Parenting Programs." http://www.nurturingparenting.com

[116] Cushnir, Howard Raphael. *Unconditional Bliss: Finding Happiness in the Face of Hardship*. Quest Books. 2000. p. 118.

[117] Seligman, Martin. *Authentic Happiness: Using the New Positive Psychology to Realize Your Potential for Lifelong Fulfillment*. Free Press, NY. 2002. p. 27.

[118] Shapiro, Francine and Forrest, Margot. *EMDR: The Breakthrough Therapy for Overcoming Anxiety, Stress and Trauma*. BasicBooks, New York. 1997. p. 29.

[119] Callahan, Roger J., PhD. *The Anxiety-Addiction Connection: Eliminate Your Addictive Urges with Thought Field Therapy*, American Academy of Psychologists Treating Addiction, Indian Wells, California Revised Edition. 1995.

[120] Bassett, Lucinda. *From Panic to Power: Proven Techniques to Calm Your Anxieties, Conquer Your Fears, and Put You in Control of Your Life*. Collins, NYC. 1997.

[121] Naparstek, Belleruth. *Invisible Heroes; Survivors of Trauma and How They Heal*. Bantam Books, NYC. 2004. p. 149.

[122] Ibid. p. 13.

[123] Ezra, Sue and Terry Reed. *Nurses Certificate Program in Imagery Handbook*. Beyond Ordinary Nursing, Foster City, CA, 1996.

[124] Ibid.

[125] Naparstek, Belleruth. *Invisible Heroes: Survivors of Trauma and How They Heal*. Bantam Books, 2004. p. 149.

[126] Childre, Doc and Bruce Cryer. *From Chaos to Coherence: The Power to Change Performance*. HeartMath. Boulder Creek, CA. 2000.

[127] Ibid. p. 74.

[128] Ibid. p. 79.

[129] Lipton, Bruce H. M.D. *The Biology of Belief: Unleashing the Power of Consciousness, Matter and Miracles*. Mountain of Love/Elite Books. Santa Rosa, CA. 2005. p. 144.

[130] Canfield, Jack and Switzer, Janet. *The Success Principles: How to Get From Where You Are to Where You Want to Be*. Harper Resource Books, New York, 2005. p. 229.

[131] Dyer, Wayne Dr. *Your Erroneous Zones*. Funk & Wagnalls, New York. 1976.

[132] *A Course in Miracles*. Foundation for Inner Peace, Tiburon, 1976. p. 25.

[133] Jacobs, Gregg. *The Ancestral Mind: Reclaim the Power*. NYC, Viking. 2003. p. 42.

[134] Ibid. p. 128.

[135] Campbell, Chellie. *The Wealthy Spirit: Daily A rmations for Financial Stress Reduction*. Sourcebooks, Naperville, Ill. 2002.

[136] Jacobs, Gregg. *The Ancestral Mind: Reclaim the Power.* NYC, Viking. 2003. pp. 12-13.

[137] Ibid. p.42.

[138] Buscaglia, Leo and Steven Short. *Living, Loving & Learning.* C.B. Slack, Thorofare, N. J. 1982. p. 10.

[139] Urdang, Lawrence. *The Random House College Dictionary.* Random House, NYC. 1973.

[140] Buscaglia, Leo and Steven Short. *Living, Loving & Learning.* C.B. Slack: Throfare, N.J. 1982. p. 9.

[141] Tolle, Eckhart. *A New Earth: Awakening to Your Life's Purpose.* Dutton/Penguin Group, NYC. 2005. p. 105.

[142] Ibid. pp. 71- 72.

[143] Lewis, Thomas, Fari Amini, and Richard Lannon. *A General Theory of Love.* Vintage Books, New York. 2001. p. 208.

[144] Buscaglia, Leo and Steven Short. *Living, Loving & Learning.* C.B. Slack: Throfare, N.J. 1982. pp. 97-98.

[145] Diamond, John, MD. *Your Body Doesn't Lie: How to Increase Your Life Energy Through Behavioral Kinesiology.* Warner Books. New York, 1979. p. 63.

[146] Childre, Doc and Bruce Cryer. *Freeze Frame: One Minute Stress Management: A Scientifically Proven Technique for Clear Decision Making and Improved Health (HeartMath System).* Planetary Publications, Boulder, CO, 1998. p. 41.

[147] Ibid. p. 42.

[148] Russek, LG; SH King; SJ Russek; HI Russek "The Harvard Mastery of Stress Study 35-year follow-up: prognostic significance of patterns of psychophysiological arousal and adaptation."

[149] Lewis, Amini, and Lennon. *A General Theory of Love.* Vintage Books, New York. 2000. p. 9.

[150] Pink, Daniel H. *A Whole New Mind: Moving from The Information Age to The Conceptual Age.* Riverhead Books, New York. 2005.

[151] Nightingale, Earl. *The Strangest Secret.* CD and MP3 file. http://www.nightingale.com

[152] Tolle, Eckhart. *A New Earth: Awakening to Your Life's Purpose.* Dutton/Penguin Group, NYC, 2005. pp. 21-22.

[153] Brehony, Kathleen. *Awakening at Midlife: Realizing Your Potential for Growth and Change.* Riverhead Books, New York, 1996. pp. 30-31.

[154] Emoto, Masaru. *The Hidden Messages in Water.* Beyond Words Publications, Hillsboro, OR. 2004. p. 51.

[155] Ibid. p.79.

[156] Ibid. p. 73.

[157] Childre, Doc and Howard Martin, *The HeartMath Solution*, HarperCollins, New York, 1999 pp. 61-62.

[158] Hawkins, David R., M.D., Ph.D., *Power Vs. Force.* Veritas Publishing, Sedona Arizona, 1995 pp. 52-53.

[159] Harris, Bill. *The Holosync Solution.* Centerpointe Research Institute, audio series, Beaverton, Oregon.

Turn Stress, Struggle & Overwhelm into JOY

Whew – life is busy, stressful and sometimes overwhelming. Peace is only a breath and a smile away. In fact, go ahead and take a couple of breaths right now. Research shows that breathing and imagery decrease the stress response and increase the relaxation response. Practicing these skills over time allows you to take charge of stress and struggle.

I invite you to visit **www.lynntelfordsahl.com** for 7 FREE audio tips that will melt away stress and overwhelm and give you the skills to shift into peace and JOY easily and effortlessly. Register under "7 Tips" on the home page.

Lots of JOY to you,

Lynn Telford-Sahl
Fall 2008

Other Products Offered

The Greatest Change of All – A Spiritual Novel (1999)

"I was completely mesmerized by the friendship and spirituality I felt just by turning the pages."
> - Tara Pettit, Sacramento, CA

"The moment I heard the title of *The Greatest Change of All,* I had that rush of energy that occurs when our spirit is deeply moved. Lynn is a gifted therapist and healer. From the enchanting cover to the last page, Lynn will inspire and support your healing journey."
> - Chryill Turner, Modesto, CA

"*The Greatest Change* is a wonderfully rich story full of great relationships, love, lessons, fun and food! I was sorry to see it end for I felt such a part of the group."
> - Teri O'Neal Boring, Modesto, CA

"*The Greatest Change of All* is like all wonderful Chicken Soup stories, it opens your heart. And, when we open our hearts we change the world."
> - Mark Victor Hanson, coauthor of Chicken Soup Series

CD's Available

How Love, Care & Compassion Heal Fear (2007)

The Five and Half Proven Factors to Reach Your Ideal Weight (2007)

Intentional JOY: Imagery to Reduce Stress & Increase Freedom (2008)

Please visit **www.lynntelfordsahl.com** to order

or call (209) 492-8745

Health, Wealth & Happiness Coaching for Women in Business

Health, Wealth & Happiness Coaching supports you to dream big, set reasonably uncomfortable goals and take lots of action to accomplish your goals in ways that works with your lifestyle. Coaching supports you to earn, achieve and be the most possible!

Coaching will teach you to:
- Expand your vision of what's possible – in business and in life
- Imagine and create your dream career
- Create a detailed 1 through 5 year vision and plan for your business
- Let go of time-wasting activities and focus your time on your most money making activities
- Take charge of stress, struggle and overwhelm with specific mind-body skills
- Create true life balance
- Listen to and follow your needs
- Say No (with less guilt)
- Make yourself a priority (you'll still give to others, but now you're included)
- ASK for what you want – from business associates, family members and friends
- Make more $$ and have more FUN

All coaching packages include a detailed health, wealth, happiness and marketing assessment designed to keep your strengths in the forefront so you can quickly work through obstacles that block you from achieving your fullest potential. The assessment will help you to be crystal clear about what's working and not working in your professional and personal life.

"If you've had your fill of stress, struggle and overwhelm, and are ready to be free, then coaching is for you."

Lynn Telford-Sahl, M.A. Psychology with Holistic Specialization

Please visit **www.lynntelfordsahl.com** for more information.

Health, Wealth &
Happiness Coaching Clients

"Lynn is a dynamic individual and remarkable coach. Her breadth of knowledge and experience in business and coaching were invaluable to my integration as business woman and metaphysician, culminating in the successful opening of The Sol Center healing center in Prineville, Oregon in 2008."

Joan Dudley, President, The Sol Center
528 SE 47th Street Prineville, Oregon 97754
(541) 306-7618

www.thesolcenter.com

"Thanks to Lynn I am attracting exactly what I asked for, clients ready to change their lives and have the money to afford my very valuable personal training service. Today's client cut me a check for the whole program."

Sonya Gonzalez,
Certified Fitness Trainer
(209) 380-5225

email: divinebody07@yahoo.com

Author Bio

At age 29, Lynn had a frightening flash of reality. She faced the fact that her own addiction to fear was driving her alcohol and cocaine abuse, and harming herself and her relationships. Lynn spent the next 25 years searching for the truth about how to heal the driving force of addiction—stress, fear, and underlying trauma.

The most meaningful result of her journey to freedom has been changing her fear-protection-control-based belief system to one bathed in the blessings of JOY with the mind-body skills she's learned and taught over the past two decades.

Lynn holds a master's degree in psychology with a holistic specialization from John F. Kennedy University, Orinda, California. She has earned a bachelor's degree in social work from Sacramento State University, Sacramento, California. A certified addiction counselor since 1989, she also became certified in integrative imagery in 2003. Before establishing a private practice in 1990, Lynn held positions as both an inpatient and outpatient counselor.

Lynn has presented and conducted dozens of workshops, trainings, and retreats, specializing in topics of stress, healing fear by choosing love, and stress and emotional and management. For four years, she was a regular guest on the radio show "Addictions & Answers" in Sonora, California. A community columnist at *The Modesto Bee* newspaper in Modesto, California, from 2006 – 2007, she wrote primarily about addiction.